"A unique and masterful blend of military p
Highly recommended for both scholars and m
see themselves as both."
—Dr. Pauline M. Shanks Kaurin,
Stockdale Chair in Professional Military Ethics,
College of Leadership and Ethics, U.S. Naval War College

"William C. Spears bridges ancient wisdom with the realities of military life, offering a clear, compelling case for Stoicism as the warrior's philosophy. This book belongs on every leader's shelf."
—Lt. Col. Thomas Schueman, USMC,
best-selling author of *Always Faithful*

"This book should be a standard text at our war colleges, service academies, for ROTC and for anyone wanting to get beyond a surface-level understanding of Stoicism as applied to the profession of arms."
—Dr. Shaun Baker, Stockdale Center for Ethical Leadership,
United States Naval Academy

"*Stoicism as a Warrior Philosophy* offers today's military a framework for thinking about the warrior ethos, how it works, and why it matters that it works on a philosophical level."
—Donald J. Robertson, best-selling author of
How to Think Like a Roman Emperor

"Spears performs the triple service of demonstrating that ancient classics are classics precisely because they can be read to good advantage centuries or even millennia after they were written, that Stoicism offers much to persons in search of such value in professional life, and that members of the profession of arms in particular owe it to themselves and to those they lead to think deeply about their vocation."
—Dr. John Mark Mattox,
U.S. National War College Chair in Leadership,
Character, and Ethics

STOICISM AS A WARRIOR PHILOSOPHY

For my sons, Jake, Eric, and Daniel. Always seek truth, wherever you go.

STOICISM AS A WARRIOR PHILOSOPHY

Insights on the Morality of Military Service

WILLIAM C. SPEARS

CASEMATE
Pennsylvania & Yorkshire

Published in the United States of America and Great Britain in 2025 by
CASEMATE PUBLISHERS
1950 Lawrence Road, Havertown, PA 19083, USA
and
47 Church Street, Barnsley, S70 2AS, UK

Copyright © 2025 William C. Spears
William C. Spears has asserted his right to be identified as author of the work.

Paperback Edition: ISBN 978-1-63624-623-9
Digital Edition: ISBN 978-1-63624-624-6

A CIP record for this book is available from the British Library

All rights reserved. No part of this book may be reproduced or transmitted in any form or by any means, electronic or mechanical including photocopying, recording or by any information storage and retrieval system, without permission from the publisher in writing.

The views expressed in this publication are those of the author and do not necessarily reflect the official policy or position of the Department of Defense or the U.S. government. The public release clearance of this publication by the Department of Defense does not imply Department of Defense endorsement or factual accuracy of the material.

Printed and bound in the United Kingdom by CPI Group (UK) Ltd, Croydon, CR0 4YY
Typeset in India by DiTech Publishing Services

For a complete list of Casemate titles, please contact:

CASEMATE PUBLISHERS (US)
Telephone (610) 853-9131
Fax (610) 853-9146
Email: casemate@casematepublishers.com
www.casematepublishers.com

CASEMATE PUBLISHERS (UK)
Telephone (0)1226 734350
Email: casemate@casemateuk.com
www.casemateuk.com

Cover image: used with permission from KA-BAR Knives, Inc.

The Publisher's authorised representative in the EU for product safety is Authorised Rep Compliance Ltd., Ground Floor, 71 Lower Baggot Street, Dublin D02 P593, Ireland.
www.arccompliance.com

Contents

Acknowledgements   xi
Foreword   xiii
Preface   xvii

1	Mission	1
2	Excellence	21
3	Discipline	51
4	Duty	91
5	Country	123
6	Warrior	165

Epilogue   205
Chronology of Key Figures   213
Bibliography   219
Index   227

Give me just one young man who has come to the school with this aim in mind, who has become an athlete in this field of action, and declares, "I for my part bid farewell to all the rest; it is enough for me to live my life free from hindrance and distress, and to be able to hold my head high in the face of events, like a free person and to look up to heaven like a friend of God, showing no fear of anything that could come about." May one of you show himself to be such a person, so that I can say, "Enter, young man, into what is your own, for you are destined to become an adornment to philosophy; yours are these goods, yours these books, yours these discourses."

EPICTETUS, *DISCOURSES* 2.17.29–30.

Acknowledgements

The first lesson a warrior learns is that nothing meaningful is achieved by an individual. The existence of this project is a testament to the generous support, insight, and encouragement of many exceptional warriors and philosophers who have profoundly shaped my thinking and enriched this work. I am specifically grateful to Shaun Baker, Brandon Booher, Ryan Broadfoot, Paul Cronk, Benelita Elie, Jason Glab, Brian E. Johnson, Michael Junge, Pauline Shanks Kaurin, Joe Leidig, Mitch Leventhal, Bradley Martin, John Mattox, Mick Mulroy, Carlos Negroni, James B. Stockdale II, Micah Sybor, Jeff Vandenengel, and Mark Welch, whose assistance and feedback reflect the shared pursuit of wisdom and service. To anyone I may have inadvertently failed to mention, please know your influence and support have not been forgotten and I remain deeply appreciative of all who have contributed to this effort.

I am also especially indebted to my wife and the light of my life, Paula, whose love and unwavering support have been my foundation throughout this journey. Her strength, kindness, and belief in me have been instrumental in bringing this project to life. My parents, Bill Spears and Mary Lynn Leach, deserve special recognition as well for teaching me what it means to live with integrity, compassion, and purpose. Their example continues to define the person I strive to be every day.

Foreword

When I first encountered an early version of William Spears's remarkable work on Stoicism, I read it with great focus and intent. At the time, I was navigating some health challenges—a fitting moment to engage with such a profound work—and I decided to revisit it closely, applying its powerful lessons to my own circumstances. It was clear to me that this was a *magnum opus*, crafted by a talented and genuine individual. Spears had poured a lifetime of research, methodical organization, and unwavering logical thought into contributing something truly meaningful to the study of authentic Stoicism.

I emphasize *authentic* Stoicism for a reason. I spent several years alongside my father, Vice Admiral James B. Stockdale, as he introduced serious Stoical study to the general public, political organizations, and military audiences. He often credited his deep knowledge and application of Stoic principles for his ability to lead, survive, and inspire those under his command, even within the depths of a dehumanizing autocratic prison system. But no matter the audience—no matter their sincerity—it was very hard for them to comprehend the levels of dedication, discipline, or devotion required to function, much less effectively lead, within the expectations of Stoicism.

He and I agreed the challenge didn't lie with any shortcomings among those in attendance. In truth, most were stepping out of a superficial, polite, commercial, sunshiny American atmosphere and into the buzz saw of a broader world—the real world—and the result for many, as best we could tell, was more disorienting than informative. We worked to adjust, softening the tone and pacing the delivery to better draw the audience into the material. Despite our efforts, it always felt as though we couldn't quite get it right. Still, the message was there—for those who chose to pursue it.

I may overstate the case, but the gap between the comforts of routine and a path that demands genuine depth and focus is undeniably vast. As a result, most attempts to introduce Stoicism are tailored to suit a relatively passing interest. Commercial realities further urge its packaging toward soft-sell modes. The result, I'm afraid, is that in cocktail party chatter or in the reductive bastions of "bro" culture, comprehension of Stoicism boils down to a marketing author's easy-listening affirmation and a Stoicism 'thought for the day' calendar. Such offerings can be torn off with little effort, inspiring superficial thinking for all of ninety seconds.

And *that* is why this book surges with importance. If Stoicism seriously attracts your attention, you need a North Star. In the life of work William Spears has invested in this text, you have a resource that provides authentic, thorough guidance. He writes it in a wonderful manner that allows you to choose your own challenges, but with the tools included to have a 'best chance' of finding both methodology and reward. And when you master an aspect of Stoicism, it allows you to 'bite off' another piece of its life-sustaining wisdom and approach any challenge with confidence.

One last item may inform your consideration of William's work. I am sometimes asked, "What does it mean to be (or to become) a true Stoic?" And my honest answer is somewhere between, "I dunno" and "I know it when I see it." Both William and I are fathers, and I think the most compelling evidence of productive Stoicism is how parents guide their children in honest give-and-take.

Two decades ago, I was afforded the opportunity to eulogize my father. Defining or even describing the Stoic ideal is beyond my reach, but I can honor relevant words of guidance and love that, while instructive, were issued with neither furrowed brow nor hint of judgment. Dad had a way of 'getting through' efficiently. The theme of any one of his twenty-second lectures was always the same: "Entitlement and privilege corrupt."

We were once doing some sawhorse work outside in sunny Los Altos Hills. It was 1961, and at age 11, I approached him about something the other kids had or something they were getting to do. I thought I had a pretty smooth presentation. Dad may have been amused by my first three sentences, but he didn't let me get far. Without even looking up from his saw he said:

"Look, Jimmy, those other kids are spoiled. They're going to be spending their parents' money getting other people to do their dirty work for years to come. They'll get away with it for a while, but then when things slip up they'll realize that in the big picture they're going to lose at life."

"Oh, they're going to have plenty of people to blame," he continued, "but they're going to lose. Is that what you want?"

End of conversation. Silence.

A few seconds passed and he kind of smiled and almost whispered, "you knew better than that…"

Back to the sawhorses. I can't give you a formula for Stoicism. The best I can do is share with you the way a Stoic speaks to his son.

This book has the potential to change your life for the better. It is deep and rich and provides an adult alternative to the contemporary superficial scurry of what passes for Stoicism these days in knick-knack bookstores. You can pass on it as you wish; you can continue to live life on your terms without advice from the ancients, without taking a plunge into deeper meaning, or wrestling with questions that have defined civilization. You can keep on walking. But at some point you may see my father's blue eyes subtly sparkle and hear his warm voice saying, "you knew better than that."

James B. Stockdale II

Preface

> This is Stoicism. It's not the last word, but it's a viewpoint that comes in handy in many circumstances, and it surely did for me.
> VICE ADMIRAL JAMES B. STOCKDALE (RET.), "THE WORLD OF EPICTETUS."

> I think if there was one book that I would read, it would be Marcus Aurelius, *Meditations*.
> GENERAL JAMES MATTIS (RET.), 26TH U.S. SECRETARY OF DEFENSE, REMARKS AT VIRGINIA MILITARY INSTITUTE.

I was 22 years old when I learned about the Stoics. It was my first year at the Naval Academy and, like many new and disoriented midshipmen, I sought my bearings in the institution's pantheon of heroes. An early favorite of mine was Vice Admiral James Bond Stockdale, a decorated fighter pilot and air-wing commander who was captured by enemy forces during the Vietnam War. He endured seven brutal years of captivity and torture, during which he served as the ranking officer and commander of the prisoners of war. For his extraordinary resilience and leadership throughout this ordeal, which is upheld today as the definitive standard of contagious moral fortitude, he was awarded the Congressional Medal of Honor.

Stockdale's story is well known, particularly his experiences in Vietnam, and I recommend it to any reader unfamiliar with this extraordinary individual. However, for this book, his later career is more relevant. In his final military role as president of the Naval War College, he personally developed a course in moral philosophy, often delivering the lectures himself. He continued to write and teach after retiring from the military and, as a midshipman, I came across his lectures in a collection at the Academy's library. While Stockdale had long emphasized the practical wisdom of classical philosophers, toward the end of his speaking career, he became particularly vocal about a former Roman slave named Epictetus.

Stoicism, the philosophy of Epictetus, teaches that while we cannot control external events—such as war, hardship, or the actions of others—we are responsible for our own thoughts, emotions, and responses. It emphasizes virtues such as courage, wisdom, justice, and self-discipline, motivating its adherents to act in accordance with reason and moral resolve, regardless of their circumstances. These principles reverberated thunderously through Stockdale's lectures, which vividly recounted how Epictetus' teachings had informed his moral decisions, fortified his resolve, and sustained his sense of freedom during his darkest moments of captivity.

Stockdale passed away before I had even completed a year in Annapolis, just months after our introduction. Through his writings, though, I was led to a way of thinking that seemed to resonate with all of my intuitions. Over the ensuing years, I consumed everything I could find on the Stoics, whose wisdom I strongly preferred to the engineering curriculum that dominated my energies. I focused especially on the statesman Seneca, whose writing style I found accessible and soothing, and Marcus Aurelius, whose fame as a Roman emperor drew me in. Epictetus, as it happens, seemed overly harsh and abrasive during these early explorations; it would be many years before I came to acknowledge him as my favorite Stoic.

After graduating and embarking on a career in the submarine service, I quickly discovered it was possible to have even less disposable time and mental energy than I'd had at the Academy. Consequently, philosophy took a back seat, as did any effective engagement with popular culture. It was not until my first shore-duty assignment that I found the Stoics again or, more correctly, they found me. Reflecting on my time at sea, I had begun thinking and writing about leadership, with particular interest in how to better train and develop new military leaders. While researching these ideas, I came across a Stoicism blog and was shocked to learn, in the years since my schooling, Stoicism had experienced an explosion in public interest, complete with online and print magazines, numerous popular books, and even an annual convention. What once felt like something of a secret I shared only with Admiral Stockdale had become a social phenomenon.

Naturally, I resented this development at first. As with any growing movement, popular Stoicism appeared to suffer its share of the inevitable abuses, misinformation, profiteering, and infighting. For every writer passionately advocating a fresh and exciting new direction for Stoicism, there seemed to be another one equally eager to criticize their approach. One would caution, "Don't commercialize it," while another would warn, "Don't trivialize it!" Others complained, "Don't secularize it" or, conversely, "Don't make it religious!" And, finally, there was the jarring appeal, "Don't militarize it!"

Something internally "clicked" when I encountered this final plea. What if we *did* militarize Stoicism—carefully and purposefully? If such a thing were even possible, what would it look like? My thoughts flashed to the famous warrior-mystics of history and fiction, from the Knights Templar to the Jedi Knights, and yet none of them demonstrated an underlying philosophy even approaching the coherence or resonance with military service as that of the Stoics. Could Stoicism, with its emphasis on self-discipline, resilience, duty, and rationality, offer a philosophical basis for the warrior ethos? Should it?

This book is the culmination of years dedicated to exploring these questions. I hope it will stand as a worthy complement to Stockdale's work on Stoicism, even if it significantly departs from his project in scope and application. To address my conclusions up front: yes, Stoicism provides a sound philosophical foundation for a warrior ethos; no, there is no need to 'militarize' it, nor should military institutions formally take any position toward it. Stoicism is, by its nature, already 'militarized' in the sense its principles align organically with the virtues and qualities required of a warrior. However, this final point remains contentious among some scholars and practitioners. This book exists, then, to explain how and why Stoicism is indeed a warrior philosophy.

Excepting a few select passages, most of the ideas presented in this text will be equally relevant to civilians as to members of the military. Furthermore, I have endeavored to ensure my sources can be easily followed by scholars. That being said, the primary intended audience for this book is serving and future warriors, specifically those invested with the capacity and the burning desire to think deeply. It is an archetype we might call the warrior-philosopher, or philosophical warrior. Naturally, this does not encompass all members of the military, but it refers to a larger population than stereotypes would suggest. Those who interact with real warriors on a regular basis understand them to be complex, intellectually capable, and exquisitely creative individuals, reflecting the depth and character of the broader society from which they are called to service.

What is a Warrior Philosophy?

Some clarification of terms is in order. When I refer to warriors in this text, I specifically mean members of the profession of arms, as opposed to athletes, first responders, or those who engage in metaphorical battles. I'm not particularly bothered by the liberal appropriation of the term—if anything, it is a compliment to those who serve—it's just not what I mean. On the other hand, I should be clear that my use of 'warrior' encompasses all uniformed members of the armed forces, regardless of specific roles or responsibilities. While there are intriguing debates to be held concerning the variance of warriorhood with technical specialty, proximity to physical danger, or individual experience, these distinctions are irrelevant to the arguments of this book. Always a collective action, warfare has evolved beyond the battlefields of popular imagination and its modern participants often do not conform to traditional notions of what a warrior does or looks like.

In this work, warriorhood is a binary status one acquires with the cloth of their nation, within which the individual is subsumed into an organ of national will. It applies regardless of one's specific position in the chain of events that delivers combat power. This status, however, is morally neutral. While certain subcultures romanticize the warrior archetype just as some others look down upon it, military service itself can be undertaken for any combination of virtuous or vicious reasons.

It is the individual's responsibility to ensure their service has moral value; I will emphasize this point throughout the book.

Having settled the meaning of 'warrior' in this text, we turn to 'philosophy', focusing on what is meant by 'a' specific philosophy as distinguished from the wider field of study. For brevity, we can compare it to similar concepts like an ethos, a code, or a creed—as in 'warrior ethos' or 'warrior code'. While these words are related and often used interchangeably, they mean different things, and a specific philosophy can belong in this set. I propose to imagine them as points along a continuum of thinking, ranging from the intuitive and organic to the deeply analytical and deliberative:

- An *ethos* refers to the naturally emerging spirit, values, and beliefs that define a particular group or culture. These principles guide the members' behavior and decision-making, contributing to a shared identity. A 'warrior ethos' might include values such as courage, selflessness, and loyalty.
- A *code* is a formalized set of rules or guidelines that govern behavior and actions within a specific context. It serves as a tangible framework individuals can refer to in moments of decision, ensuring their actions are consistent with collective ideals. A 'warrior code' might include statements like "I will never surrender of my own free will," as stated in the Code of Conduct for Members of the United States Armed Forces.
- A *creed* is a statement of belief or faith that outlines the fundamental tenets held by a group. It serves as a declaration of identity and purpose, encapsulating the core convictions that unite its members. A 'warrior creed' might include repeatable oaths such as "I will support and defend the Constitution of the United States of America," as stated in the Sailor's Creed of the United States Navy.

In contrast to the above, a *philosophy* involves a broader approach to thinking, even potentially incorporating fundamental ideas about psychology, ethics, and the nature of reality. It necessarily involves the exercise of *reason* to get at the 'whys' behind values or norms of behavior. A 'warrior philosophy' might encompass mutually reinforcing claims about the meaning of honor, the nature of conflict, and the tensions between individual and collective identity. It should say something about *why* one should be selfless, *why* one should never surrender of one's own free will, and *why* one should support and defend the Constitution.

Approach to Stoicism

Although some within the popular Stoicism movement identify as modern Stoics, adopting a tailored interpretation of Stoic teachings as a core aspect of their identity, this is not the approach I promote here. While I have no issue with those who find philosophical labels useful, I have found them to be restrictive and prone to creating more problems than they solve. Therefore, while this book can be justifiably considered a contribution to the literature of popular Stoicism, it adheres to the academic convention that Stoics exist only in antiquity. When I refer to Stoics, then, I refer specifically to the ancient Stoics.

Furthermore, I do not present Stoicism as an alternative religion or its adjacent, a 'philosophy of life'. As a practicing—albeit gleefully heterodox—Roman Catholic, Stoicism is neither of those things to me. Instead, I see it as a powerful framework for thinking through moral and existential problems, applicable to life in the same way strategic-planning frameworks are applicable to problems of national security. As such, it offers a degree of philosophical coherence I find unparalleled in other systems, including those belonging to religious orthodoxy. However, it is not without flaws, and I firmly believe that, like all systems of thought, Stoicism must be engaged critically and selectively.

Therefore, I recommend an eclectic approach to philosophy, taking what works and leaving the rest. Ideas must stand on their own merits and what is worth adopting should withstand scrutiny both rationally and practically. However, there is a catch to this approach. When engaging with a cohesive system of ideas like Stoicism, effectively assessing its soundness requires us to consider the full scope of the system, as many of its claims are dubious in isolation, but mutually reinforcing in concert. To fully appreciate these relationships, we have to play a kind of game—a thought experiment in which we provisionally adopt the ideas as they are introduced, proceeding 'as if' we accept the Stoics' claims at face value. This book is written with that mode of thinking in mind.

Synopsis

All presentations of philosophy are inevitably shaped by the priorities of the author; this work is no exception. Nevertheless, I have endeavored to remain faithful to the sources and to support my assertions with appropriate references. Although at first some readers might find the level of detail daunting, the academic rigor is necessary because there's no other reason to accept my word on the material presented here. I can speak with professional authority on topics like nuclear propulsion or torpedo employment but, as a philosopher, I am just a motivated amateur. I therefore encourage skeptical readers to engage with the references provided, examine the same sources I have, and draw independent conclusions. In my ideal world, some readers might even feel inspired to carry the philosophical task forward in entirely new directions.

If I allow myself one significant liberty, it is in often portraying Stoicism as if it were a unified and monolithic school of thought, which helps to provide clarity and accessibility. This simplification is necessary for exploring what are widely considered orthodox Stoic positions relevant to the aims of this book, though it inevitably omits some internal disagreements and evolving views within the tradition. In reality, Stoicism developed considerably over its 500-year history, encompassing three separate periods whose distinction we should briefly acknowledge.

Stoicism's founding in Athens around 300 BCE marked the beginning of the early Stoa, which established the fundamental principles of the Stoic school. Although it was founded by a shipwrecked merchant named Zeno, its most influential figure was Chrysippus, who codified the doctrines that remain the core of Stoic belief. The school thrived in Athens for several generations but began to lose cohesion as philosophers like Panaetius and Posidonius introduced ideas drawn from other traditions, many of which would be unrecognizable as Stoicism today. This eclectic phase of Stoicism is known as the middle Stoa, and it effectively ended with the dissolution of Athens' philosophical community during periods of war and upheaval.

Stoicism reemerged approximately a century later as a mainstream philosophical force in Rome. This late Stoa lacked formal organization and leadership but still generally represented the core doctrines established by Chrysippus and the early Stoa. Its primary focus, however, shifted toward the practical application of moral principles, with comparatively little attention given to theoretical details. Most surviving ancient Stoic texts come from this period and almost all modern works on Stoicism rely on the writings of the late Stoics—specifically Seneca, Epictetus, and Marcus Aurelius. The three periods are visually represented at the end of this book, accompanied by brief biographical descriptions of key figures for easy reference.

Common to all periods of Stoicism is the belief only virtue is inherently good, whereas external circumstances—wealth, health, reputation, and the like—are indifferent in determining a person's well-being. Stoics argued happiness stems from living in alignment with nature and reason, cultivating self-discipline, and accepting events outside one's power with equanimity. For the Stoics, the key to a meaningful life lay in developing inner character and adhering to moral principles, regardless of external challenges or misfortunes.

In the text that follows, I will step through ideas like these to explore their basis and implications, including the connecting points that bind them into a system. Building on this foundation, I will extrapolate Stoic moral theory onto questions of patriotism and war, specifically examining modern political and moral questions from a Stoic perspective. These discussions are organized across six chapters, which include the following:

Chapter 1: Mission. To begin the discussion, this chapter explores metaphysical notions of fate, nature, and causality, which are deeply intertwined with the pantheistic view that the universe itself is God. I will introduce key concepts such as determinism, the belief all events are fated to unfold exactly as they do, and teleology, which explains phenomena by the purposes they serve. I will also discuss the concept of cosmopolitanism, a key Stoic idea that appears to conflict with ideas like patriotism and the moral permissibility of war—topics examined more closely in later chapters.

Chapter 2: Excellence. In this chapter, I will explore the Stoic theory of virtue, defining it as moral perfection and situating it within the broader tradition of Hellenistic philosophy. I will consider the Stoic perspective on the cardinal virtues, their pre-Stoic origins, and key principles such as the idea virtue is a form of knowledge. I will discuss the profound claim that virtue is both necessary and sufficient for happiness, tying it to the teleological concept of nature introduced in the previous chapter. Finally, I will identify Stoic equivalents to modern military concepts of honor and integrity.

Chapter 3: Discipline. This chapter introduces the adjacent concepts of discipline and attention, emphasizing their centrality to a life properly lived. I will proceed deeply into the Stoic theory of mind, which envisions an internal command center that regulates thoughts, emotions, and actions through various governing processes. Throughout the chapter, I will tie in Epictetus' unique perspective on moral choice, which emphasizes distinguishing between what is within our power and what is not—a principle represented in the metaphor of a 'Stoic knife' that has many important applications.

Chapter 4: Duty. Building on ideas laid out in previous chapters, I will examine the mechanics of moral obligation to present a Stoic theory of duty, then introduce Epictetus' framework of role ethics, which grounds duty in the various roles one fulfills, both as a reasoning human and as an individual member of various social spheres. I will also grapple with the relationship between conformity and moral independence, recognizing the tensions that arise when duties come into conflict.

Chapter 5: Country. Drawing upon writings from the lesser-known philosopher Hierocles, this chapter concerns the complex relationship between moral progress and patriotism. I will show how Stoicism leads to a nuanced form of patriotism that harmonizes communitarian and cosmopolitan impulses. I will touch upon Stoic political theory, showing how ideals of just governance evolved among Stoics over time. Finally, I will also propose a Stoic theory of collective duty, in which communities themselves act with intentionality and bear moral responsibility.

Chapter 6: Warrior. This chapter opens by surveying the nearly unbroken cycle of imperial warfare that defined the reign of Roman emperor Marcus Aurelius. I will confront its tensions with Stoic cosmopolitanism, considering how the Stoics, had they endured as a distinct philosophical movement, might have independently developed a theory of just war. The focus will turn to the warrior archetype as a unique moral role, reflecting on how military obedience might coexist with the Stoic ideal of moral freedom. Finally, I will return to the concept of the philosophical warrior, drawing on principles from each preceding chapter to refine and articulate this archetype as the embodiment of idealized moral virtue.

A brief epilogue adjusts focus to recommend modern resources for further reading on Stoicism. This will be explored through the lens of the current mental health crisis, examining Stoicism's influence on contemporary psychotherapy and its potential impact as a growing movement within both the armed forces and society at large. Additionally, I will offer suggestions for deeper scholarly investigation and outline the recommended response of military institutions to the rise of popular Stoicism.

Notes on Academic Conventions

To maintain consistency with the broader body of existing literature on the Stoics, I have opted to use commonly accepted translations of terms and sources in the majority of cases. Except where otherwise noted, I use the Gummere translation of Seneca's *Moral Epistles*, the Hard translation of Epictetus, and the Waterfield translation of Marcus Aurelius. Sources for other translated items are available in the bibliography.

I have strived to keep the main text as reader-friendly as possible without oversimplifying. Footnotes are provided for the benefit of scholars, while casual readers are invited to ignore them. Citations follow standard academic conventions with Latin abbreviations. Some recurring conventions include:

- DL: Diogenes Laertius (an ancient biographer of philosophers).
- LS: Long and Sedley (editors of *The Hellenistic Philosophers*, an important collection of Stoic texts).
- SVF: *Stoicorum Veterum Fragmenta* (a collection of fragments of early Stoic works).
- Cf.: Confer (i.e., compare to).
- Ff.: Folio (i.e., and the following pages).
- Ibid.: Ibidem (i.e., in the same place, referring to a source cited immediately before).
- N.B.: Nota bene (i.e., note well, used to emphasize an important point).
- Trans.: Translator (used before the name of the translator).
- Pace: With due respect to (used when disagreeing with an author).

Gender-neutral language is used in most illustrative examples. In some instances, gendered examples are included to enhance readability. I have alternated the genders in these cases to reflect that warriors, like philosophers, come in male and female varieties, while the arguments themselves remain agnostic of gender. On the other hand, the ancient authors referenced in this work wrote within the conventions of their time, so quoted passages often reflect male-gender normativity. Nevertheless, their arguments should be regarded as equally applicable to individuals of either gender.

Finally, in keeping with philosophical tradition, I discuss past thinkers in the present tense. I do not refer to what they 'said' but to what they 'say', emphasizing philosophy is not a final truth handed down through time but a conversation between mortals that never ends.

CHAPTER I

Mission

> Matter lies sluggish, a substance ready for any use, but sure to remain unemployed if no one sets it in motion. Cause, however, by which we mean reason, molds matter and turns it in whatever direction it will, producing thereby various concrete results. Accordingly, there must be, in the case of each thing, that from which it is made, and, next, an agent by which it is made. The former is its material, the latter its cause.
>
> SENECA, *LETTERS* 65.2.

One of the most striking features of military organization is that everyone and everything has a mission—a fundamental reason for existing. The mission of an early warning radar system, for example, is to detect and track airborne threats. The mission of an attack submarine is to destroy hostile ships.[1] In this context, mission does not refer to a particular task or assignment, such as moving to a specific location or securing an objective. Instead, it refers to an overarching purpose that is only comprehensible with reference to a larger system.

This concept is observable at every level of organization. An individual combat medic's mission, for instance, is to provide lifesaving care, while the mission of a tourniquet is to stop severe bleeding. Lower-level missions inevitably support and reflect the mission of the higher echelons to which one belongs, whether that is a field hospital, a brigade combat team, or a larger army, fleet, or joint force.

The philosophical term for mission, as it is used here, is *telos*, which can also translate to "purpose," "end," or "goal." Many ancient philosophers, particularly the Stoics, were committed to the idea that everything has a *telos* that ties it to larger systems and processes within the natural order. Even a lifeless rock has an important role to play in this view, whether as part of the physical landscape, a tool in human hands, or simply as a mass-laden constituent of a wider gravitational system of unfathomable complexity. This principle extends to every echelon of existence, where civilizations, continents, and celestial bodies must serve some purpose. Even the universe itself is invested with a grand and logical *telos* that governs its design and operation. This claim naturally leads to contemplation of what—or *who*—might be implied in an intelligent cosmic order.

---

[1] *SSN-688 Class Ship Systems Manual*, Vol. 1, Ch. 1, Section 1.1.

The mission, or *telos*, of this book is to provide information, present an argument, and, ideally, inspire a spirit of philosophical inquiry in the modern warrior. Supporting and reflecting this mission, the *telos* of this chapter is to lay down the fundamentals of Stoic metaphysics, describing an interconnected structure of reality and a purposeful nature of existence. The concepts introduced here are foundational and necessary for understanding the arguments presented in later chapters. These concepts are also rather esoteric. To grasp how the system works, we must venture deeply into the jungle of first principles.

With unease, some readers may detect the presence of a God-sized elephant in the room. "I didn't sign up to be proselytized," one might think, "nor to be inducted into a pagan religion." Rest assured, that is not what I'm doing here. The *telos* of this book does not involve creating converts to a philosophical school that faded nearly two thousand years ago nor to any contemporary imitation thereof. Instead, what I am engaging in is akin to a thought experiment—a deliberate, provisional adoption of certain beliefs to understand better how they interconnect and function within a larger framework.

However, I must acknowledge few topics are as divisive, discomfiting, or burdened with cultural baggage as claims about the existence or nature of God. It would be very convenient if we could neatly separate philosophy from such sensitive issues; many modern interpreters of Stoicism have attempted to do just that. The purpose here, however, is to present Stoicism as a model, not to modernize it, sanitize it, or force it into conformity with anyone's prior commitments. Therefore, there is no good reason to avoid the God talk; given the importance of the Stoics' metaphysics to their wider system, it would be irresponsible to do so.

Instead of tiptoeing around Stoic theism, then, I shall address it early and directly as an essential pillar of Stoic physics. I have dual purposes in choosing to begin here. The first is practical: the foundation this chapter provides is essential for later chapters to make any sense. We cannot comprehend the Stoics if we don't grasp their understanding of nature, and that is inseparable from their understanding of God. This relationship reverberates throughout all Stoic thinking, early and late, Greek and Roman. It cannot be painted over, compartmentalized, or postponed for a later discussion that may never happen.

The second reason I have chosen to lead with this chapter is more confrontational, with the most enthusiastic of would-be orthodox Stoics specifically in mind. I aim to place before the reader an assortment of claims one cannot possibly accept in full, even if those ideas are held by one's most admired figures. This, I hope, will drive home the point that, to be properly engaged, a philosophy should be approached not like a faith but *like a philosophy*—that is to say, as an ongoing discussion between imperfect mortals. There are no prophets here, no sacred texts—just seekers of wisdom feeling around in the dark. It is not just acceptable, but positively essential that we can say our teachers are sometimes wrong.

On contact with a discrete idea, one should adopt it provisionally, weighing it against one's prior beliefs. What hinges on its truth and what prior truths support it? What might be undermined by it? What structures would collapse if the claim were proven false—or true? With these questions in mind, the reader should engage with the philosophers as equals—demand they convince you. Or let them fail to do so. As Cicero, an admirer of the Stoics, a key source for their views, and a worthy model for the eclectic approach, might advise, "You must exercise your own judgment on the content without pressure from me."[2]

Fields of Knowledge

Unlike modern university professors, whose disciplines have evolved through centuries of specialization, the ancient philosophers were polymaths. For them, all kinds of knowledge were facets of philosophy, and it was the business of philosophers to catalog, study, and teach it to others. Thus, an ancient philosopher might explore mathematics, provide legal counsel, design architectural structures, analyze animal behavior, or practice medicine. The schools of that era were not formal institutions like modern universities but small bands of intellectuals who gathered to discuss and debate such knowledge. The Stoics began as one such group, taking their name not from their founder, Zeno, but from the *Stoa Poikile*, or "painted porch," where they gathered. They categorized all knowledge into three interdependent domains: physics, logic, and ethics—each a vital part of the wider system.

> Philosophic doctrine, say the Stoics, falls into three parts: one physical, another ethical, and the third logical. … They liken philosophy to a fertile field: Logic being the encircling fence, Ethics the crop, Physics the soil or the trees … No single part, some Stoics declare, is independent of any other part, but all blend together.[3]

In addition to the analogy of a "fertile field" as described above, Stoics also compare the categories of knowledge to the parts of an egg (Figure 1), or of a living animal.[4] In each model, "logic" is represented by something providing structure to an otherwise shapeless whole—the bones and sinews of a body, the shell of an egg, or the fence around a field. It represents the boundaries and frameworks of human reasoning, and it encompasses all subjects dealing with the interplay of knowledge and language. In all cases, neither "physics," "logic," nor "ethics" can exist alone without the other

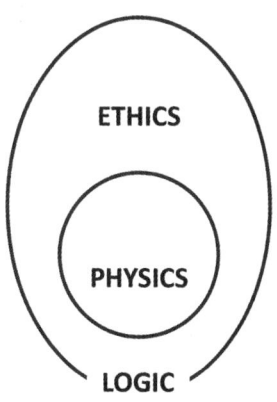

Figure 1. The 'Stoic Egg'.

---

2 Cicero, *On Duties* 1.2.
3 DL 7.39–40.
4 DL 7.40.

two. Regardless of which model is discussed, or which philosopher proffers it, their overriding purpose is to show an interdependence between the three fields of knowledge.

Most of the principles commonly associated with Stoicism today fall within the domain of "ethics." This includes guidance on how individuals ought to think and act—not solely because such behavior is morally required, as ethics is often understood in modern terms, but also because it is believed to lead to a state of happiness. In the various analogies described above, "ethics" is represented as the white of an egg, the crop of a field, or the flesh and blood of an animal. In addition to concerns of moral right and wrong, it comprises the Stoic understanding of emotions and moral choice, the importance of duties and personal relationships, and the connections between virtue, nature, and reason.

"Physics," as understood by the ancient Stoics, is a broader—albeit less developed—field of study than the empirical science bearing this label today. It concerns all theories about how the world *works*, not just the natural sciences but also the social sciences and metaphysics. Stoic ideas about causality and the divinity of nature, of which this chapter is expressly concerned, are considered concepts of physics. In the Stoics' various metaphors for knowledge, physics is compared to the soul of an animal, the yolk of an egg, or the soil and trees of a field, delivering the 'fruit' of knowledge, which is ethics.

A common misconception about Stoicism is that all its salvageable wisdom—those ideas promoted by Seneca and Epictetus, contemplated by Marcus Aurelius, and repackaged by modern bloggers and self-help authors—belongs exclusively to Stoic ethics. This perspective mistakenly interprets the terms "Stoic logic" and "Stoic physics" as antiquated precursors to modern disciplines bearing the same names. More importantly, this framing overlooks the entire point of presenting knowledge as an interconnected whole, where logic, physics, and ethics are inseparable components of a system.

Certainly, the Stoics made many claims that can be disregarded at no great cost to the coherence of the broader system. For example, some suggested earthquakes were caused by trapped air or that thunder was the sound of clouds breaking apart.[5] Notoriously, early Stoics claimed the human faculty of reason was physically located in the heart, though by Marcus Aurelius' time, Stoics had correctly identified the brain as its seat.[6] The perpetual challenge, however, lies in distinguishing wheat from chaff. This dividing line does not align neatly with the original three fields of knowledge. *Virtue*, for instance, may primarily belong to the field of ethics, but *reason* is more likely to be associated with logic while *nature* is rooted in physics. Furthermore, we will increasingly come to understand virtue, reason, and nature as inseparable concepts, much as the fields of knowledge are inseparable.

---

5   DL 7.154.
6   Galen, *On the Formation of the Foetus* 4.698, 2–9 (SVF 2.761, part) = LS 53D.

The late Stoics' overwhelming emphasis on ethical matters was largely a reflection of their culture and motives in practicing philosophy. The Romans were a pragmatic people, and philosophy in their time was expressly meant to teach one how to live. While the *discussion* of philosophy could be divided into parts, philosophy itself could only be realized in practice and this required the application of knowledge as a coherent system.[7] Therefore, physics and logic were not discarded by the Romans, they were 'baked in' to the foundations that underlie the most interesting and important discussions.

Of Plan and Planner

As a precept of physics, Stoics believe every event or situation, including every human decision and action, is the consequence of preceding events according to the laws of nature. There are no uncaused events; every occurrence must follow from an incalculable chain of antecedent causes ranging back for eternity. The inflexibility of this causal chain suggests, given a specific set of conditions or events, only one outcome can naturally follow, and this will have been destined to occur since the beginning of time. The inevitability of any given event can be called fate, as Cicero articulates:

> By "fate," I mean what the Greeks call destiny—an ordering and sequence of causes, since it is the connection of cause to cause which out of itself produces anything. It is everlasting truth, flowing from all eternity. Consequently nothing has happened which was not going to be, and likewise nothing is going to be of which nature does not contain causes working to bring that very thing about. This makes it intelligible that fate should be, not the "fate" of superstition, but that of physics, an everlasting cause of things—why past things happened, why present things are now happening, and why future things will be.[8]

The appropriate attitude toward fate, Cicero suggests, should be one of dispassionate acceptance. Anything else would be wasteful. Early Stoics illustrated fate's irresistibility, and the proper attitude toward it, with an analogy of a dog tied to a horse-drawn cart. If the dog walks along willingly with the cart, it will arrive at its destination without the suffering that comes from resisting the inevitable. If the dog resists the direction of the cart and tries to pull away or stop, it will be dragged along the same path painfully. In either event, it will end up at the same place. "So it is with men too," the Stoics argue, "even if they do not want to, they will be compelled in any case to follow what is destined."[9]

In the broader philosophical tradition, the idea events are destined to occur exactly as they do, or are predetermined, is called *Determinism*. The Stoics, therefore, are early determinists. Outside of Stoicism, this concept has a rich and vigorously

---

7 See Hadot, *The Inner Citadel*, 81–82.
8 Cicero, *On Divination* 1.125–6 (SVF 2.921) = LS 55L.
9 Hippolytus, *Refutation of All Heresies* 1.21 (SVF 2.975) = LS 62A.

debated history, particularly in its implications for ethics and human behavior. If every action is the unavoidable result of preceding causes, then the notion of free will—understood as the ability to have genuinely chosen to do something other than what one does—comes into question. This challenges traditional views of moral responsibility, suggesting to some we are not truly responsible for our actions in the conventional sense, as our decisions are predetermined by events beyond our power. For their part, the Stoics reject the idea *Determinism* conflicts with free will or moral responsibility. Furthermore, Stoics deny a predetermined future implies one should not plan or work toward desired future outcomes. We will revisit these particulars in future chapters.

What matters for our present discussion is the way Stoic determinism naturally fits together with the adjacent concept of *Teleology*. As a generic philosophical approach, *Teleology* is the explanation of phenomena by the *telos*—the missions served—rather than by antecedent causes. Teleological explanations consider the design, purpose, or goal-oriented aspects of objects and processes, especially in contexts where these aspects are believed to be inherent or intrinsic. In contrast are causal explanations; for example, a causal explanation for why trees have leaves is that ancestors of modern trees with leaf-like structures were more successful in surviving and reproducing, thus passing on the genes for leaf development. A teleological explanation would be that trees have leaves to optimize surface area for photosynthesis, which is essential for the tree's survival.

Teleological explanations often proceed naturally into *theological* explanations, or claims about God. In the case of the Stoics, this is seen when *Determinism* coincides with a generally reverent disposition toward the natural order in the universe, or what today we would call the laws of physics. This powerful concoction of ideas manifests as what we might call an 'attitude of gratitude' toward this same universe, a posture emphasized repeatedly throughout all the ancient Stoic sources. It can be distilled into a general teleological principle, wherein fated events occur only in accordance with a rational purpose which collectively constitutes a providential cosmic plan. But a plan implies a *planner*, thus, a claim about God emerges.

Without some specificity in what is meant by 'God', theological discussions are rather unproductive. For example, the question of God's existence would be entirely wasted on an omniscient oracle, who could answer in the affirmative or the negative as desired merely by assenting to a tailored definition of God. Suppose, for example, that God is synonymous with nature. In that case, we must agree God exists because we must agree nature exists. Substantial issues like immortal souls, eternal bliss and damnation, the reality of angels, or the historicity of sacred texts, might never enter the discussion.

As to the Stoics, what is perfectly clear is they believe in something and this something is translatable as God. Both the early and late Stoics refer to it frequently, however, their God-concept differs markedly from the speaking, emotional, miracle-creating, and prayer-answering God featured in the Abrahamic faiths of Judaism, Islam, and Christianity. Rather, Stoics are *pantheists*, meaning they hold that God or divine reality is identical to the cosmos and everything in it. In the Stoic view, God is the universe and the universe is God, "a living being, rational, endowed with a soul, and intelligent."[10] All materials, objects, and living creatures are a part of it. Time, causality, and the laws of physics are as well. By proceeding according to a chain of events destined to occur exactly as it has since the beginning of time, this universe effectively manifests a divine plan and benevolently exercises providence in executing that plan. As Epictetus puts it, "The first thing that needs to be learned is the following, that there is a God, and a God who exercises providential care for the universe, and that it is impossible to conceal from him not only our actions, but even our thoughts and intentions."[11]

The Stoic concept of God is simultaneously limited and infinite. It is limited in that the universe is fully *corporeal*, meaning God consists of nothing outside of matter and natural phenomena. This constraint is a key point of departure from most monotheistic or polytheistic traditions, where gods are conceived as ethereal, immaterial personalities that create or act *upon* the universe from beyond its physical limits. In contrast, the Stoic God-concept acts *as* the universe—not just the watchmaker, but also the watch.

Although the pantheistic universe consists only of matter and natural phenomena, it is also infinite in that it consists of all matter and natural phenomena *through time* as well as all natural laws governing the same ... therefore God can be simultaneously described as nature, the universe, reason, causality, providence, or any of the traditional names assigned to deities:

> For they call him Dia because he is the cause of all things; Zeus, insofar as he is the cause of life or passes through the living; Athena because his ruling part extends into the upper air (aether); Hera because it extends into the air; Hephaestus because it extends into the designing fire; Poseidon because it extends into the watery domain; and Demeter because it extends into the earth. Likewise, they give him other titles by fastening onto particular aspects of his nature.[12]

By connecting to the polytheism of their time, Stoics do not intend to endorse a literal interpretation of classical Greek myths. They clearly recognize these stories as human inventions, crafted to explain the world through narrative and symbolism. Well-versed in metaphor, the Stoics interpret the Olympian gods not as literal beings but as personifications of various natural phenomena.

With their expansive concept of God encompassing all things and events, the Stoics view everything traditionally represented by the gods as expressions of the

---

10 DL 7.142–3.
11 Epictetus, *Discourses* 2.14.11.
12 DL 7.147.

same universal intelligence. For them, the divine does not describe individual deities but is instead the underlying order and reason inherent in the phenomena they symbolize. This perspective allows the Stoics to engage with the cultural and religious frameworks of their day while maintaining coherency with the prevailing theories of physics. Seneca explains:

> Nor did they believe that Jupiter throws lightning-bolts with his hand, like the one we worship on the Capitol and in other temples. They recognize the same Jupiter as we do, the ruler and guardian of the universe, the mind and breath of the world, the master and the craftsman of this creation, for whom every name will be appropriate. Do you want to call him fate? You will not be mistaken: he it is on whom everything depends, the cause of causes. Do you want to call him providence? You will be right: he it is by whose deliberation provision is made for this world, so that it can advance unhindered and unfold its actions. Do you want to call him nature? You will not be wrong: he it is from whom everything is born, by whose breath we live. Do you want to call him the world? You are not mistaken: for he himself is all this that you see, contained in his own parts, sustaining both himself and his creation.[13]

It would seem the Stoics can agree to almost any description of a higher power so long as there is one. Today, pantheism is even sometimes characterized as a lightly mystical angle on atheism, whereby the universe proceeds in mindless accord with the laws of physics, and the metaphorical God does not actually possess life or consciousness. Because it is loosely compatible with modern secular sensibilities, this model of pantheism is popular among those who wish to identify as contemporary Stoics but don't want any superstitious baggage. It serves to smooth over the mystical edges of the ancient philosophy, but it also diverges from the beliefs of the ancients with non-trivial impacts on the ethical system.

On the surface, an atheistic abstraction of a pantheistic God into metaphor is of little practical consequence. After all, the living universe neither speaks to individuals, sends prophets, nor inspires the creation of holy texts. As there is no consensus on what life or consciousness even look like at a cosmic scale, it is possible for pantheists and atheists to loosely agree these terms describe natural phenomena in a spiritual way. However, what cannot be easily dismissed or abstracted away is the pantheistic tenet that nature exercises forethought, a claim that follows from Stoic determinism when viewed in light of a living universe.[14]

As committed determinists, the Stoics define fate as the "causal chain of the universe" or a "rational principle according to which the cosmos is administered."[15] If the universe is an omniscient being, then the fates of all its creatures must be elements of an elaborate, divine plan. As rational participants in this divine plan, Stoics are compelled not just to accept their fate, but also to imbue a love of it—often expressed as *amor fati*—manifesting a spiritual thankfulness deeply entrenched in

---

13 Seneca, *Natural Questions* 1.45.
14 DL 7.147.
15 DL 7.149.

Stoic thinking.[16] Without a living, planning, and *providential* universe, the Stoics' distinctive gratitude for their circumstances would necessarily become deflated if not neutralized entirely.

In the early Stoics' time, the atheistic concept of an unplanned universe governed only by physical laws was well represented in the teaching of Epicureans, a rival school to the Stoics. As deists, Epicureans assented to the existence of gods but effectively denied them any significance beyond the universe's creation. They saw the resulting universe as an assortment of randomly interacting 'atoms' that lacked any teleological organizing principle or intelligence. Stoics and Epicureans, like pantheists and atheists today, could agree there is no anthropomorphic, emotional personality intervening in human affairs from the heavens. They could agree nothing 'supernatural' exists as all matter and phenomena are parts of nature. They would have to disagree, though, about the existence of a divine teleology. The Stoics disputed the Epicurean view vigorously and unambiguously, as Seneca does here:

> So what is the difference between God's nature and our own? The mind is the superior part of us; in him there is nothing apart from mind. He is nothing but reason, although such great error grips the mortal sphere that human beings think that the most beautiful, the most organized, the most reliable thing that exists is subject to accident, at the mercy of chance, and therefore disorderly, with all the lightning-bolts, clouds, storms, and other things that batter the earth and the neighborhood of the earth. And this foolishness is not confined to the uneducated, but it also affects those who profess wisdom. There are people who think that they themselves have a mind, one that has foresight, administering in detail both its own and other people's affairs, but that this universe, in which we too find ourselves, is carried along without any plan by some haphazard process or by a nature that does not know what it is doing.[17]

The late Stoics were well acquainted with the Epicurean model of nature, which posits a universe governed by random, mindless atomic interactions. Seneca, Epictetus, and Marcus Aurelius each reject this view in their own distinct ways. Among them, Marcus employs the most elliptical approach, reflecting with a tone of mock objectivity on the consequences of the two models. He presents the choice as a stark dichotomy: a universe teleologically organized by "providence" or one ruled solely by the chaotic interplay of atoms. This tension, encapsulated in the phrase "providence or atoms," underscores his analysis.[18]

Contrary to how it is sometimes interpreted, the "providence or atoms" dichotomy does not suggest the Epicureans offer an equally plausible explanation of nature as

---

16 While it aptly describes a particular attitude among Stoics, the Latin phrase *amor fati* does not appear in any ancient text and was actually coined by 19th-century philosopher Friedrich Nietzsche. Its more recent association with the Stoics is most attributable to the 20th-century scholar Pierre Hadot. See Hadot, *The Inner Citadel*, 129–82.

17 Seneca, *Natural Questions* 1, Preface 14–15; cf. Epictetus, *Discourses* 1.12.1–9, 2.14.26–7.

18 E.g., Marcus Aurelius, *Meditations* 4.3. Cf. *Meditations* 4.27, 6.4, 6.10, 6.24, 7.32, 8.17, 9.28, 9.39, 10.6, 11.18, 12.14.

the Stoics' teleologically organized cosmos. Marcus' writings demonstrate regular cycles of skepticism and self-examination but also a clear preference for the Stoic position.[19] Viewed in context with the entirety of his writings, his "providence or atoms" refrain is apparently a drill employed to reinforce his own Stoic training, driving home that even if the universe were truly chaotic, it would still not follow that humans should behave chaotically: "The choice is between divine intervention, in which everything is as it should be, or mere chance, in which case you must still not be ruled by chance yourself."[20] Like his Stoic forebears, Marcus believes the philosophical mind gravitates to a disciplined and dignified existence, consistent with that prescribed by reason, and expressive of an intelligent state of nature.

Pneuma

The Stoic commitment to a *corporeal* universe means everything in existence is composed of physical matter. In wider philosophical tradition, this perspective is generally termed *Materialism*, making the Stoics early materialists. It implies thoughts, perceptions, and even beliefs are inseparable from the physical state of the body and brain, with no abstract or immaterial entities existing independently. Even emotions and mental states must have a physical basis.[21] Accordingly, Stoics assert abstract concepts do not exist independently of the individual objects and events we experience. For example, Mickey Mouse *subsists* as a fictional concept, but he does not *exist*.[22]

Similarly, universals—general descriptors or categories that apply to multiple individual things—do not have any reality beyond the particular things that instantiate them. For example, the concept of roundness cannot exist as an abstract *thing* but is merely a term we use to describe certain characteristics shared by round objects.[23] Likewise, the concept of war has no independent existence beyond a series of actions collectively assigned a name. I cannot physically hold a war in my hand or measure its gravitational field. Furthermore, I cannot confer existence to this concept just by assigning a name to the amalgam of events that comprise it.

This notion, where universals and abstract concepts exist only as 'names' in language, is known today as *Nominalism*. Thus, the Stoics are considered early proponents of both *Materialism* and *Nominalism*, much like several other philosophical

---

19 Hadot, *The Inner Citadel*, 147–49.
20 Marcus Aurelius, *Meditations* 9.28.
21 See Long and Sedley, *The Hellenistic Philosophers*, 1: 162–64; Sextus Empiricus, *Against the Professors* 10.3–4 (SVF 2.505, part) = LS 49B; Brunschwig, "Stoic Metaphysics," 210–19. Cf. Lossky and Duddington, "The Metaphysics of the Stoics," 481–89.
22 See Long and Sedley, *The Hellenistic Philosophers*, 1: 164 for more on "subsist" versus "exist."
23 See Long and Sedley, *The Hellenistic Philosophers*, 1: 179–83; and De Harven, "How Nothing Can Be Something," 405–29.

'isms'.[24] While these views may seem overly abstract and irrelevant to practical concerns, I will return to them when I consider how Stoics might think about war.

A commitment to materialist and nominalist precepts leads the early Stoics to a place of intriguing speculation. Building upon the idea that only physical things exist, they suggest the purposeful universe operates through two principles in constant interaction—a *passive* principle and an *active* principle. The former comprises matter: anything that physically exists and which is acted upon. The latter comprises causation or reason, the link between cause and effect, which at the cosmic scale becomes the *Logos*, or the intelligence of nature.[25] Passive and active principles can be articulated as *matter* and *cause* respectively, as in this chapter's epigraph; alternatively, they can be expressed as *matter* and *God*.[26]

In a simple model, we might describe these principles by visualizing an asteroid floating around in space. It would not be as simple as saying this rock is made up of only passive principle, even though it is nothing but lifeless matter. Its material properties like hardness or weight are aspects of passive principle, but its propensity to spin or tumble in a certain way when pushed is an internal property expressing latent active principle. Once subjected to an impulse, it continues to spin due to its own internal nature.

Unaware of asteroids, Chrysippus illustrates active and passive principle through the different behaviors of a cylinder and a cone when pushed. As inanimate matter, both require an initial 'push' (i.e., a cause) to begin moving, but the cylinder will roll or the cone will spin in different ways as a function of intrinsic properties.[27] If we increase the complexity of our model to include dynamic phenomena and life forms, the internal properties include life processes like circulation, digestion, and respiration, all examples of the active principle at work.

---

24 The specifics of Stoic ontology (the study of what exists) remain a contentious topic among scholars. As cited in the preceding footnotes, Long and Sedley argue the Stoics are more conceptualist than nominalist, while Nikolay Lossky suggests Stoics promote "ideal-realism" rather than strict materialism. These discussions, however, are beyond the scope of this project. For practical purposes, we will adhere to the conventional view the Stoics are nascent materialists and nominalists.

25 The term *logos* in ancient Greek translates to "word," "reason," or "principle." It applies in various contexts to signify logic, discourse, or the underlying structure of the universe. For instance, in classical rhetoric, *ethos*, *logos*, and *pathos* represent the three modes of persuasion: the credibility of the speaker, the logic of the argument, and its emotional appeal. As it is used here, in contrast, (capital L) *Logos* represents divine and perfect reason, or intelligence, in the workings of the universe.

26 Seneca, *Letters* 65.2; See Long and Sedley, *The Hellenistic Philosophers*, 1: 271 for more on "matter and God."

27 Cicero, *On Fate* 39–43 (SVF 2.974) = LS 62C. As Chrysippus deploys it, the "cylinder and cone" analogy is apparently intended as a defense of free will and moral responsibility in a predetermined universe. Like the cylinder and cone, different people will respond to the same stimulus in different ways as a function of their own internal qualities. See also Frede, "Stoic Determinism," 192–200.

If the Stoics insist everything in existence must have corporeal (i.e., physical) substance, then the concept of an active principle poses a challenge. The early Stoics address this by proposing the active principle itself must have a physical form, which they call *pneuma*. Meaning "breath" in ancient Greek, *pneuma* existed as a philosophical concept long before the Stoics, but under their custody it is invested with new and distinct meaning, like many other ideas they inherited. Stoics envision *pneuma* as a "designing fire, proceeding methodically on its course—that is to say breath that is fiery and endowed with designing power."[28] It is the *Logos* in physical form: a force of life, breath, warmth, and soul. Through their possession of *pneuma*, all living beings are said to possess an element of divinity.

The soul, say the early Stoics, is distinct from the body, consisting of pure *pneuma* and providing for 'psychic' qualities like personality and personal identity. They say the soul can temporarily survive the body's destruction before *pneuma* dissipates, but it is unclear how long this might take, and Stoics expressly deny any concept of an afterlife or an immortal soul.[29] For example, Marcus Aurelius muses upon the infeasibility of an ever-growing crowd of immortal souls around us, concluding souls must dissipate like bodies returning to the soil: "After remaining there for a while, transformation and disintegration occur, and then they're turned to fire when they're received back into the seminal principle of the universe."[30] These ideas are probably best interpreted as an expression of the Stoics' commitment to a fully corporeal universe while still making room for a personal identity separate from the physical body.

In a concept that bears more than a passing resemblance to the modern theory of the "Big Crunch," whereby the universe may someday contract upon itself and explode into a recurring series of Big Bangs, the Stoics theorized the universe would ultimately pull all matter (passive principle) into a point of pure energy (active principle)—pure *pneuma*. This fiery event, called *ekpyrosis*, or "the conflagration," would see the universe transform into a perfect 'God-phase' where "no evil at all remains, but the whole is then prudent and wise."[31] During *ekpyrosis*, the elements of matter are annihilated such that only the active principle remains:[32]

> They use the term "cosmos" in three senses: of God himself, whose proper quality is derived from the whole of substance; he is indestructible and ungenerated, since he is the craftsman of the world's orderly arrangement, at set periods takes all substance back into himself, and generates it again from himself. They also speak of the world-order itself as a cosmos. And in a third sense, the cosmos is that which is composed of both.[33]

---

28 DL 7.156.
29 See Long, "Soul and Body in Stoicism," 34–57. Cf. Eusebius, *Evangelical Preparation* 15.20.6 (SVF 2.809) = LS 53W; Nemesius, *On the Nature of Man* 78.7–79.2 (SVF 1.518, part) = LS 45C.
30 Marcus Aurelius, *Meditations* 4.21.
31 Plutarch, *On Common Conceptions* 1067a (SVF 2.606) = LS 46N.
32 See DL 7.134.
33 DL 7.137.

Through *ekpyrosis*, even the God-universe can execute a natural cycle of expiration and rebirth, exhibiting in broad strokes the circle of life at a cosmic scale. This theory also permits Stoics to maintain their commitment to corporeality while still allowing for a kind of creation event.[34] The implications of this are significant. Because humanity and, indeed, all life must be periodically annihilated, it follows there is no rule that fated events must ultimately support the immediate benefit of humanity, as we might perceive it. Rather, events occur for the greater benefit of the universe according to its own divine wisdom. If tomorrow a natural disaster were to obliterate all life on earth, it would not contradict the teleological thesis wherein events are driven by a providential and rational purpose.

The ancient theories of *pneuma* and *ekpyrosis* are not central to the Stoic ethical system, but they are relevant. Such ideas were promoted by a number of the early Stoics, especially in defense against rival philosophers, but, by the Roman imperial period, such ideas had begun to give way to the prevailing physical models of the time.[35] That said, the implications of these ancient theories, in which all life contains an element of God, reverberate throughout the late Stoic ethical writings. It never ceases to be a Stoic position that God is everything and, therefore, everything must be God. As Seneca observes, "All this universe which encompasses us is one, and it is God; we are associates of God; we are his members."[36]

Cohesion

While every part of the universe reflects some aspect of the *Logos*, not all parts manifest it to the same degree. Inanimate matter, for example, exhibits mostly passive principle, providing the raw material to be acted upon by various natural causes. Dynamic events, such as weather or the motion of planets, are manifestations of active principle and are the life processes of an animate universe. Plants and animals inhere life at an observable scale; plants exhibit growth and a cyclical nature that returns them to inanimate matter, whereas animals add warmth, breath, and an 'impulse' to seek what preserves life and avoid what endangers it. Finally, humans express all of life's aforementioned qualities but are also uniquely endowed with the ability to reason. Epictetus observes, "All other animals have been excluded from being able to understand the divine governing order, but the *rational animal* possesses resources that enable him to reflect on all these things, and know that he is a part of them, and what kind of part, and that it is well for the parts to yield to the whole."[37]

---

34 White, "Stoic Natural Philosophy (Physics and Cosmology)," 129–30.
35 Lapidge, "Stoic Cosmology," 183–84.
36 Seneca, *Letters* 92.30.
37 Epictetus, *Discourses* 4.7.7, emphasis mine.

Humanity's special gift of intellect is no small thing to the Stoics. The degree of separation between an ability to reason and the basic behavior of an animal is at least as great as that between that of an animal and a plant.[38] Wisdom facilitates virtue and, in many contexts, it *is* virtue, such that someone who is fully possessed of it would necessarily be a model of perfection—what Stoics call a 'sage'. It is of this ideal that Seneca writes when asserting "he in whose body virtue dwells and spirit ever present is equal to the gods."[39] Because rationality is a kind of divinity, the perfectly wise sage is a transcendent and godlike ideal.

As for us modestly rational mortals, we are thought to possess a fragment of the *Logos*, or that rational principle animating the universe. That makes each of us a miniature representation of the cosmos—a microcosm. Thus, Epictetus suggests the divine is present in all aspects of our lives; in our social relationships, physical activities, and conversations, we are continuously feeding and exercising this inner divinity. True to form, he turns this observation into a critique: "You carry God around with you, poor wretch, and yet have no knowledge of it."[40] Reason, then, is a kind of godliness that confers enormous responsibility. Insofar as we express it, we model God.

Viewed conversely, the universe itself is a 'macrocosm' of an individual organism, hence the claim that it exhibits life at a cosmic scale. This relationship of microcosm to macrocosm, where natural systems share common features at vast differences of scale, is not unique to Stoicism. As a property of nature, it is called 'Self-Similarity', which appears in fields like art, math, and the natural sciences.[41] Self-Similarity is observed in the branching patterns of trees, the logarithmic expansion of a nautilus shell, repeating structures of snowflakes and coastlines, and even certain types of music and architecture. Fractal theory represents it mathematically, whereby geometric patterns repeat themselves ad infinitum, such that a microscopic sample of a pattern effectively provides a blueprint for systems of enormous complexity (Figure 2).

Figure 2. A Barnsley Fern, a mathematically generated fractal image modeling Self-Similarity in nature.

---

38 See Seneca, *Letters* 124.14. Cf. DL 7.86.
39 Seneca, *Letters* 92.30.
40 Epictetus, *Discourses* 2.8.12.
41 Mandelbrot, *The Fractal Geometry of Nature*, 1–24ff.

The principle of Self-Similarity is observable in the tiers of community and human organization. Humans form families, towns, countries, and an entire species, each reflecting the features and behaviors of a living organism. As the lowest echelon still possessed with reason, the individual human represents a microcosmic blueprint of cosmic intelligence. Among all life forms, only humans enjoy this particular status; from this shared nature, the Stoics derive reasons for human interconnectedness—both as explanations for relationships and motivations to nurture them. Seneca states, "All that you behold, which comprises both God and man, is one—we are parts of one great body. Nature produced us related to one another, since she created us from the same source and to the same end. She engendered us in mutual affection, and made us prone to friendships."[42]

From this perspective, humanity is not merely a collection of individuals but a living, interconnected system, greater than the sum of its parts, with each component reflecting the wisdom of the whole. Flocks and herds within the animal kingdom exhibit similar impulses toward collective identity. Observing these patterns, Marcus Aurelius notes behaviors of attraction and community are not merely a function of living beings but extend across the spectrum of existence, from the simplest of creatures to massive celestial bodies, which exhibit a self-similar organization spanning the greatest conceivable distances.[43]

For an individual within this system, progress begins when the primal instinct for self-preservation evolves to encompass the interests of others as self-interest. Social creatures, like those reflected upon by Marcus, transition from a self-serving infancy to an adulthood oriented toward their offspring and the broader species. Among humans, endowed with reason, this natural progression manifests in social structures like "states, friendships, families, groups, their treaties and truces," each reflecting an inherent *telos* to cooperate.[44] For the individual member of this species, a progression from simple to complex forms of moral consciousness can be visualized as an ever-expanding horizon, beginning from the self and extending outwards to family, community, and ultimately to the entirety of humanity.

If the logical culmination of this process is transcendent and godlike sagacity, we might ask how the sage is envisioned to exist in a social context. There are many possibilities, but we can definitively say the ideal wise person is not some hermit in a loincloth issuing platitudes from atop a mountain. On the contrary, membership in the species entails membership in the community, and that requires active participation. Seneca quotes Zeno, "The sage will engage in public affairs unless he cannot."[45] Cicero is more specific, arguing:

---

42 Seneca, *Letters* 95.52.
43 Marcus Aurelius, *Meditations* 9.9.
44 Ibid.
45 Seneca, *On Leisure* 2.2.

> ... since we see that man is designed by nature to safeguard and protect his fellows, it follows from this natural disposition that the wise man should desire to engage in politics and government, and also to live in accordance with nature by taking to himself a wife and desiring to have children by her. Even the passion of love when pure is not thought incompatible with the character of the Stoic sage.[46]

We should be careful to understand Cicero within the context of the late Roman Republic, when political service was seen as a natural responsibility for those with the requisite knowledge and oratory talent. His endorsement of political activity is a general injunction to participate in social processes as befits one's specific environment, not for personal gain but for the common good. Furthermore, his promotion of marriage and family is a comment on the prosperous and flourishing life, clearly refuting the trope that wisdom involves a solitary existence on the fringes of society. Such separation is unnatural; as Epictetus observes, "Don't you know that in isolation a foot is no longer a foot, and that you likewise will no longer be a human being?"[47]

The communitarian impulse of Stoics is not just about what one should do. It is also about how one should perceive oneself, not as a lone spirit but as a vital organ of one's respective social group. "Our relations with one another are like a stone arch," remarks Seneca, "which would collapse if the stones did not mutually support each other."[48] A mature individual should feel this responsibility with the full weight of those affected by any failure to meet it. Community membership is therefore not just about belonging and fellow-feeling, but also the duties that one should perform, and the faculty of reason is salient in the interdependence of these two forces. It is a regulatory dynamic that subsists throughout the entire life of wisdom, as Seneca opines:

> We shall remain in active service right up to the very end of life, without ceasing to apply ourselves to the common good, to help the individual, and to give assistance with an aged hand even to our enemies. We Stoics are the ones who grant no exemptions from service at any age, and as that most eloquent of poets puts it, "We clamp down the war-helmet on our gray hair." We are the ones who hold so strongly that there is no inactive moment before death that, if circumstance allows, death itself is not inactive.[49]

The crux of Stoic communitarianism is that one's moral identity is inherently embedded within both a social and cosmic context, evolving as a function of intellectual maturity to encompass broader perspectives. As one's sense of community expands, so too do moral obligations and self-interest, integrating local duties into an ethical awareness of global scope. This expanding sense of affinity is both natural and essential for the effective functioning of individuals and societies. A proclivity to

---

46 Cicero, *On Ends* 3.68.
47 Epictetus, *Discourses* 2.5.26.
48 Seneca, *Letters* 95.53.
49 Seneca, *On Leisure* 1.4.

work together in communities, rooted in human rational faculties, is thus a defining feature of Stoic thought; I will explore its implications more fully in later chapters.

Tension

When the moral horizon expands to encompass the entire world, a sense of global community naturally follows. This idea is one of the most recurrent themes in Stoicism, championed by all its prominent thinkers. Seneca, for instance, encourages adopting the motto: "I am not born for any one corner of the universe; this whole world is my country."[50] Similarly, Cicero highlights the Stoic belief "that the universe is governed by divine will; it is a city or state of which both men and gods are members, and each one of us is a part of this universe; from which it is a natural consequence that we should prefer the common advantage to our own."[51] Connecting global citizenship to the divinity of reason, Epictetus goes even further, comparing one's nationality to the corner of a room where they were born—an arbitrary and insignificant point of identity when measured against the vastness of a divine and ordered cosmos.[52]

No Stoic figure reflects upon the common nature of humanity with such regularity or under such intensely trying circumstances as the wartime emperor Marcus Aurelius. Perhaps reflecting the constant moral stressors of the battlefield, his journal entries record what occupied his mind at the close of each day. He frequently seems to be reminding himself—if not convincing himself—of core Stoic doctrines. Consider, for example, the systematic argument he presents below:

> If intelligence is something we have in common, then reason too, which makes us rational beings, is something we have in common.
>
> If so, then the reason that dictates what we should and shouldn't do is also something we have in common.
>
> If so, then law too is something we have in common.
>
> If so, then we're fellow citizens. If so, then we have some form of society in common.
>
> If so, then the universe is a kind of community, since the universe is the only shared society that anyone could describe as common to the entire human race.
>
> And it's from there, from this shared community, in fact, that we get intelligence, reason, and law.[53]

Marcus' syllogism is effectively a checksum of the argument that a living universe compels universal human communion. Marcus reverses it, deducing all humans must be countrymen and therefore the universe must be their country. Either way,

---

50 Seneca, *Letters* 28.4.
51 Cicero, *On Ends* 3.64.
52 Epictetus, *Discourses* 1.9.1–5.
53 Marcus Aurelius, *Meditations* 4.4.

all human beings are connected by a shared rational nature; this claim is represented in the wider principle of *Cosmopolitanism*. Cosmopolitan literally means "citizen of the universe," an expression used by Diogenes the Cynic, a legendary predecessor to the Stoics.[54] Like the Cynics before them, Stoics insist humans should not view themselves merely as members of a particular society—some tiny backwater in the cosmic order—but as part of the uniquely endowed human species, bearing responsibilities that reflect this elevated position.

Cosmopolitanism, as a distinct intellectual tradition, emphasizes all human beings, regardless of nationality or origin, belong to a shared global community. In contemporary political discourse, cosmopolitans champion global justice and universal moral principles, arguing that individuals have obligations to humanity as a whole, not just to their immediate or national communities. They advocate for dismantling barriers and eliminating discrimination based on nationality, ethnicity, or culture, while promoting policies that encourage global understanding and respect for diverse ways of life.

Much like Stoic determinism, Stoic cosmopolitanism offers an early, measured approach to these principles, distinguished from later thinkers who, from a Stoic perspective, may have extended such ideas beyond the bounds of reason. Within Stoicism—like any moral framework—cosmopolitan values encounter natural limits, as an excessive emphasis on global obligations risks compromising obligations to one's immediate companions. I will explore these tensions intensely in Chapter 5. In the meantime, for this book's intended audience of serving and future warriors—readers who may have expected a straightforward guide to becoming more formidable and efficient in their craft—the Stoics' cosmopolitanism is likely to give pause. Moreover, their tendency to downplay the importance of national allegiance may seem difficult to reconcile, if not outright antithetical, to traditional warrior values like patriotism and loyalty.

And what of Marcus Aurelius? Rome's brutal military campaigns against rebellious tribes would seem fundamentally at odds with Stoic ideals of human unity and shared citizenship. Was Marcus a philosophical hypocrite, championing lofty principles of universal brotherhood while overseeing campaigns of imperial domination? Alternately, was he merely a weak man constrained by his circumstances, unable or unwilling to halt the relentless machinery of empire? Perhaps, as is often the case with both history and philosophy, the truth is more complicated. I will return to these questions in Chapter 6.

The tension between cosmopolitan ideals and moral obligations to kin and country represent the core dilemmas facing a theoretical Stoic warrior—when is it appropriate to refuse combat and when is it appropriate to seek it? Over the coming pages, I will ultimately address these challenges and others, as their resolution lies

---

54 DL 6.63.

at the heart of this book's mission. However, before going on the attack, we must equip ourselves with the proper kit and the knowledge to use it effectively. As usual, there is more work to do.

Why Study the Ancients?

At the outset of this chapter, I warned the terrain might become difficult, not due to the complexity of the subject matter per se, but because some readers might find the discussion of metaphysics to be uncomfortable or unwelcome. If you're still reading, take comfort in knowing you've made it through the most theologically charged material of this book. I trust the reasons for presenting it early are evident. At the very least, these reasons will become inescapable in the next chapter, which explores the Stoic concept of virtue. As the Stoics insist upon describing it as life "in harmony with nature," it is fully necessary to clarify what is meant by "nature."[55]

To that end, I explained in this chapter that the Stoics' metaphysics integrates the physical laws of the universe with a deep reverence for reason as a kind of divine human capability. I outlined several essential principles that encapsulate this view of the universe, which is imbued with causality, purpose, interconnectedness, and rational community:

- *Materialism*: Everything that exists is part of the physical world and operates under its laws.
- *Nominalism*: Universals—qualities or conditions shared by existing things—do not have an independent existence; rather, they are merely names we apply to groups of things.
- *Determinism*: All events result from preceding causes, which have been set in motion since the beginning of the universe.
- *Teleology*: All events occur for a reason and together they form an intelligent cosmic plan.
- *Communitarianism*: Life forms are impelled by nature to cooperate within communities.
- 'Self-Similarity': Natural systems, including communities, reflect the characteristics of their individual parts across various echelons or scales.
- *Cosmopolitanism*: All human beings are connected by a shared rational nature, creating a global community that includes all of humanity.

When we refer to the wisdom of the ancients, we should be mindful of a natural human tendency to grant them more authority than deserved simply on account of their 'ancientness'. We must avoid treating them as prophets or gurus, even as we try to determine what constitutes a 'doctrinally Stoic' belief. One way to check ourselves

---

55 DL 7.87.

for this bias is to imagine the Stoics had never existed and that our society is otherwise exactly the same. How would we respond if a modern philosopher presented these ideas today? Would we find them compelling or dismiss them as the ramblings of a crank? By considering the ancients' ideas in light of what we know today, we can engage with them not like cultists or ideologues, but like philosophers; they would expect no less of us. As Seneca remarks:

> He who follows another not only discovers nothing but is not even investigating. What then? Shall I not follow in the footsteps of my predecessors? I shall indeed use the old road, but if I find one that makes a shorter cut and is smoother to travel, I shall open the new road. Men who have made these discoveries before us are not our masters, but our guides.[56]

Perhaps the Stoics' metaphysical claims, and the pantheistic awe pervading them, amount to a heap of prescientific gibberish. On the other hand, perhaps these ideas reflect important truths as articulated by history's most seminal minds, who carved out the foundations of intellectual tradition with little more than their bare hands and the human faculty of reason. Both can be true in a way. The ancient ideas betray a certain proclivity, which we might call the philosophical impulse, that is discernable in the great minds of any age. Consider the words of modern philosopher Bertrand Russell, a thinker as far removed from mysticism or superstition as one can imagine, yet even he approaches the majesty of the unknown with a tone of metaphysical humility, asserting we engage in inquiry "because, through the greatness of the universe which philosophy contemplates, the mind is also rendered great, and becomes capable of that union with the universe which constitutes its highest good."[57]

The philosophical impulse entails an unquenchable thirst for wisdom, which is regarded as an unalloyed good; a deep respect for humanity as the sole natural possessor of certain cognitive capabilities; and an appreciation for the negligible speck current human understanding represents against an infinite unknown. In service of that impulse, then, we study the ancients not just to compile the facts of history, but also to identify stable signals within the noise, those common threads of truth that define the human experience across past, present, and future. We are not dismayed by a lack of clear-cut answers to our questions, as we pursue philosophy for the questions themselves. We recognize there is incredible power and freedom in identifying what we don't know, breaking down the walls of our self-constructed prisons and confronting what is possible. It becomes our mission, then, to take up the tools of our forebears and continue the endless work of our species, uniquely equipped as we are to realize and refine our own rational nature.

---

56 Seneca, *Letters* 33.10.
57 Russell, *The Problems of Philosophy*, Ch. 15.

CHAPTER 2

Excellence

O ye, who learned are in Stoic fables,
Ye who consign the wisest of all doctrines
To your most sacred books; you say that virtue
Is the sole good; for that alone can save
The life of man, and strongly fenced cities.
But if some fancy pleasure their best aim,
One of the Muses 'tis who has convinc'd them.

ATHENÆUS, DL 7.30 TRANS. YONGE.

Always fight bravely, and be superior to others.

POSIDONIUS TO POMPEY MAGNUS, STRABO, *GEOGRAPHY* 11.1.6.

The central claim of the Stoic philosophy is "virtue is the sole good."[1] With clarity and force, it serves as the keystone concept in a vast arc of Stoic moral reasoning, without which the entire system collapses into a heap of motivational quotes and folk wisdom. Stoicism cannot stand as a coherent philosophy without it. And yet, in most popular portrayals of Stoicism, virtue receives little attention, crowded out by preoccupations with emotional resilience and self-control—qualities that, as we shall see, are simply specific expressions of virtue. When virtue is discussed at all, it is typically assumed everyone understands what it means. But is that a safe assumption?

The purpose of this chapter is to clarify exactly what the Stoics mean when they say virtue is the sole good. First, we must recognize we are relying on translations, and some meaning may inevitably be lost in that process. The Greek word we render as virtue is *aretē*, which refers broadly to qualities of goodness, excellence, or perfection.[2] The Merriam-Webster English dictionary describes virtue as "conformity to a standard of right," which seems to fit the contexts in which *aretē* is employed. However, we must bear in mind that virtue, so defined, is not solely a human quality; for instance, a horse can have virtue if it runs well and a knife can have virtue if it cuts well.

---

1   DL 7.30 trans. Yonge.
2   E.g., DL 7.89.

Virtue, then, must be understood broadly as goodness in a descriptive sense, and it is well to have clarified this point. With this understanding in hand, we return to the keystone concept, which can now be rephrased with a straightforward substitution. We arrive at the profound claim that … *goodness* is the sole good? Now, that is not helpful at all. Something must be missing.

Aretē, or virtue, must refer to something a bit more specific than goodness. We may say it is goodness, but goodness at what? Goodness to what end? Let us return to our examples: a horse could demonstrate virtue if it runs well and a knife if it cuts well. On the other hand, let us imagine a horse that produces excellent milk. This would not be a reason to say it is a good horse. Likewise, a particular knife may be very effective in striking blunt objects, but that would not make it a good knife. Virtue, as befits our examples, appears to mean something like goodness *toward a specific mission*, or goodness at *being* what something is *supposed to be*.

The next question practically leaps out at us: by what criteria can we say a human is being what one is supposed to be? Stoics would say we can start by ruling out anything a human cannot control. For example, physical attributes, like height or skin color, are not really up to us, so they can have no bearing on whether or not we are being what we are supposed to be. Extending this reasoning, we can rule out wealth, reputation, companionship, and anything else not really up to us. Our actions may influence such things, but in the end they are *external* to us; they can be taken away at any moment for any reason. Because our virtue refers to *us*, and not these features external to us, what remains as the virtue of a human are *internal* factors, or what we might otherwise call *moral* factors.

The word *moral* warrants further clarification. In popular perception, morality frequently calls to mind values such as forgiveness or chastity, a reflection of the deep influence religious traditions have had in shaping (real or perceived) social values. While such priorities are not without merit, some individuals may associate morality with a kind of 'softness' or naivety, reminiscent of the lessons we teach to children. As a result, some readers may be inclined to dismiss discussions of morality as an irrelevant or even undesirable regression.

However, there is much about morality that is not taught in children's books. In the sense that I use it, morality refers to all traits of character that make up who we are and who we aspire to be. It captures every kind of 'hardness' a warrior might wish to cultivate, excepting perhaps the literal density of muscle tissue, but not excepting the personal discipline required to achieve it. Qualities like fortitude, work ethic, wisdom, and reliability under stress—hallmarks of an effective human, but especially of an effective warrior—are therefore moral factors. Insofar as Stoicism is useful or interesting at all for application within the modern world, it is as a moral philosophy.

Virtue, as befits a human being, is moral perfection. In the language of the Stoics, then, moral perfection is the sole good. That is to say, it is *internal* perfection, or a human's propensity to be what one is supposed to be, which is the exclusive aim or goal that will ostensibly lead to happiness. In the words of the Stoics, this means to live "in harmony with nature." In the pages that follow, I will explore what that means.

I will begin with the fundamental claim that virtue is a form of knowledge, a concept that predates the Stoics by centuries. We will see how Stoics adapt it and combine it with other inherited ideas, such as the cardinal virtues of prudence, courage, moderation, and justice. Within these discussions, I will isolate three key ideas that become uniquely Stoic when fitted together: that all virtues are ultimately the same thing, that this thing is a specific form of knowledge, and that it is either fully possessed or not possessed at all.

This third idea, that virtue is an all-or-nothing proposition, has far-reaching implications within the Stoic view of moral progress and its objective of perfect wisdom. Exploring these will lead us to a peculiar distinction between so-called "right actions" and "appropriate actions," which will be important in later discussions about behavior and duty. Finally prepared, I will transition to the essential Stoic claim that virtue is both necessary and sufficient for happiness, which presents the Stoics at their most extreme.

The latter portion of this chapter will explore the concept of indifferents, including a brief detour into the philosophical problem of value as it applies to morally neutral terms. These discussions will lay the groundwork for future investigations into the Stoic theory of mind. Before concluding the chapter, however, I will compare the modern warrior values of integrity and honor with similar Stoic concepts, arguing these 'martial virtues' are fully represented within the Stoic moral framework.

Virtue as Knowledge

The Stoic theory of virtue is traceable to a specific Athenian war hero. This individual was a hoplite, or heavy infantryman, who served during the Peloponnesian War. Renowned for his physical strength and personal discipline, he was said to be impervious to cold, hunger, or other hardships and appetites. He fought bravely in several notable battles, including Delium, Amphipolis, and Potidaea—the latter being a site where he saved the life of a young officer.[3] Even in later life, after his military service had ended, he continued to wear the simple cloak of a soldier through winter and summer. Although he was admired in his time as an exemplary warrior, it is for his later contributions that he is remembered today. Perhaps the reader has heard of him: a peculiar and unassuming questioner, often portrayed as a funny little man, known as Socrates.

---

3 See Plato, *Apology* 28e; *Symposium* 219e–221b; Copleston, *Greece and Rome*, 97.

Although he left no writings of his own, the life and ideas of Socrates are recorded in the works of thinkers like Plato and Xenophon.[4] His signature approach, the Socratic method, emphasizes that wisdom is about questions, not answers. In the famous Socratic dialogues, he typically meanders through a discussion, systematically dismantling his interlocutors' confident opinions without providing definitive conclusions. He further deepens their frustration and humiliation by insisting it is he who knows nothing. Despite this professed ignorance, legend has it the Oracle at Delphi pronounced no man was wiser than Socrates—a paradox widely interpreted to mean that, unlike those who arrogantly claimed wisdom, he possessed a rare insight into the vastness of what was still left unknown.

Socrates produced a tectonic shift in the philosophical tradition, effectively clearing the intellectual battlefield with his relentless and disarmingly humble questioning. Many Hellenistic schools, including the Stoics, regarded themselves as his true intellectual descendants. In the Stoics' case, Socratic ideas were inherited through Crates, a Cynic philosopher under whom Zeno, the first Stoic, was instructed. The Cynics were founded by Antisthenes, a protégé of Socrates, who, following his teacher, emphasized the primacy of virtue and the irrelevance of prestige or material possessions—core Stoic values throughout their history. Considering this lineage, when attempting to piece together the Stoic theory of virtue amid the surviving scraps and fragments of early Stoic writing, we are invited to go straight to the source of their ideas.

As discerned from various dialogues, it appears Socrates perceives virtue as a form of knowledge. More specifically, it is a special kind of scientific knowledge, or *epistêmê*, that, once acquired, compels a person to act rightly. According to this view, it is impossible for someone possessing this knowledge to act otherwise.[5] This creates what is often regarded as a paradox in Socratic thought as it suggests anyone who commits injustice or wrongdoing does so involuntarily. Notably, this is a recurring theme in the teaching of Epictetus. However, it seems to contradict the observable reality that some people knowingly and willfully choose to do wrong.[6]

Surely, the possibility of a 'knowing evildoer' did not elude the sharp intellect of Socrates. There must be a plausible explanation; generations of scholars have

---

4 Scholars generally agree the Socrates portrayed by authors like Plato and Xenophon reflects their authors' ideas to a large extent, prompting debate over who depicts him more authentically. See Copleston, *Greece and Rome*, 99–104. The 'authentic' Socrates remains eternally elusive but, for our purposes, this matters less than how his intellectual descendants, namely the Stoics, understood him.

5 This is known as the "strong" version of the claim that virtue is knowledge. It is contrasted with a "weak" (non-Socratic) version where the maxim means a given act can only be called virtuous or vicious if the performing agent first has knowledge of what is right and wrong. See Houlgate, "Virtue Is Knowledge," 142–53.

6 Santas, "The Socratic Paradoxes," 147–64.

debated what it might be. One interpretation is that Socrates was using a particular definition of 'knowledge'. In this view, the 'knowledge of virtue' is less about the passive accumulation of facts or information and more akin to a transformative mastery of a skill or technique. This kind of knowledge would imply an internalized understanding so profound it inevitably shapes one's actions, making deliberate wrongdoing impossible.[7]

To elaborate, consider that human beings are not fixed objects; we are constantly changing due to physical, biological, and environmental processes. The acquisition of knowledge is among the most profound forms of personal change we experience. To learn even the most trivial fact is to be altered in a lasting way. A perfect assimilation of knowledge, then, must result in a perfect transformation of whatever form a specific brand of knowledge compels. In the case of moral knowledge—virtue—this implies any remaining capacity for wrongdoing constitutes an incomplete assimilation of the knowledge.

Another interpretation involves what is called an *egoistic theory of motivation*.[8] This is the assumption one is always attracted to what one thinks is good, that is, what is in their own interest.[9] In effect, a human always behaves *egoistically*, or selfishly, and virtue is developed by acquiring the *knowledge* it is against one's interests to do wrong. In this view, the knowing evildoer may recognize what they do is wrong, but they would have to be confused about where their interests actually lie. Because no one desires what is bad for them, the evildoer would be compelled to do right if only they really understood that virtue is in their interest.[10] Whether Socrates genuinely held this view remains a matter of debate, but it is undeniably reflected in Stoic thought.

As a general philosophical concept, the belief all behaviors, including altruistic behaviors, are motivated by self-interest is called *psychological egoism*. The extreme version of this view, where all human behaviors are ultimately and unequivocally selfish, has been rejected by nearly all modern philosophers.[11] However, in the Stoic view, the human relationship to 'the good', however it is perceived, is characterized by an inexorable attraction that cannot be resisted. For example, Epictetus describes 'the perceived good'—anything one believes is to their benefit—as a kind of currency that cannot be turned away.[12] This attraction is a function of nature observable in all living things, such as plants are attracted to light and animals are attracted to food and mates.[13] We can call it 'Stoic egoism' and it emerges as an important underlying principle within the Stoics' wider theory of virtue.

---

7 Houlgate, "Virtue Is Knowledge," 146–48.
8 Ibid., 145.
9 Shaver, "Egoism," *The Stanford Encyclopedia of Philosophy* (Spring 2023).
10 Santas, "The Socratic Paradoxes," 150–57.
11 Singer, *The Expanding Circle*, 126–27.
12 Epictetus, *Discourses* 3.3.3–4, 2.22.15–19.
13 See DL 7.85–6.

This view has important implications for how we should interpret the actions of others. Those who do evil, or who otherwise do things that anger, irritate, or frighten us, do so out of ignorance. Our emotional reactions to their behaviors are our responsibility, especially since those behaviors can do us no real harm. The unwise individuals who perform them are not to be despised or even pitied, they are to be taught or otherwise led to truth through example.[14]

Closely related to this equivalence of virtue with knowledge is another important Socratic contribution. Although, true to form, he never directly states this, Socrates demonstrates through various arguments that virtue is indivisible. This does not mean Socrates denies the existence of 'discrete' virtues like courage or discipline, but rather that he views them as context-dependent expressions of the same underlying knowledge.[15] For him—and certainly for the Stoics after him—courage, discipline, and other desirable qualities are all facets of a broader concept, which I will call virtue *proper* to distinguish it from *discrete* virtues like courage. Going forward, I will reserve the terms 'virtue proper' and 'discrete virtues' for instances where the context may not clearly differentiate between the overarching concept of virtue and discrete virtues.

Consistent with the prevailing wisdom of their time, the Stoics identify four specific qualities as the cardinal or primary virtues, from which all other positive traits are derived: prudence, courage, moderation, and justice.[16] While their definitions are clear enough on the surface, it is worth acknowledging translations from ancient Greek are imperfect and sometimes inconsistent in the scholarship. For example, the virtue *phronesis* is translated here as "prudence," though some sources render it as wisdom or the more precise 'practical wisdom' to distinguish it from mere factual knowledge or intellectual capacity.[17]

Similarly, *sōphrosýnē* is translated here as "moderation," though it is also often called "temperance." In practice, however, neither term fully conveys the empowering essence of *sōphrosýnē*, which emphasizes personal character and self-discipline. By contrast, the common use of "temperance" can imply a stuffy and puritanical

---

14 Epictetus, *Discourses* 1.18.3–4, 2.21.1–25; *Handbook* 46; Marcus Aurelius, *Meditations* 6.27, 7.22.
15 While Socrates never directly asserts virtue is indivisible, he illustrates it through various discussions, each addressing the concept from a unique angle. For instance, in *Protagoras*, he implies discrete virtues such as courage, justice, and moderation share a common opposite—folly—suggesting these are all expressions of the same principle. Similarly, in *Meno*, he questions whether virtues can be divided into distinct parts, likening such division to breaking a useful object into fragments, thereby reducing its functionality. In *Euthydemus*, he argues that so-called good things, such as health or wealth, can become harmful if misused, indicating it is the knowledge of how to use them properly that constitutes true goodness. See Plato, *Protagoras* 329b–333b; *Meno* 77a; *Euthydemus* 278e–281e.
16 I have adopted Long and Sedley's preferred translations for *phronesis, andreía, sōphrosýnē,* and *dikaiosýnē*, however common alternatives are acknowledged in the following paragraphs. See Long and Sedley, *The Hellenistic Philosophers*, 1: 377–86.
17 E.g., Pamela Mensch, whose translation of Diogenes Laertius is used throughout this text.

disposition, as seen in the 'Temperance movement' of the American Prohibition era, while 'moderation' may connote ambivalence or lack of conviction. The translations of *andreía* as "courage" and *dikaiosýnē* as "justice" are less contentious, though 'just-ness' would capture the latter's meaning more precisely. These cardinal virtues are not uniquely Stoic; rather, they represent an inherited framework, most clearly attributable to Plato, whose influence shaped numerous philosophical traditions.

The cardinal virtues work like the primary colors of red, blue, and yellow, providing base ingredients to the countless shades and hues of excellence that may comprise a specific individual's good character. An infinite number of derivative qualities—such as honesty, endurance, or industriousness—contain elements of the cardinal virtues. What sets the cardinal virtues apart is that they cannot be reduced further.

Table 1. A Stoic Taxonomy of Virtues[18]

Cardinal Virtue:	*Prudence*	*Moderation*	*Courage*	*Justice*
Derived Virtues:	Good Sense	Good Discipline	Endurance	Piety
	Good Calculation	Seemliness	Confidence	Honesty
	Quick-Wittedness	Sense of Honor	High-Mindedness	Equity
	Discretion	Self-Control	Cheerfulness	Fair-Dealing
	Resourcefulness		Industriousness	

Like Socrates, the Stoics recognize all virtues as facets of a single concept. But while Socrates identifies this concept as *epistêmê*, or scientific knowledge, the Stoics identify it as *phronesis*—practical wisdom, or prudence. Specifically, Stoics say courage is prudence applied to what should be endured, moderation is prudence in what is chosen, and justice is prudence in what is to be distributed to others.[19] Intriguingly, Stoics also reserve a "special perspective" for the virtue of moderation, which is "the theory of what falls under the other virtues" and is the antithesis of ignorance.[20] Moderation, then, captures the regulatory effect where one virtue checks and stabilizes the others.

To put this stabilizing effect of moderation in context, it would be helpful to compare it to an alternative view, such as the concept of the 'philosopher's mean'. Proposed by Aristotle, whose Lyceum rivaled the Stoics as a philosophical school, the philosopher's mean suggests virtue lies in a middle ground, specifically between

---

18 Stobaeus 2.59,4–60,2; 60,9–24 (SVF 3.262, 264, part) = LS 61H; Jedan, Stoic Virtues, 158–9, 163. Note this table merges translations: specifically, Long and Sedley translate the discrete virtue *aidēmosyne* as "modesty," while Jedan translates it as "sense of honor." This merging is intended to distinguish *aidēmosyne* from the rational emotion *aidōs*, which is also sometimes translated as "modesty." *Aidōs* is discussed at the end of this chapter and plays an important role in the overall argument of this book.
19 Plutarch, *On Moral Virtue* 440E–441D = LS 61B; *On Stoic Self-contradictions* 1034C–E = LS 61C.
20 Stobaeus, 2.63,6–24 (SVF 3.280, part) = LS 61D; 2.68,18–23 (SVF 3.663) = LS 41I.

extremes of excess and deficiency. For example, Aristotle would argue courage is the mean between the excess of recklessness and the deficiency that is cowardice.[21] The Stoics, however, would see it differently: one can never have an excess of prudence. Recklessness is a form of imprudence, and since courage is prudence applied to what should be endured, an excess of courage is not possible. Whatever we may call recklessness, it is not courage.

Interestingly, the later Stoics do not speak much about the cardinal virtues. One plausible explanation for this reluctance is that cardinal virtues are not a uniquely Stoic concept. Epictetus, for instance, appears to intentionally avoid referencing the cardinal virtues as a combined set.[22] Instead, he emphasizes that a virtuous person is free, trustworthy, and self-respecting—qualities that carry layered meanings, which later chapters will explore in greater detail.[23] These qualities are the practical outcomes of a holistic-virtue concept, each worthy of examination as distinct effects, though Stoics never explicitly frame them as virtues.

The Problem of Progress

From the idea all virtues are expressions of prudence, another perplexing tenet of Stoicism follows—virtue does not admit of degrees. This principle applies both vertically and horizontally; vertically, for a virtue to be possessed, it must be possessed in its entirety without qualification, as anything less would entail some degree of imprudence. Thus, there is "nothing in between virtue and vice."[24] Horizontally, the possession of any one particular virtue necessarily entails the possession of all virtues, "whoever has one has all."[25] Thus, virtue takes on a binary status; one cannot be somewhat virtuous any more than one can be somewhat absent, pregnant, married, or deceased:

> Therefore the power and the greatness of virtue cannot rise to greater heights, because increase is denied to that which is superlatively great. You will find nothing straighter than the straight, nothing truer than the truth, and nothing more temperate than that which is temperate. Every virtue is limitless; for limits depend upon definite measurements. Constancy cannot advance further, any more than fidelity, or truthfulness, or loyalty. What can be added to that which is perfect? Nothing otherwise that was not perfect to which something has been added. Nor can anything be added to virtue, either, for if anything can be added thereto, it must have contained a defect.[26]

---

21 Aristotle, *Nicomachean Ethics* 2.6–7.
22 Epictetus does discuss each of the cardinal virtues individually; e.g., prudence in *Discourses* 1.20.6; courage in *Discourses* 1.6.28, 1.6.43, and 4.1.109; moderation in *Discourses* 3.1.8 and 4.9.17; and justice in *Discourses* 2.7.5, 2.22.30, and 3.1.8.
23 Kamtekar, "ΑΙΔΩΣ in Epictetus," 136; Bonhöffer, *The Ethics of the Stoic Epictetus*, trans. Stephens, 30–2.
24 DL 7.127.
25 DL 7.90, 7.101; Stobaeus 2.63,6–24 (SVF 3.280, part) = LS 61D.
26 Seneca, *Letters* 66.9.

From the tenet that virtue must be possessed fully or not at all, the concept of the Stoic sage naturally follows. If virtue is moral perfection and cannot exist in degrees, then a sage is what we would call someone who has actually achieved a state of virtue. This is not someone who struggles with indecision or anxiety or fear, or who otherwise must deal with everyday human flaws. Rather, it is a person who has attained complete and unassailable wisdom, making them a transcendent and godlike ideal. In this way, the sage represents a logical conclusion of the Stoic belief that virtue is indivisible and absolute.

This all-or-nothing binary conception of virtue is viewed by both critics and admirers of the Stoics to be paradoxical, as it does not clearly accommodate a transition from mere moral progress into sagacity. The problem is famously illustrated in an analogy of a drowning man, wherein the progress of an imperfect individual is compared to someone swimming to the surface from deep underwater. The drowning man's condition is equally perilous to those deeper than him until the exact moment he breaks the surface.[27] Likewise, while all sages are equally perfect, all non-sages are equally imperfect, such that vice is never reduced along the path to virtue. The transition from progress to sagacity, then, must be instantaneous and, some argue, imperceptible to the new sage.[28]

Even if this is the Stoics' doctrinal position on virtue and sagacity, it is evident it was controversial from the outset. As much as we discuss the topic indirectly, we must bluntly ask whether the Stoics truly considered sagacity attainable. It seems the early Stoics did, even if they considered true sages "rarer than the phoenix."[29] For the middle and late Stoics, however, the issue is more ambiguous and it might matter which Stoic you ask. For example, the middle Stoic Panaetius seems to have denied the existence of sages.[30] Seneca speculates a sage might appear once every 500 years and, in his advice, he frequently acknowledges human limitations.[31] Epictetus addresses the issue pragmatically: "Is it possible thenceforth to be entirely free from fault? No, that is beyond us, but this at least is possible: to strive without cease to avoid committing any fault."[32]

Thankfully, no essential Stoic arguments depend upon the historical existence of sages. Applying a bit of common sense, we can conclude, for all of its usefulness as an instructive concept, sagacity exists only in theory. We might also infer the late Stoics thought along these lines as well. Epictetus, for example, clearly recognizes his students would be frustrated by entreaties to pursue the unachievable and he

---

27 Plutarch, *On Common Conceptions* 1063A–B (SVF 3.539, part) = LS 61T; Cicero, *On Ends* 4.48.
28 Plutarch, *On Common Conceptions* 1062B = LS 61U.
29 Alexander, *On Fate* 199.14–22 (SVF 3.658, part) = LS 61N; cf. Sextus Empiricus, *Against the Professors* 9.133–6 = LS 54D.
30 Copleston, *Greece and Rome*, 421.
31 Seneca, *Letters* 42.1.
32 Epictetus, *Discourses* 4.12.19.

confronts the issue directly. Using himself as an example, he reasons an irreparably flawed agent should still strive endlessly to improve:

> And then, because I'm not naturally gifted, shall I therefore abandon all effort to do my best? Heaven forbid. Epictetus won't be better than Socrates; but even if I'm not too bad, that is good enough for me. For I won't ever be a Milo either, and yet I don't neglect my body; nor a Croesus, and I don't neglect my property; nor in general do I cease to make any effort in any regard whatever merely because I despair of achieving perfection.[33]

Whatever the endeavor, the fact a higher level of achievement will always be possible is still no reason to abandon the effort. Epictetus' use of "neglect" here is telling—he views it as a responsibility to 'strive without cease', regardless of the imperfect outcome. Yet, it remains unclear how we can claim this striving accomplishes anything if we must deny virtue increases or vice decreases through our efforts. How is it possible to move from black to white in a world that allows no room for gray?

Although this 'problem of progress' has provided fodder for the Stoics' adversaries since Zeno first walked the painted porch, it is not as complicated as it might appear. It is really just a language problem masquerading as a conceptual problem. After defining virtue as a state of perfection, Stoics struggle to describe any state of progress along the path to virtue. This is not the same thing as saying progress does not or cannot occur. To illustrate, let us imagine progress represented as a mathematical asymptote (Figure 3).

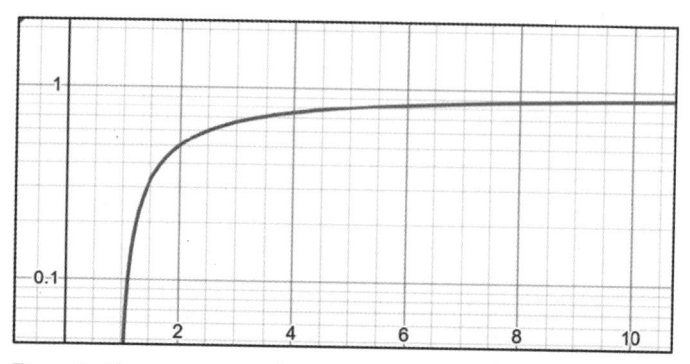

Figure 3. The asymptote $y = (x - 1)/x$, or what moral progress might look like as a calculus problem.

---

33 Ibid. 1.2.35. "Milo" refers to a legendary athlete, and "Croesus" refers to a man of great wealth. What Epictetus means by "I don't neglect my body" is an intriguing question. A minor debate in the discourse of popular Stoicism concerns the question of physical fitness as a Stoic value. In my view, if a Stoic sage existed today, they would almost certainly exercise frequently and follow a restrictive diet, reflecting prudence in a world of caloric excess. As a model of human perfection, they would be disciplined and self-respecting, never slothful nor gluttonous. At the same time, they wouldn't be vain, judgmental, or concerned with arbitrary or cosmetic standards. As always, what constitutes a properly 'Stoic' value should be measured against the virtues of prudence, courage, moderation, and justice. See additional discussions on Stoic *askēsis* near the end of Chapter 3.

On this graph, the line plotted shows that for any value of x there is a corresponding y value. As x approaches infinity, y approaches 1 by ever-smaller increments, never quite reaching it. This graphically illustrates the concept of a diminishing return in an improvement effort, where early efforts yield significant improvements, or what weightlifters call beginner gains. However, as effort continues, the returns gradually decrease, making further improvements increasingly difficult to achieve. This phenomenon can be observed in nearly any progressive effort, be it physical fitness, academic study, or the honing of skill. If we say the value of 1 represents perfection, then as effort approaches infinity, performance approaches perfection.

In this framing, if the value of 1 represents perfection, then on a plot of *moral progress* it corresponds to virtue. It would not make sense, therefore, to suggest virtue itself increases along the path of moral progress—just as it would not make sense to say 1 increases as x increases. One is not a variable; it is a fixed point, representing a binary quality either attained or not. Likewise, virtue—as moral perfection—is not a variable. One either attains it, or one does not, but this says nothing about whether moral progress, as depicted through changes in the value of y, is possible.

Consider a more concrete example. If an aircrew reduces their response time to scramble a bomber from seven minutes to six minutes, we can objectively say their progress toward perfection has improved, even though we cannot say they are perfect. The fact we cannot call them a more-perfect aircrew has nothing to do with their improvement, or lack thereof, and everything to do with our choice of words and the definition of 'perfect'. Likewise, our inability to say vice is reduced on the path to sagacity is purely a consequence of our defining virtue as moral perfection, and vice as the absence of perfection.

To answer the question of how moral progress is possible, Epictetus cuts directly to the results:

> So where is progress to be found? If any of you turns away from external things to concentrate his efforts on his own power of choice, to cultivate it and perfect it, so as to bring it into harmony with nature, raising it up and rendering it free, unhindered, unobstructed, trustworthy, and self-respecting; and if he has come to understand that whoever longs for things that are not within his power, or seeks to avoid them, can neither be trustworthy nor free, but must necessarily be subject to change, and be tossed in all directions along with those things, and is inevitably placing himself under the domination of other people, namely, those who can secure or prevent such things; and if, finally, when he gets up in the morning, he holds in mind what he has learned and keeps true to it, if he bathes as a trustworthy person, and eats as a self-respecting person, putting his guiding principles into action in relation to anything that he has to deal with, just as a runner does in the practice of running, or a voice trainer in the training of voices—this, then, is the person who is truly making progress; this is the person who hasn't travelled in vain![34]

---

34 Ibid. 1.4.18.

Critics, both ancient and modern, have cited Stoicism's unattainable perfectionist standard as a serious flaw in its viability as a livable philosophy. For example, an ancient critic likens the Stoics' endless striving to the absurdity of an archer who "does everything in his power not for the purpose of hitting the mark, but for the purpose of doing everything in his power."[35] His critique might be persuasive if moral progress—like an archer futilely aiming at nothing—produced no improvement in the individual, revealed no wisdom, eliminated no falsehoods, inspired no courage, reinforced no discipline, or demanded no justice in actions toward others. However, moral progress specifically consists of and compels these very things, which are themselves virtuous and good. While a person may not achieve virtue in the perfectionist sense, their thoughts and behaviors progressively align more closely with a virtuous disposition, benefiting both the individual and all who know them.

Right and Appropriate Actions

Our difficulties with a perfectionist definition of virtue do not end with the problem of progress. If we are to define virtue as moral perfection, then we will struggle to find anything we can unequivocally call virtuous. If we concede sages only exist in theory, then we may find nothing at all that meets this standard. On the other hand, if we remain rigidly committed to Stoic theory in our use of language, then we will be left without a descriptor for real thoughts or behaviors that meet a conventional standard of virtuousness. In such a case we will inevitably find ourselves reaching awkwardly for alternatives just to say what we mean.

Consider how we might describe the way a sentry stands his watch. If we say the sentry stands his watch virtuously then, by a strict interpretation, we must mean he performs the duty perfectly. But this still requires clarification—we could simply mean the act of standing watch is perfect in the technical sense, such that he remains perfectly alert, formally reports any irregularities, and executes all protocols with precision. In the more likely case that we refer to virtue in the moral sense, we would mean the sentry has a virtuous disposition when standing his watch—that is, he does so with perfectly pure motives, fully committed to his duty, and perfectly contented in fulfilling his role. In other words, we would mean the sentry is a sage.

The corollary is that if the sentry is not a sage, then we cannot say his watchstanding is virtuous, at least not in the strict moral sense as the Stoics use it. This is true even if he resists the temptation to relax his vigilance or let his mind wander to more pleasant activities, such as sleeping or playing games. The very existence of such impulses, even if not acted upon, would imply something short of a perfectly virtuous

---

35 Plutarch, *On Common Conceptions* 1071C = LS 64C.

disposition. The same rule applies to any action, no matter how conventionally virtuous it may seem. In effect, it precludes us from calling any action properly 'virtuous' when it is performed by a living human, no matter how well the action itself aligns with nature.

Once again, we are confounded by the limits of our language. It would be helpful if we had separate and distinct terms for actions that are virtuous in the strict sense, which is to say these actions are performed by a sage, and actions that are virtuous in the conventional sense, which is to say performing them aligns with virtue, or nature. It so happens the Stoics did use such separate and distinct terms. *Katorthōma*, or what are most commonly translated as "right actions," are actions that are virtuous in the sense they originate from a perfectly virtuous disposition.[36] *Kathēkonta*, normally translated as "appropriate actions," are actions that are morally correct (as observed from outside) despite originating from an imperfect disposition, or, in other words, actions performed by a non-sage that nonetheless align with nature.

The importance of a distinction between right actions and appropriate actions is not immediately apparent. All but the most obscure and theoretical discussions can proceed intelligently without acknowledging it. In some key explanations, though, a distinction is essential, as will become apparent later on. Notably, there are no adverbial translations for *katorthōma* and *kathēkonta* which enjoy widespread use. Even in academic literature relating to Stoicism, 'virtuous' and 'virtuously' are sometimes used in ways that only meet a conventional standard, as in saying a non-sage can do a virtuous thing or do a thing virtuously. Without this allowance, discussion of moral progress can become tedious to the point of impossibility. I suggest, then, that the use of 'virtuous' to describe mere appropriate actions can be acceptable and even preferred to awkward linguistic workarounds, so long as we recognize it does not necessarily imply the perfection of a sage.

An essential takeaway here is that, from an external viewpoint, right actions and appropriate actions appear indistinguishable; they might be called 'observationally identical'. The distinction lies solely in the moral disposition of the actor. This perspective illuminates the evolution from *prokoptôn*—a "progressor"—to a sage; although a progressor might perform all the appropriate actions, they do not attain the sage's happiness until these actions become habitual and consistent, reflecting an internal peace and confidence in their rightness. Chrysippus describes this as the actions gaining "their own particular fixity."[37] I will examine right and appropriate actions in much more detail in Chapter 4.

---

36 Stobaeus 2.85,13–86,4 (SVF 3.494) = LS 59B. We could eliminate some confusion by rendering *katorthōma* as "perfect" or "sagacious" actions, but to align this project with current literature we will stick with "right actions."
37 Ibid. 5.906,18–907,5 (SVF 3.510) = LS 59I.

Necessity and Sufficiency

Following the Cynics' interpretation of Socrates, Stoics hold that virtue is both necessary and sufficient for happiness. Like the idea virtue is indivisible, these conclusions are inferred from various observations and arguments, never directly articulated by Socrates himself.[38] It was by making sense of these ideas—and refining them into defensible claims—that Socrates' successors developed their core positions.

The claim that virtue can deliver happiness even in the absence of basic necessities is truly extraordinary. It implies a sufficiently wise person—a sage—could remain content even while imprisoned, tortured, or facing execution. This apparently fantastical assertion has two sides that must be understood together. On one side is the idea that virtue, once attained, is so fulfilling it overrides all other desires, including the natural inclination to avoid pain or discomfort.[39] However, this view is insufficient on its own, as it attributes all satisfaction to virtue's capacity to provide fulfillment, without considering the personal transformation involved in acquiring moral knowledge. While virtue is indeed good and fulfilling, the reason it brings contentment is not merely because it satiates desires, but because moral knowledge itself is the conquering of desire. This is the other side of the argument. As Seneca writes:

> Does virtue alone suffice to make you happy? Why, of course, consummate and God-like virtue such as this not only suffices, but more than suffices: for when a man is placed beyond the reach of any desire, what can he possibly lack? If all that he needs is concentrated in himself, how can he require anything from without?[40]

As we explore virtue's purported sufficiency for happiness, it may be worth refining our understanding of happiness itself. The original Greek term we clumsily translate as "happiness" is *eudaimonia*. More precise translations might include "flourishing," "well-being," or "the good life." The word 'happiness' fails to fully capture the depth of *eudaimonia*, which refers not merely to emotional satisfaction but to a life lived in accordance with virtue and reason. While happiness in conventional usage can refer to fleeting emotional states—failing to exclude, for example, the euphoria of a drug user or the amusement of a torturer—*eudaimonia* represents a deeper, more enduring sense of fulfillment. It encompasses an entire way of life characterized by virtuous actions, rational thought, and harmony within oneself and with the

---

38 For example, in Plato's *Gorgias*, Socrates equates living well with living honorably or justly; in *Crito*, he argues justice is essential for the health of the soul; and in *Apology*, he insists no harm can come to a truly good person. See Plato, *Gorgias* 48b; *Crito* 47d–e; *Apology* 28b, 28d, 30c, 36c, 41c–d.
39 DL 7.94.
40 Seneca, *On the Happy Life* 16.3.

community. *Eudaimonia* is not just about feeling good, it is about living well in a truly holistic sense.[41]

Many Hellenistic schools—Stoics, Cynics, Aristotelians, and others—hold the pursuit of *eudaimonia* to be the natural goal of human activity, though each school disagrees on the specifics of how it should be achieved. Epicureans, for example, believe *eudaimonia* can be attained through the pursuit of pleasure. Aristotelians, like the Stoics, hold that *eudaimonia* results from virtue but, unlike the Stoics, Aristotelians believe certain external goods—such as food, shelter, and good health—are prerequisites for achieving it. The Stoics, on the other hand, stubbornly insist *eudaimonia* is an internal matter, determined solely by the individual's moral character. For the Stoics, it is essential that *eudaimonia* cannot be affected by anything external; individuals are entirely responsible for their own well-being. External circumstances can affect how easy or hard it is to *feel* happy, but one whose happiness depends on something external is living in a precarious illusion.

This brings us to the necessity of virtue: if no external agent can deprive someone of *eudaimonia*, no external agent can provide it either. The idea is straightforward—there is no substitute for virtue as the source of happiness, understood holistically as we have defined it. As Seneca aptly stated, "Virtue is the only good; at any rate there is no good without virtue."[42] No amount of wealth, prestige, power, companionship, or achievement can deliver happiness—*eudaimonia*—on its own.

This claim is not nearly as radical as virtue's sufficiency. It echoes a common-sense belief found in many of the world's religions and moral philosophies, which recognize worldly pleasures as fleeting and ultimately unsatisfying. The uniquely Stoic nuance to this idea lies in their unwavering commitment to moral perfectionism. Once again, this depends on how we define our terms. If vice is understood as the absence of virtue, then it necessarily entails ignorance, envy, vanity, or other forms of inner turmoil. Insofar as any worldly aim is achieved without virtue, it must be accompanied by vice and the misery that follows.

Indifferents

By saying virtue is both necessary and sufficient for happiness, the Stoics effectively deny the importance of any worldly concern. Specifically, anything that is not 'up to us' is decided from outside of the self and therefore its outcome or realization must depend on something other than our own virtue. The Stoics call these matters *indifferents* (sometimes *externals*) and maintain that the only proper attitude toward

---

41 Martha Nussbaum considers "happiness" a misleading translation of *eudaimonia*, clarifying that "Not only virtuous actions but also mutual relations of civic or personal love and friendship, in which the object is loved and benefited for his or her own sake, can qualify as constituent parts of a person's *eudaimonia*." Nussbaum, *Upheavals of Thought*, 32.
42 Seneca, *Letters* 71.32.

them is emotional indifference. These are not good or bad things, but merely *things* that can be used to good or bad ends. These include properties like innate talents or disabilities, wealth or poverty, health or sickness, fame or ignominy, and the like.[43] Purely trivial matters, like the number of hairs on one's head, are also considered indifferents, as are external events, like weather or war.[44]

The sufficiency of virtue for *eudaimonia* thus serves as a robust affirmation of moral autonomy, shielding the dignified individual against forces of corruption and extortion. In comparison to true goods, for instance, the trappings of wealth and station amount to mere trinkets and playthings, and ridiculous pursuits as such. As Epictetus derides, "They're scattering nuts and figs. The children scramble to pick them up and fight among themselves; but men don't do so."[45] For one equipped with moral knowledge, an extortionist would have nothing to offer or to withhold.

Unmodified by the arguments that follow, what I have described above essentially aligns with the teachings of the Cynics, intellectual predecessors to Stoics. Extreme in their rejection of indifferents, the Cynics deliberately impoverished themselves to focus on the pursuit of virtue. Their philosophy was centered on the belief that anything external to virtue, including wealth, comfort, and social status, held no inherent worth. This radical stance led them to dismiss both material goods and social conventions as irrelevant distractions to a good life.

Where the first Stoic, Zeno, broke from his Cynic mentors was by allowing for a distinction between some indifferents as either preferred or dispreferred.[46] According to Zeno, although indifferents are not goods and should not be the object of desire, a fit and mature Stoic can and should still prefer one indifferent (e.g., health) over its alternative (e.g., sickness), as would seem to agree with nature, when given the choice. As a function of said nature, Stoics are not merely permitted but are required to pursue preferred indifferents and avoid dispreferred ones, as long as their actions remain consistent with virtuous motives.

A key distinction between a good and a preferred indifferent is that an indifferent can be used in either positive or negative ways. Take wealth, for example. Wealth is something we might naturally regard as a good—unless, of course, it belongs to a wicked criminal who uses it to bribe politicians and consolidate power. The same test could be applied to health, as both "wealth and health can be put to both good use and bad; therefore wealth and health are not goods."[47] In contrast, moral knowledge is something that could never be misused for evil. If a criminal were to acquire moral knowledge, as we discussed earlier, they would necessarily come to

---

43 Stobaeus 2.79,18–90,13; 18–20,1 = LS 58C.
44 DL 7.104.
45 Epictetus, *Discourses* 4.7.21–22.
46 These are the most common translations of the original *proêgmena* and *apoproêgmena*, however, these may also be translated as "promoted" and "demoted," or "advanced" and "relegated" respectively.
47 DL 7.103.

recognize benevolence and lawful behavior as being within their own interest and would be *egoistically* compelled to act accordingly. Moral knowledge is inherently good, while health and wealth are merely preferred indifferents.

By this standard, it would seem almost all concerns and decisions are swept into the bin of indifferents, leaving very little conceptual space for virtue. The catch is that virtue has a role to play in the choices we make when selecting indifferents. Even though the indifferents are themselves devoid of moral valence—that is, a positive or negative quality—virtue may yet compel preference for one indifferent over another. For example, all else being equal, it would almost always be imprudent, and therefore vicious, to choose sickness over health, or poverty over wealth. Virtue might then weigh upon conflicts between preferred indifferents; for example, although academic knowledge and personal companionship are both normally preferred indifferents, a wise and disciplined student may forgo companionship to stay home and study.

What we see, then, is that, in the constant process of selection, indifferents provide the raw material for virtue to work upon, much like a potter shapes clay. But does this mean we are always compelled to follow conventional wisdom when choosing between indifferents? Must we always choose the high-paying job over the lower-paying one, or the safe and comfortable path over the dangerous one? Can we never opt for quiet solitude over the company of friends and family?

Of course not. The Stoics neither say nor imply such things. On the contrary, Stoics repeatedly emphasize that even the most naturally preferred indifferents—even the preservation of one's own life—can become dispreferred under certain circumstances.[48] The capacity to navigate such situations systematically and with virtue must be a defining feature of a warrior philosophy. Therefore, to understand how reason directs the selection process amid such complexities, it is necessary to examine what makes one indifferent preferable to another.

The Problem of Value

Much like the concept of virtue as an all-or-nothing proposition, the Stoics' allowance for preference among indifferents is controversial. For example, if we show preference for one indifferent over another, then there must be something 'about' that indifferent making it choice-worthy, no matter how emphatically we insist it is not a genuine 'good'. 'Preferred' and 'good' might be a distinction without a real difference. So, how do the Stoics resolve this apparent contradiction?

This question, which we will call the 'problem of value', has sparked debate among Stoics since the very beginning, just like the problem of progress. Unfortunately, the surviving fragments of Stoic writings do not offer a clear or easily satisfying doctrinal answer to these critiques. Nevertheless, scholars tend to converge around

---

48 DL 7.109.

several common interpretations regarding the relationship between indifferents and value. Some of these views are more convincing than others, while a few are likely based on misunderstandings. To distinguish between them, and to keep this foray into theory as concise as possible, I will compare the most common interpretations.

The first interpretation I shall consider is the view preferred indifferents are valued not because they are good, but because they can support or facilitate the good, i.e., virtue. For example, it must be easier to think and act virtuously when one's basic needs are met, as the correlation between crime and poverty would seem to attest. A healthy billionaire could surely deliver more positive outcomes than a sickly and destitute peasant. It would seem, then, that a Stoic should select health over sickness and wealth over poverty to ensure the best possible preconditions to perform virtuous actions. Framed this way, preferred indifferents would be *instrumental* to virtue.

This instrumental interpretation, then, sees preferred indifferents as a means to an end, with virtue being the end. Although this is intuitive, it is not compatible with the Stoics' greater theory of virtue. To explain, let us compare two imaginary individuals: a wealthy philanthropist who builds charity hospitals and a laborer who supports a family. We might want to say the philanthropist has more opportunity for virtue than the laborer, but virtue does not require a specific opportunity. It cannot be a luxury reserved for the well-off. What differs between the philanthropist and the laborer are the instantaneous choices before them, which manifest as different sets of appropriate acts.

The instrumental interpretation misrepresents Stoic virtue theory in that it conflates virtue with the so-called positive outcomes of appropriate acts.[49] The wealthy and powerful may have more choices before them than others, some of which will be appropriate acts and some of which may alter the world in ways most would prefer, but these may not be the same. Furthermore, their choices will also include more options to act wrongly. A philanthropist and a laborer will each lead an existence comprising moral decisions, wherein every juncture will offer a morally optimal path whether the alternatives number in the tens or in the thousands. Among crooked paths of any number, there can be "nothing straighter than the straight," as Seneca puts it.[50] Virtuous individuals will simply choose appropriate acts, within their own unique situations. Our capacity for choice is *always* within our power; therefore, virtue can have no external means.

An instrumental view of indifferents can actually be harmful in that it provides an avenue to talk ourselves into bad choices. For example, we may be tempted to compete dishonestly for promotion under the rationale that, if successful, we

---

49 Note that this instrumental reading has been supported by important modern scholars such as Pierre Hadot. See Hadot, *The Inner Citadel*, 215. Cf. Brennan, *The Stoic Life*, 182–202, for criticism of this view.
50 Seneca, *Letters* 66.9.

would later make better, more morally conscious decisions than our competitors. Wicked people with wealth and power do this all the time, excusing their injustices as service to a so-called greater good. Note I am not denying the existence of real moral conflicts, as the life of a moral practitioner is filled with them. What I am saying is by understanding that virtue can have no external means, we can be better prepared to avoid this particular moral trap.

Another intuitive but flawed interpretation treats preferred indifferents as a kind of *lesser good*, possessing a tiny measure of goodness desirable in its own right yet negligible in comparison to virtue. In this view, it's fine and normal to think of preferred indifferents as if they are good, as long as virtue is never compromised in their pursuit. This appears to be a practical way to understand it, and it seems to be what Cicero is getting at here:

> For as the light of a candle is obscured and put out by the light of the sun; and as a drop of brine is lost in the magnitude of the Aegean sea; or an addition of a penny amid the riches of Croesus; or as one step is of no account in a march from here to India; so, if that is the chief good which the Stoics affirm is so, then, all the goods which depend on the body must inevitably be obscured and overwhelmed by, and come to nothing when placed by the side of the splendor and importance of virtue.[51]

However practical this lesser-good interpretation may seem, it simply doesn't jibe with the Stoics' uncompromising position on virtue and the good. It places indifferents, which can be misused for wrongdoing, on the same scale as virtue, which cannot. It also doesn't really address the matter of desire, which Stoics regard as irrational when applied to anything that isn't explicitly moral in nature. Thankfully, this reading wasn't widely promoted by classical commentators and is more accurately viewed as a misunderstanding that sometimes arises from simplified accounts of Stoicism. It is not quite what Cicero describes.

What Cicero attempts to explain is a nuanced definition of "value" (*axia*), which we can isolate as a third perspective—a *selective value* interpretation. In this view, the value possessed by preferred indifferents is simply a different thing than the value held by virtue. Even though health is an indifferent, and therefore it is not a 'good' or an 'end' that anyone should *desire*, a rational human would normally *select* it over the alternative of sickness if given a simple choice. If not value in the moral sense, health still possesses *something* making it choice-worthy, and that something is "selective value" (*axia eklektikê*). This selective value is not cumulative with the value of virtue; it is a different concept altogether:

> In truth, if to be wise be a desirable thing, and to be well be so too, then both together must be more desirable than wisdom by itself; but it does not follow, if each quality deserves to be esteemed, that therefore, the two taken together deserve to be esteemed more highly than wisdom does by itself. For we who consider good health worthy of any esteem, and yet do not

---

51 Cicero, *On Ends* 3.13.45.

rank it among the goods, think, at the same time, that the esteem to which it is entitled is by no means such as that it ought to be preferred to virtue.[52]

An important caveat to selective value is it only pertains to future-oriented impulses.[53] For example, all else being equal, it is usually prudent to select promotion in rank over career stasis. Promotion, in this case, would be said to have selective value. If already possessed, though, the higher rank is purely indifferent. When the act of selection occurred, any selective value attached to the new position became irrelevant, just as a future reduction in rank would be equally irrelevant. We may prefer what merits selection, but we must not become attached to any of it.

The selective value interpretation is similar to the others in that it supports the seeking of preferred indifferents, so long as their pursuit does not involve some compromise of virtue along the way. It differs by characterizing preferred indifferents as morally neutral assets possessing no 'goodness' but still possessing a distinct and separate quality of preferability. Early critics of Stoicism cried foul at this intrusion of invented terms. Specifically, critics from Plato's Academy, a competing school of ancient Athens, thought Stoics had painted themselves into a corner with absolutist claims and were attempting escape through word games, using preferred indifferents as "goods under another name."[54] Unfortunately, since we must rely on scraps and third-party accounts to discover what the early Stoics believed, we don't have a convincing, consolidated rebuttal from the Stoics themselves.

However, it is possible to infer an explanation. If we examine preferred indifferents alongside the Stoics' teleological theory of nature, it seems the selective value interpretation, as I have presented it above, is simply incomplete. The Stoics argue virtue compels the selection of certain indifferents over others, just as it compels life in harmony with nature. These activities must be one and the same. To correctly recognize that a given indifferent should be selected, then, is itself an appropriate action that comports with nature, which is to say it is an act with positive moral valence. This view, characterized as *epistemic* because it deals with the mechanics of human knowledge, is effectively a fourth interpretation. It shifts the focus from indifferents themselves to the rational assessment of their compatibility with the natural order.

The epistemic interpretation, then, describes the idea an indifferent becomes preferred not because of its intrinsic moral worth but because of the justified belief its selection aligns with nature's overarching design.[55] Similarly, an indifferent is deemed dispreferred if there are grounds to believe it is consistent with nature's

---

52 Ibid. 3.13.44.
53 Tad Brennan suggests translating it "planning value" for this reason. Brennan, "Stoic Moral Psychology," 263–4.
54 Klein, "Making Sense of Stoic Indifferents," 231; Long and Sedley, *The Hellenistic Philosophers*, 1: 406–10.
55 For a defense of this view, see Klein, "Making Sense of Stoic Indifferents," 231.

design to avoid it, and the discernment of this fact is what has moral valence. In either case, the selective value is not assigned to the indifferent, which can only be morally neutral, but to the *belief* it is choice-worthy, which resides in the deciding individual and is morally correct. Seneca exhibits this view when he asserts, "If I have the choice, I shall choose health and strength, but … the good involved will be my judgment regarding these things, and not the things themselves."[56]

A particular strength of the epistemic interpretation is it elegantly accommodates a case-by-case assessment of preference among indifferents by examining them within their specific contexts. Compared to other approaches, this seems more practical for everyday life, which we know to be a maelstrom of conflicting priorities and moral dilemmas. Even a typically preferred indifferent such as health or safety may need to be sacrificed when it becomes clear that nature—meaning virtue—requires something else of us in a specific situation. Epictetus, paraphrasing Chrysippus, highlights this very point, stressing the interconnectedness of fate, subordination to the whole, and the proper selection among indifferents:

> So Chrysippus did well to say, "As long as the consequences remain unclear to me, I always hold to what is best fitted to secure such things as are in accordance with nature; for God himself, in creating me, granted me the freedom to choose them. But if I in fact knew that illness had been decreed for me at this moment by destiny, I would welcome even that; for the foot, too, if it had understanding, would be eager to get spattered with mud."[57]

Of the four approaches to the problem of value—the *instrumental*, the *lesser good*, the *selective value*, and the *epistemic* interpretations respectively—which is most correct? We can definitively say the first two are incoherent. To say virtue can depend on something external to an individual, or that anything other than virtue can be a 'good' to any degree, is contrary to fundamental Stoic claims. On the other hand, the third interpretation, which establishes selective value as a special quality making something choice-worthy without making it a 'good', is well-supported in the evidence. Many ancient sources talk about selective value but fail to explain how it works. The *epistemic* interpretation, then, provides a more complete explanation consistent with other key Stoic claims. If we were able to ask Zeno or Chrysippus, they would probably agree with it. On the other hand, if we were to ask Epictetus, he would probably chastise us for wasting time with indulgent theorizing when we could be getting on with a virtuous life.

Selection as Self-Interest

Selective value, we have said, refers to the justified belief the choice of a particular indifferent aligns with nature's overarching design. While this helps explain how

---

56 Seneca, *Letters* 92.13.
57 Epictetus, *Discourses* 2.6.9.

something can be preferred without being considered a 'good', it does not address the deeper question: what is the source of this value and why is it assigned to one indifferent over another? Additionally, I have acknowledged that virtue plays a role in the selection of indifferents, but not yet fully articulated just how relevant this is to the greater Stoic theory of virtue. Cicero, for one, seems to regard it as central: "The final good is a life in which one applies knowledge of those things that happen by nature, selecting those in accordance with nature and rejecting those contrary to nature, that is—a life in agreement and consistent with nature."[58] As he describes it here, life in agreement with nature—the defining aim of the *eudaimon* life—does not just involve but fully consists of the rational selection of indifferents.

Not all indifferents possess selective value. Some are purely trivial, such as "having an odd or even number of hairs on one's head" or "extending or bending one's finger."[59] Indifferents of this kind "excite neither impulse nor aversion," meaning they impose neither an urge nor an obligation to act in any particular way toward them.[60] In contrast, what makes an indifferent preferred is that its selection aligns with nature, thereby creating an obligation to choose it which should be accompanied by a corresponding impulse.

Like many Stoic concepts, the theory of selective value originates in observations of animal behavior. It is the natural tendency of a living creature to be *egoistically* attracted to what it perceives as beneficial to its survival and well-being, while avoiding what it perceives as harmful. This is the most basic level of evaluating indifferents, driven by the force of nature through rational self-interest. At this level, we can say certain indifferents—such as food, shelter, or safety—are normally preferred because these things naturally seem to support the creature's inherent purpose or mission in life. Without any additional information, it is safe to assume they should be selected over their alternatives.

As with most things, the situation becomes more complicated when humans are involved. Unlike animals, whose choices are driven by instinct and survival, humans must navigate the complex moral, functional, and social frameworks that emerge as a function of reason, whose attendant obligations may come into conflict. As I have said, the Stoics recognize this complexity and are careful to specify that selective value is always conditional. No preferred indifferent is universally preferred; for example, if a healthy body might cause one to be pressed into military service for a wicked tyrant, a sage might rationally prefer to be sick.[61] Health is normally a preferred indifferent, but it may become dispreferred as "conditioned by the circumstances."[62]

---

58 Cicero, *On Ends* 3.31 = LS 64A.
59 DL 7.104.
60 Ibid.
61 Sextus Empiricus, *Against the Professors* 11.64–67 = LS 58F.
62 DL 7.109.

Earlier, I established we are not just morally permitted but morally obligated to select what accords with nature. However, considering the reference to animal self-interest, it seems the Stoics might be promoting a contradiction. What is to stop me from pillaging my neighbors to take their belongings? Would that not be my natural impulse? Indeed, we observe such ruthlessness in animals at least as much as we observe the prosocial behaviors of flocks and herds. Cicero, at least, offers a partial answer: "The Stoics define the highest good as 'being in conformity with nature', and what I think this means is that we must always align ourselves with virtue, and *choose all else which accords with nature* so long as it does not militate against virtue."[63]

We are to pursue our self-interested aims, but only within the bounds such pursuits must not conflict with virtue. With this tidy qualifier, I could declare the question settled and leave it at that. But something still feels unresolved: it seems we would behave as violent brigands and would be justified in doing so, if not for this nebulous concept of virtue holding our animal impulses in check. Yet is it not also virtue (specifically prudence) that compels us to select self-interested indifferents in the first place? Does virtue, then, contradict itself?

The missing piece in this discussion is the concept of a human's 'purpose' or 'mission'—the idea of 'being what one is supposed to be'—which is fundamentally different from the purpose of an animal. Observing that human beings are inherently and uniquely driven to form complex societies, and that *reason* is humanity's distinctive province within the animal kingdom, the Stoics conclude reason compels humans to act justly. Destructive animal instincts doubtless exist in all creatures but, uniquely in humans, there is also the impulse to outgrow them.

Zeno states "the goal is to live in harmony with nature, which means to live according to virtue; for nature leads us to virtue."[64] Thus, when the Stoics say we should live in accordance with nature, they are referring to humanity's natural drive to transcend primal urges and embrace reason, which manifests as virtues like prudence, courage, moderation, and justice. We are not meant to act like animals; we are meant to act like reasoning humans, *in spite of* our animal instincts, thereby bridging the gap between unreasoning animals and the intelligence of a rational universe. As Epictetus expands, "it is thus shameful for a human being to begin and end where the irrational animals do," leaving the higher faculties unrealized. Rather, the 'rational animal' should end "with contemplation, and understanding, and a way of life that is in harmony with nature."[65]

Rational selection among indifferents is not merely about choosing preferences but is a fundamental expression of life in accordance with nature. This process

---

63 Cicero, *On Duties* 3.13, emphasis mine.
64 DL 7.87.
65 Epictetus, *Discourses* 1.6.19–21; cf. *Discourses* 2.9.2–7; Seneca, *Letters* 76.9–10.

involves navigating the complexities of human social reality, where normal preferences and obligations may be overridden by the circumstances. These circumstances can include laws, social customs, and a growing recognition the interests of others are commensurate with one's own. Through alignment of personal choices with the universe's overarching design—understood through the assignment of selective value—human nature is fully realized as an integral element of universal nature.

Integrity and Honor

The complexity of moral problems compounds when we introduce the perspective of a warrior. What becomes of my so-called natural impulses toward harmony and global community when another human stands ready to kill me or my countrymen? If his death or suffering—what Stoics would identify as dispreferred indifferents—are justified or 'conditioned by the circumstances' that govern my actions, can I still assert I am acting within the bounds of a universal moral system?

Such questions would seem to suggest a separate moral system for warriors. For as long as the warrior has stood apart as a discrete social role, some warriors have believed they are held to a different, if not 'higher', moral standard than the broader societies they serve. A common rationale for this belief is discussed in military ethics as the "functional argument."[66] According to this perspective, the functions a warrior must perform are uniquely demanding of moral character in a way other professional tasks are not.[67] The logical conclusion of this perspective is that a liar or coward might make a fine merchant or farmer, for example, but they could not perform the duties of a warrior effectively.

However, Stoics would deny there are separate moral standards, much less separate systems of evaluation, regardless of one's social role. We are not yet ready to contend with the complexities of role ethics, collectivized morality, or justified warfare. For now, it will suffice to emphasize that Stoics would subject warriors to the same universal moral framework as everyone else. The actions of warriors, like those of any other individual, must withstand rational scrutiny against a single standard of right and wrong.

Contrary to the functional argument, a high-performing warrior might still betray their spouse or act dishonorably toward their neighbor. Furthermore, history provides countless examples of abhorrent individuals who were nonetheless effective in a warrior's role—a problem for the functional argument we might call the 'wicked warrior'. Because wicked warriors exist, it cannot be true that

---

66 See Ficarrotta, "Are Military Professionals," 59–75; French, *Code of the Warrior*, 8–9.
67 See Hackett, "The Military in the Service of the State," 119; Wakin, "Ethics of Leadership I," 191; "Ethics of Leadership II," 208.

warriors are necessarily good people in a holistic sense. While certain virtues may be specifically necessary for military effectiveness, this alone does not establish a separate 'warrior morality'.

However, the functional argument is not without value. Specifically, it highlights that what is good about an effective warrior would be good in any human, and what is bad about a wicked warrior would be bad in any human.[68] This further supports the existence of a single standard of virtue. Put differently, it refutes the existence of 'martial virtues' as qualities uniquely relevant to warriors. In this view, which the Stoics would support, martial virtues are simply virtues.

This point is reinforced by the existence of traditional warrior ideals embedded within the Stoic moral framework. For example, *integrity* and *honor* are universally promoted in military culture—if not as virtues themselves, then as important guiding principles that express virtue and encourage military effectiveness. Although Stoic literature often does not translate them as such, integrity and honor are well-represented in Stoicism, not just as specific qualities of an effective warrior but as essential features of an effective human.

Notably, modern military institutions often use the terms integrity and honor imprecisely, at times treating them as interchangeable. For example, all United States service academies enshrine similar concepts of honor, the oldest and most concise of which is the Cadet Honor Code of the United States Military Academy at West Point: "A cadet will not lie, cheat, steal, or tolerate those who do." And yet as it is described in the U.S. Army's own value statement, integrity "requires that you do and say nothing that deceives others."[69] Similarly, under the banner of integrity in a statement of core attributes, the U.S. Navy declares "conduct must always be upright and honorable both in public and when nobody's looking."[70] Integrity and honor, then, are deeply intertwined and are often informally treated as synonymous with honesty. While this simplification can convey a general impression, it obscures a deep well of meaning beneath the surface.

Of the two terms, integrity is the more straightforward to define. Whether referring to personal character or a ship's hull, integrity describes a state of being sound, whole, and undiminished. For an individual, it does not refer to any specific personal quality or virtue, but rather the consistency and coherence among one's various attributes. It has been expressed as "loyalty to oneself," meaning conformity

---

68   Savagery, belligerence, or bloodthirst might be proposed as traits desirable in a warrior but not in an ordinary person. However, when these traits are found in recruits to an unusual degree, they often constitute a specific kind of military liability. If not addressed through effective training, they can sometimes result in errors of tactical or even strategic consequence.
69   "Army Values," accessed October 21, 2024.
70   "U.S. Navy: Core Attributes," accessed October 21, 2024.

to one's own moral standards.[71] A person lacking integrity is internally conflicted, with actions that do not align with their values or with misalignments among the values themselves. Conversely, someone who possesses integrity is fully whole. Such persons are resilient in the face of unforeseen hardship, finding strength in mutually reinforcing capabilities, and knowing what to do when "perspective seems to blur, when rules and principles seem to waver."[72]

The equivalent Stoic concept, often translated as "consistency" or "agreement," is *homologia*. To Stoics, moral and intellectual consistency are integral to virtue, which is described as "consistent, firm, and unchangeable reason."[73] Happiness, or *eudaimonia*, is itself understood as "living in agreement," which involves harmony on multiple levels: agreement with nature, agreement with virtue *proper*, and agreement between one's own discrete virtues as an independent and rational being.[74] Consistent with the Stoic model of virtue as an all-or-nothing proposition, possession of integrity in one dimension implies its possession in all others.

Integrity, as *homologia*, also serves as a crucial test of philosophical validity. Philosophers, both ancient and modern, challenge one another's claims by highlighting inconsistencies, treating internal coherence as the ultimate proof of a sound system. Such activity is precisely what made Chrysippus so influential, as he authored numerous works in an effort to clarify the Stoics' positions and defend them against misrepresentation. This is part of what distinguishes a philosophy from an ethos or a code. An emphasis on philosophical integrity naturally extends into personal integrity, where consistency in thought, word, and deed validates an individual's intellectual and moral grounding. As Seneca writes:

> Philosophy teaches us to act, not to speak; it exacts of every man that he should live according to his own standards, that his life should not be out of harmony with his words, and that, further, his inner life should be of one hue and not out of harmony with all his activities. This, I say, is the highest duty and the highest proof of wisdom, that deed and word should be in accord, that a man should be equal to himself under all conditions, and always the same.[75]

---

71 Olsthoorn, *Honor in Political and Moral Philosophy*, 105–8. Cf. Malham M. Wakin, who amends Alfred Thayer Mahan to suggest it is integrity, not obedience, that "may well be 'that one among the military virtues upon which all of the others depend.'" Wakin, "Ethics of Leadership I," 191.
72 Stockdale, "The World of Epictetus," in *War, Morality, and the Military Profession*, 12.
73 Plutarch, *On Moral Virtue* 440E–41D = LS 61B. Note that while I have drawn a direct connection between integrity and the ancient concept of *homologia*, other scholars have viewed it differently. For example, A. A. Long sees integrity as one of four core concepts that unify Epictetus' philosophy (the others being freedom, judgment, and volition), but he equates it to a cluster of Epictetus' favorite terms including shame, reverence, trustworthiness, conscience, and decency. See Long, *Epictetus*, 27–31.
74 Stobaeus 2.75,11–76,8 = LS 63B.
75 Seneca, *Letters* 20.2. Cf. *Letters* 82.22 and Epictetus, *Discourses* 2.20.26, where Seneca and Epictetus each indicate the quality of a philosophy can be judged by the qualities it inspires.

Modern thinkers debate whether integrity should be considered a virtue, given that its desirability is contingent upon which specific traits are said to be in agreement.[76] One might imagine a scoundrel who is harmoniously deceitful, manipulative, violent, and cruel; the aforementioned 'wicked warrior' might fit this description. However, the military performance of such an individual would still suffer, as their abilities to provide accurate reports or to work well within a team would misalign with their other qualities. Stoics, for their part, would suggest such a person is fundamentally at odds with their own human nature, which compels progress toward justice and other virtues. Notably, the Stoics do not include *homologia* within any set of discrete virtues; instead, they present it as a foundational principle of consistency within the greater theory of virtue.

Compared to integrity, the modern concept of honor is much harder to isolate, complicated by a variety of distinct but interrelated senses of the term. For example, there is the aforementioned service academy definition of honor, which is effectively indistinguishable from honesty or personal integrity. But honor also carries a variety of meanings oriented toward external perspectives, such as those related to station or reputation. These include recognition through awards, titles, and courtesies, where one may *be* honored or *receive* certain honors. Alternately, honor can refer to emotions of pride or shame, where one may *feel* honored or dishonored respectively.

Traditionally, this latter sense can encourage certain activities deemed necessary to uphold, defend, or restore one's honor, often through violence or exposure to physical danger. These behaviors have earned honor the scorn of some academics, who view it as an outdated concept associated with dueling aristocrats of the past and violent criminal gangs of the present. In contrast, such scholars promote *dignity* as a more modern ideal that emphasizes the inherent worth of the individual and encourages the resolution of conflict through dialogue and negotiation.[77] The accompanying contrasts between "honor cultures" and "dignity cultures" are then deployed to explain various social phenomena, such as an elevated rate of homicide among whites in the American South.[78]

Still, an externally oriented concept of honor has a few defenders in academia, who emphasize its regulative effects on behavior, particularly in fostering community and group cohesion.[79] This is especially relevant in environments where personal accountability is essential. For example, in the military, concern for the esteem of one's comrades often serves as a powerful motivator for positive action. This sense of honor—rooted in a duty to protect and support those around one, to 'pull one's

---

76 Olsthoorn, *Honor in Political and Moral Philosophy*, 116–19.
77 E.g., Taylor, "Politics of Recognition," 27; Berger, "Obsolescence of Honour," 151.
78 E.g., Nisbett and Cohen, *Culture of Honor*.
79 E.g., Sommers, *Why Honor Matters*, 80–97.

weight'—is integral to the achievement of collective goals. In such contexts, honor acts as a stabilizing force, encouraging individuals to perform their respective duties to the standard of their peers.

There is a particular interpretation of honor that captures these regulative effects while avoiding unproductive preoccupations with external opinions or status. In this view, honor is understood as a sensitivity to being *deserving* of censure or respect—an inner impulse to act as if one's actions were constantly observed from an outside perspective.[80] Rather than relying on the judgment of others, this form of honor encourages individuals to self-enforce moral standards by internalizing the concept of accountability. It is informally expressed as 'doing the right thing even when nobody is looking', which emphasizes a sense of self-respect independent of external validation.

It is expressly in this sense that the Stoics conceive of honor. Seneca, for example, advises that, when alone, one should imagine being in the company of admired moral figures.[81] The relevant term is *aidēmosyne*, usually translated as "modesty" but also rendered as a "sense of honor."[82] It is a discrete virtue, distinguished alongside discipline and self-control as a subordinate species of moderation. When Epictetus describes the virtuous person as "free, trustworthy, and self-respecting," it is specifically the virtue *aidēmosyne* to which "self-respecting" refers. In his usage, the implied "external observer" is one's own internal share of universal reason, the "God within" manifested as personal conscience.[83]

While *aidēmosyne* is a virtue, it is most often expressed in the form of an emotion. Specifically, this is the "rational emotion" of *aidōs*, a species of "caution" against the danger of deserving moral criticism.[84] It is usually translated as "shame" or "modesty." *Aidōs* is the appropriate emotional response to the prospect of justified censure and, as such, serves as a regulative force on behavior.

Frequent references to shame can lend the ancient sources a stigmatizing tone but, when the Stoics speak of shame, they are really referring to an impulse to do what is right for the right reasons. This is contrasted with the passion of fear, which manifests in various ways, including the impulse to modify behavior out of concern for superficial matters like reputation or reward.[85] I will examine the intricacies of rational emotions and their counterpart, passions, in the next chapter.

Honor, understood as both emotional self-regard and a discrete species of virtue, depends upon higher faculties of reason unavailable to simpler creatures. Epictetus highlights this distinction, stating, "And what is our nature? To be people who are

---

80 Olsthoorn, *Honor in Political and Moral Philosophy*, 48–51.
81 Seneca, *Letters* 25.4–6.
82 E.g., Jedan, *Stoic Virtues*, 158–59, 163.
83 E.g., Epictetus, *Discourses* 1.14.6, 2.8.11–2; Seneca, *Letters* 41.1.
84 Kamtekar, "ΑΙΔΩΣ in Epictetus," 138–42.
85 Ibid.

free, noble-minded, and self-respecting. For what other animal blushes; what other animal has a sense of shame?"[86] This capacity for independent self-evaluation is part of what distinguishes humans as such. However, the self-respecting state, once obtained, is not unassailable—it can be forfeited if one fails to live up to their own standards.[87] Dishonorable activities—whether observed by one's peers or not—should be forbidden by a properly functioning sense of shame.

While volumes have been written on integrity and honor, and very good ones at that, my purpose here is not to provide an exhaustive treatment of these concepts.[88] Rather, by identifying their Stoic counterparts, I aim to show that these concepts are not only present but also deeply integrated into the Stoic theory of virtue, which captures every quality one might desire in a warrior. To summarize, the concept of *homologia*, or consistency, captures the essence of integrity as a state of being whole and undiminished, with coherence in thought, word, and deed. Supporting this idea are the virtue of *aidēmosyne* and the rational emotion of *aidōs*, which together comprise a Stoic concept of honor. This form of honor encourages individuals to act as if their actions were constantly observed—not by others, but by their own conscience, the "God within" that compels one to do what is right for the right reasons.[89] Finally, there is no separate system of 'warrior morality' apart from the conventional concept of virtue. What are called 'martial virtues' are, in fact, just virtues, and a warrior's actions must hold up to scrutiny under reason like those of any other human.

Making Progress

The wider arc of this chapter is divisible into three general themes: first, I examined the origins of the Stoic theory of virtue, particularly in the thought of Socrates; second, I have sought to define virtue as the Stoics themselves understood it; finally, I have explored the implications of this definition, especially through the concepts of moral progress and indifferents. These discussions ultimately reconnect the theory of virtue to the concept of rational nature, which bears importantly upon the morality of a warrior.

---

86 Epictetus, *Discourses* 3.7.26–7. Cf. Epictetus, *Fragments* 14.
87 Epictetus, *Discourses* 4.9.6–10; cf. *Discourses* 2.4.3, 2.10.18, 3.18.7.
88 E.g., Malham M. Wakin, *Integrity First: Reflections of a Military Philosopher* and *War, Morality, and the Military Profession*; and Peter Olsthoorn, *Honor in Political and Moral Philosophy*.
89 Consider the reflections of J. Glenn Gray: "We all figured we might be dead in the next minute, so what difference did it make what we did? But the longer I was over there, the more I became convinced that it was the other way around that counted—that *because* we might not be around much longer, we had to take extra care how we behaved ... We had to answer to something, to someone—maybe just to ourselves." Gray, *The Warriors*, xvii.

In summary, modeling Socrates, Stoics maintain all virtues are essentially aspects of the same thing—prudence, or moral knowledge. This supports the claim virtue is both necessary and sufficient for happiness, which is why it is called the "sole good." Because all creatures are inexorably attracted to what they perceive as 'good', a belief I introduced in the previous chapter as Stoic *egoism*, it is the natural tendency of a human being to make moral progress as they grow and learn what is actually good. To live in agreement with nature, then, entails fulfilling this virtuous *human* nature as distinguished from the unreasoning nature of an animal.

Because virtue is moral perfection, it is either possessed fully or not at all, and one cannot be 'somewhat' perfect. This gives rise to the concept of the Stoic sage or wise person, a theoretical model of moral perfection that serves as a vision of 'what right looks like'. The 'point' of studying philosophy is not to become a sage, which is probably not realistic, but to make as much progress toward moral perfection as possible. Progress is achieved by habituating appropriate patterns of thought and action.

Everything that is external to the moral 'self'—that is, beyond one's ability to control—is considered indifferent by the Stoics. However, it is natural and appropriate to prefer some indifferents to others, given the choice. Virtue is expressed through the rational selection of preferred indifferents and the avoidance of dispreferred ones. Stoics are not merely allowed but are required to select indifferents that are preferred, as reason would recommend in agreement with nature.

Although some indifferents, such as health or comfort, may be normally preferred, specific circumstances—such as a duty to face physical danger—may supervene to displace them as the morally correct choice. No particular indifferent is always preferred or dispreferred, just like no particular action is always appropriate or inappropriate. As always with Stoicism, there is no 'rulebook' to cover every situation, no set of 'thou shalt' injunctions to fall back upon. Instead, there is a general imperative to become the kind of person who makes the right decisions for the right reasons.

To advance the conversation, then, we must ask how one is supposed to go about this task. Specifically, how does one habituate appropriate patterns of thought and action? Answering this question in earnest will require a deep dive into the recesses of Stoic theory, particularly as it pertains to the workings of the human mind. The next chapter will explore these ideas in detail, wherein self-mastery, emotional resilience, and dutiful attention to the present will coalesce as both the starting point and the end results of personal discipline.

CHAPTER 3

Discipline

> Pay careful attention, then, to your impressions; watch over them unceasingly. For it is not something of little importance that you're trying to preserve, but self-respect, fidelity, impassibility, freedom from distress, fear, and anxiety, and in a word, freedom. At what price will you sell that? Consider how much it is worth.
>
> EPICTETUS, *DISCOURSES* 4.3.6–8.

In the previous chapter, I explored the Stoic theory of virtue, which posits that reason is the natural and defining characteristic of a human being. To live in accordance with nature, then, means to obey reason in both thought and action. This is not only a moral obligation but also the path to a happy and fulfilling life. However, to make use of this knowledge requires much more than mere comprehension of the underlying principle which, on its own, is of no more use than simply knowing diet and exercise are essential to physical health. To consistently think and act according to reason, as a Stoic sage would, demands what most would consider an unrealistic degree of self-control.

If reason is an inherent human faculty, then following reason is essentially an act of self-obedience. Why, then, is it so hard? How can it be made easier? Do the Stoics offer specific practices to encourage it? As a matter of fact, they do.

The core themes of this chapter will be familiar to a modern reader. For example, discipline, as widely understood today, is the ability to control one's behaviors, desires, and emotional reactions in the face of external circumstances, as necessary to achieve specific goals or adhere to certain standards. This often requires self-regulation and commitment, with a conscious effort to pursue long-term objectives even if it means postponing immediate gratification. It manifests through habits like regular exercise, consistent routines, and maintaining healthy boundaries in various aspects of life. A growing body of scientific evidence suggests discipline works like a muscle, in that it can be developed and improved through training, and that it can become fatigued or depleted throughout a given day.[1]

Closely related to discipline, in modern thinking, is the concept of mindfulness. Both a cultural movement and a personal practice, mindfulness entails being fully conscious and engaged in the current moment, maintaining a non-judgment awareness of

---

1   Baumeister and Exline, "Virtue, Personality, and Social Relations," 1165–94.

one's thoughts, feelings, and surroundings. It requires paying attention to the present experience without becoming overwhelmed or reactive. The popular mindfulness movement has roots in traditions like Zen Buddhism—where it is reinforced through techniques such as meditation, deep breathing, and self-reflection—but today it stands independent of its Eastern origins. Mindfulness is now a key component of *performance psychology*, a loose collection of mental exercises and strategies taught in pressurized enterprises such as business leadership, professional sports, and the military. These practices help high-performance individuals maintain a sense of calm and clarity despite highly demanding and stressful conditions.

Performance psychology identifies a harmonious relationship between mindfulness and discipline. When we are mindful, or conscious of our present state, we are more likely to recognize and regulate impulsive thoughts and behaviors. Conversely, strong personal discipline supports the habituation of mindfulness by steering mental effort toward self- and present-consciousness, as well as by fostering exercises that encourage such efforts. For example, setting aside time for meditation, journaling, or physical exercise requires discipline; routinely engaging in such activities further reinforces that same discipline.

Both discipline and mindfulness have clear equivalents within the Stoic framework and these concepts are central to the substance of this chapter. Specifically, discipline is distinguished as a discrete virtue, subordinate to the cardinal virtue *sōphrosýnē*—what we call "moderation," "temperance," or "self-control," depending on the translator. Mindfulness, on the other hand, aligns with the Stoic concept of *prosochē*, which differs from discipline in that it is not considered a virtue, but rather an activity or disposition.

Although *prosochē* could just as easily translate to "mindfulness," it is most often rendered as "attention." This term captures the practice of observing one's thoughts, actions, and surroundings in the moment, as emphasized in this chapter's epigraph. For consistency, this project will adhere to the convention of translating *prosochē* as "attention." Thus, while discipline represents a discrete virtue within the Stoic tradition, attention is better understood as an *activity* that manifests this virtue.

Stoic concepts of discipline and attention are the thematic topics of this chapter. I will examine their harmonious relationship as the Stoics conceive it. But this is where the similarity to modern thinking will end. To understand how discipline and attention interact—how discipline is to be achieved and attention is to be sustained—requires a deep dive into the Stoic theory of mind, including phenomena like emotions, judgments, and decision-making processes. I will introduce esoteric ideas like the *hegemonikon*, or a reasoning 'command center' of the mind, and the distinct processes by which it governs *phantasiai*, or sensory information. This will lead us to the Stoic theory of emotions, which are described as the byproduct of judgments about the information one receives.

The discussions above will transition toward a powerful concept of moral choice. While the focus so far has been on the foundational theories of early Stoics, this excursion will veer directly into the teachings of the late Stoic Epictetus, placing him at the forefront of the broader narrative. Epictetus uniquely connects moral choice to the division of what does and does not lie within one's power; as I will demonstrate, this framing is far more versatile than the intuitive wisdom to which it is often reduced. As Epictetus conceives it, moral choice is central to personal identity; the latter passages of this chapter will explain how this is so.

All of this is encapsulated in the imperative to pay attention, specifically to what is going on in the present moment. Both the focus on one's internal state and the careful examination of moral choice lead one to recognize their immediate situation as preeminent, although each approach arrives at this understanding through different logical paths. Therefore, I will demonstrate how concentration on the present is not merely a stereotype of the wise philosopher but is, in fact, the logical culmination and convergence point for some of the Stoics' most important ideas.

One other matter will be addressed before moving on to the next chapter: throughout the ancient sources, and especially as evidenced in the material here, it is implicit a Stoic should take responsibility for their internal state regardless of what they can or cannot control, or what they believe they can or cannot control. This obligation applies to both external circumstances and the internal activities of the mind, and it explains why it is not especially important whether sagacity—the achievement of moral perfection—is or is not realistic. One should strive for perfection in any event. This principle starkly parallels a practical concept of responsibility that pervades military culture; I will briefly explore this connection at this chapter's end.

Let us step off, then, onto the iceberg's tip that is Stoic moral choice.

Unsheathing the Knife

"Some things are within our power" declares Epictetus in the *Enchiridion*'s first line, "while others are not."[2] It is important to note the *Enchiridion*, or "handbook," was not written by Epictetus himself, but rather was compiled by Arrian, his devoted student. Arrian carefully selected key excerpts from his more extensive records of Epictetus' lectures, the *Discourses*, to create a concise and easily accessible handbook that would capture the essence of his teacher's philosophy. It is possible we would not select exactly the same excerpts as Arrian if we were to compile an *Enchiridion* today, but we could hardly choose a more powerful opening passage.

That we have power over some things and not others is a deceptively straightforward claim. Its substance is compelling without elucidation, its factual correctness

---

[2] Epictetus, *Handbook* 1.

undeniable, its implications deep and far-reaching even from a surface view. It 'feels' philosophical. In popular literature, Epictetus' dictum is sometimes described as "the dichotomy of control," an either/or sorting function where all factors and events must be categorized one way or another.[3] The simplicity and practical utility of this model, especially when facing emotionally challenging situations, have been key drivers in the recent revival of popular Stoicism.

For reasons that will soon become apparent, I prefer instead to think of Epictetus' dictum as a very sharp blade, whose infinitesimally fine edge tolerates no in-between condition. This 'Stoic knife' cuts through conceptual knots with extreme efficiency, separating the sticking parts completely and leaving moral indifferents on the cutting-room floor. It functions as a philosophical razor, which, at its simplest, represents the Epictetan principle: 'that which is not up to us is not ours'. In the pages that follow, I will explore the full implications of this puzzling assertion.

For the time being, it will suffice to say that a knife is a tool designed for frequent and practical use and easily carried upon the person. If we were to reduce this powerful instrument to a mere dichotomous sorting function, then we would misrepresent Epictetus and overlook almost the entirety of his point. We would really just be repackaging common sense; indeed, any village elder might tell us we should not worry about what we cannot control. However, I propose that just underneath this veneer of folk wisdom lies a sophisticated metaphysical claim with profound moral implications.

It would be worthwhile to say what I mean by profound. An idea is profound if it addresses complex existential, ethical, or epistemological questions that resonate deeply within the human experience or, in other words, questions as relevant today as they were thousands of years ago. Profound concepts may transcend specific contexts and resonate across various scenarios and disciplines, offering insights applicable to individual choices, societal structures, or the nature of reality itself. They may challenge us to rethink familiar ideas and potentially change our perspectives.

A perennial challenge in philosophy is that true profundity is unrecognizable without the right equipment. When we lack the vocabulary or haven't been exposed to foundational concepts, the authentically profound is indistinguishable from nonsense or irrelevant conjecture. Ironically, from that same vantage point, rather mundane or hackneyed propositions can also appear to be profound. A mark of genius in Epictetus' approach is that he encapsulates a truly profound idea within the palatable shell of an apparently profound platitude. Who can deny we have power over some things and no power over others? Who could dispute we must not forget which is which? Such wisdom, such depth. We will see there is a bit more to it.

---

3   This phrase, "dichotomy of control," was coined by the popular author William B. Irvine, and it has since propagated throughout the pop-Stoicism blogosphere. "Negative visualization," discussed later in this chapter, originates in the same work. See Irvine, *A Guide to the Good Life*, 85–101.

To properly appreciate the scope of Epictetus' thinking, we should first review his dictum in full:

> Some things are within our power, while others are not. Within our power are opinion, motivation, desire, aversion, and, in a word, whatever is of our own doing; not within our power are our body, our property, reputation, office, and, in a word, whatever is not of our own doing. The things that are within our power are by nature free, and immune to hindrance and obstruction, while those that are not within our power are weak, slavish, subject to hindrance, and not our own. Remember, then, that if you regard that which is by nature slavish as being free, and that which is not your own as being your own, you'll have cause to lament, you'll have a troubled mind, and you'll find fault with both gods and human beings; but if you regard only that which is your own as being your own, and that which isn't your own as not being your own (as is indeed the case), no one will ever be able to coerce you, no one will hinder you, you'll find fault with no one, you'll accuse no one, you'll do nothing whatever against your will, you'll have no enemy, and no one will ever harm you because no harm can affect you.[4]

Reflecting his origins in slavery, Epictetus frames moral issues in terms of 'possession' or 'ownership'. In his construct, what we own is what we can control with absolute certainty. Not even our physical bodies meet this standard, and whatever we cannot control absolutely can defy us, deteriorate, or disappear in front of our eyes—it is not truly ours. Frustration and misery, including coercion by others, are all traceable to the confusion about what is and is not within our power. The crux of Epictetus' approach is to recognize a distinction that excludes nearly everything from our sphere of power, and then to elevate what remains to a status of extreme, almost transcendent importance.

When all superfluity has been cut away, that sole remaining, supremely important thing is the moral power of 'choice'. It is not just a capability to make decisions but also to employ faculties like judgment and perception, as informed by reason. As a completely *internal* faculty, it is always available and cannot be threatened by any exterior factor; even a prisoner can decide how to react to his situation. As Epictetus scoffs at a hypothetical jailor, "What are you saying, man, chain *me* up? You can chain my leg, but not even Zeus can overcome my power of choice."[5]

Despite its apparent versatility, it is not yet clear how this power is actually supposed to work. It seems rather unhelpful and dismissive to tell someone who is suffering they should just choose to be happy. Further, it's unclear whether choice has anything to do with the virtue of discipline or the activity of attention. A simple sorting function—distinguishing what is within our power from what is not—can only do so much and, in fact, it is better understood as a vital mechanism within a much wider system. To appreciate these interrelationships, we will need to go deeper, examining the Stoic theory of mind at a systematic level.

---

4 Epictetus, *Handbook* 1.
5 Epictetus, *Discourses* 1.1.23, emphasis mine.

One Mind, Three Processes

As the Stoics conceive it, the conscious mind is constructed around an energetic core called the *hegemonikon*, or what effectively translates as the "ruling center." The *hegemonikon* functions as an internal 'headquarters' and the seat of reason from which one's thoughts, emotions, and actions are orchestrated. Moral progress entails imposing rationality and order throughout this busy facility; as Epictetus puts it, "the material that the good and virtuous person works upon is his own ruling center, as that of a doctor or wrestling master is the human body, and that of a farmer is his land."[6] Virtue, as a 'disposition' of the ruling center, is found in the habituation of such discipline so that it might occur effortlessly and consistently.[7]

The ruling center governs an individual through three discrete yet interdependent processes. First, it judges, or grants and denies *assent* to thoughts as they occur. Second, it *desires*, attracting an individual to what is perceived as good and repelling from what is thought to be bad. Third, it compels *action*, providing impulses for the body to behave in a certain way. These three governing processes—assent, desire, and action—operate continuously and in harmony, akin to the circulatory, respiratory, and musculoskeletal systems of an organism. Epictetus, much like a physical trainer, argues a proper philosophical regimen should specifically target each aspect for balanced development:

> There are three areas of study in which someone who wants to be virtuous and good must be trained: that which relates to desires and aversions, so that he may neither fail to get what he desires, or fall into what he wants to avoid; that which relates to our motives to act or not act, and, in general, appropriate behavior, so that he may act in an orderly manner and with good reason, rather than carelessly; and thirdly, that which relates to the avoidance of error and hasty judgement, and, in general, whatever relates to assent.[8]

This division of an internal headquarters into three processes is an explicitly Epictetan take. Before Epictetus, Stoics discussed the ruling center in terms of two functions, assent and action, with desire regarded as a species of the latter.[9] Epictetus, and Marcus Aurelius after him, indicate desire as a third discrete process, thereby creating a tripartite model that maps conveniently onto the early Stoics' division of knowledge into the three major fields of logic, physics, and ethics. This connection between the two models then supports a comprehensive curriculum where all human knowledge can be described as facilitating a balanced and morally mature human mind.

Neither Epictetus nor Marcus explicitly lay out these connections or directly describe a tripartite model in the sources we have available today. Instead, these ideas

---

6   Ibid. 3.3.1.
7   Sextus Empiricus, *Against the Professors* 11.22–6 = LS 60G; Plutarch, *On Moral Virtue* 440E–41D = LS 61B.
8   Epictetus, *Discourses* 3.2.1.
9   B. Inwood, *Ethics and Human Action*, 116–26.

emerge from repeated statements like the quote above, and they have been picked out by modern scholars who strain to discern the specifics of their unique philosophies within our painfully limited original sources. As he is preserved, Epictetus avoids systematic theoretical digressions in general. Despite their omission from the *Discourses*, it is plausible Epictetus' full curriculum included the intricate details of early Stoic theory. If so, it may have been Arrian who chose not to document these lessons, rather than Epictetus who chose not to teach them. In any event, it is clear from the *Discourses* that Epictetus is fully versed in early Stoic theory and he expects his students to be as well.

Influential scholars have described the Epictetan imposition of control over the ruling center's processes as a set of "disciplines."[10] Logically, these are the "discipline of assent," the "discipline of desire," and the "discipline of action." Achievement within a given discipline, then, corresponds to mastery of a given field of knowledge:

- The discipline of assent (sometimes called judgment) consists of controlling one's internal thoughts to reject whatever does not comport with reason. This discipline is closely related to the comprehension of logic, encompassing the structures and limits of knowledge. The bulk of this chapter will explore the inner workings and implications of this process.
- The discipline of desire involves refusing to want anything other than what is already decided by fate, encapsulating Stoic acceptance. This discipline is tied to the understanding of physics, or how the universe operates. This reveals the Stoics at their most mystical, a topic thoroughly explored in Chapter 1.
- The discipline of action involves doing what one ought to do and is connected to the understanding of ethics. This will be examined in detail in the next chapter.

Like the three fields of knowledge, each discipline reinforces and is mutually supported by the others, ultimately making the three processes inseparable. We should note 'discipline' can be confusing in the way it is used here, as it is a peculiar translation of the ancient Greek term *askēsis,* which might also be rendered "exercise" or "training." In English, a 'discipline of' prefix usually implies the context of an art or skill, such as the discipline of carpentry or the discipline of Jiu Jitsu. As the term is employed here, though, it might be better read as a 'domestication of' or

---

10 Note that this interpretation of Epictetus is controversial among scholars. On this matter, I take as my bellwether the French philosopher Pierre Hadot, upon whose work this section leans heavily. Intriguingly, psychotherapist Donald Robertson suggests the interlocking systems of Cognitive-Behavioral Therapy (CBT) and Rational Emotive Behavioral Therapy find their origin in the same tripartite model Hadot describes, associating assent, desire, and action with "thoughts/cognition," "feelings/affect," and "actions/behaviour" respectively. See Hadot, *The Inner Citadel,* 73–100ff; Robertson, *Philosophy of CBT,* 61–65ff.

'control of' statement. Achievement of the disciplines, then, represents perfected mental functionality (i.e., virtue) as total command and control of the mind's ruling center.

Our difficulties with translated language do not end with the competing contexts of discipline. As helpful as translators can be, sometimes they paint over important details whose significance only becomes clear in a particular light. For example, let us revisit the passage from earlier, where Epictetus articulates the moral faculty of choice. As translated in the passage we read, Epictetus says, "Within our power are opinion, motivation, desire, aversion, and, in a word, whatever is of our own doing."[11]

This sentence, as it appears in a popular rendering of Epictetus, is straightforward—a mere list with no particular room for deeper implications. But if we look past this one translator's interpretation, we find some important meaning has been left on the table. Let us specifically consider what things Epictetus says are in our power. In his language, they are *hypolēpseis*, *orexis*, and *hormē*. The specific meanings of these terms are context-dependent, but they can be roughly approximated as follows:

Hypolēpseis: Assumption, premonition, recognition, comprehension.

Orexis: Appetite, striving, inclination, intention.

Hormē: Drive, momentum, impulse, attack.

In other words, Epictetus is talking about assent, desire, and action. So if we consider a different rendition of this passage, one sensitive to the Epictetan postulate of a ruling center with three distinct processes, then a different picture comes into focus: "What depends on us are value-judgments (*hypolēpseis*), impulses toward action (*hormē*), and desire (*orexis*) or aversion; in a word, everything which is our own business."[12]

In essence, what depends on (i.e., what is 'up to') us are, and only are, the three governing processes of the ruling center—those are what we can control and nothing else. That we even can control them is a profound claim; that we can control nothing else is a separate, but no less profound, claim. Choice, then, can be understood as the decision to assume command of the ruling center. That is to say, it is the choice to take full responsibility for one's own behaviors and internal state, cutting away distractions and excuses.

We have not yet grappled with the full implications of Epictetus' dictum, but cracks are forming in the folk-wisdom shell. There are glints of sophisticated machinery lying just underneath. At the very least, the colossal task of living in accordance with nature can be broken into three preeminent Stoic aims: to think what is true, to desire what is one's own, and to do what is right.

---

11 Epictetus, *Handbook* 1.
12 Epictetus, *Handbook* 1, trans. Hadot, *The Inner Citadel*, 83.

Impressions

In modern academic language, *epistemology* is a branch of philosophy that deals with the nature and limits of knowledge. When theorists like Alvin Goldman or David Chalmers work to clarify boundaries between knowledge and feelings, or when they debate what is possible for a computer to 'know', they are attempting to solve epistemological problems. The eternal challenge of epistemology is producing a reliable definition of knowledge; for example, its classic characterization as 'justified, true belief' has been continuously challenged since its emergence.[13] Like many problems in philosophy, this debate may never find a resolution, but considering the diversity and merit of ideas it has generated, we may hope it never does.

Like most philosophers of their time, the early Stoics developed their own unique brand of epistemology which informs the wider system I describe in this chapter. Theirs is based on perception, attempting to trace a path from sensory input to absolute certainty by way of reason. Eternal fans of tripartite models, Stoics identify three discrete levels of comprehension on this path: *fantasia, doxa, and epistêmê*, or what we will call "impressions," "opinions," and "knowledge" respectively. Each category calls for a different standard of rigor and, as we will see, each is relevant to the Stoic ethical system in different but important ways.

Impressions are undeveloped mental reactions and are what Stoics consider to be the starting point for all thought and understanding. Opinion and knowledge, the higher forms of comprehension, both begin as impressions before being processed by higher mental faculties. The term 'impression' suggests the imprint of stimulus on the mind is like a seal in hot wax, changing its shape indelibly (that is, permanently) to conform to a subject's contours. Like marks in the wax, the impression then becomes a subject of interpretation by higher faculties.

While all sense data necessarily become impressions, not all impressions originate in the senses. Non-sensory impressions are those "apprehended through thought, as is the case with incorporeal [immaterial] things and everything else that is apprehended through reason."[14] These can simply be ideas, or they can also be impulses to perform actions, called 'impulsive impressions'.[15] The discipline of action, then, would be an imposition of control or filtering over those specific impressions.

In modeling consciousness, the analogy of a seal on wax reaches its limitations as, unlike wax, the mind can—and indeed must—accommodate an endless

---

[13] The most widely accepted origin of 'justified, true belief' as a definition for knowledge is Plato's Socratic dialogue *Theaetetus*. The most influential challenger of the 'JTB' convention is Edmund Gettier, whose 1963 paper "Is Justified True Belief Knowledge?" sparked an ongoing debate over thought experiments now known as 'Gettier cases'. See Ichikawa and Steup, "The Analysis of Knowledge," *The Stanford Encyclopedia of Philosophy* (Fall 2024).

[14] DL 7.51.

[15] Brennan, *The Stoic Life*, 87.

variety of impressions on the same beleaguered surface.[16] Everyday consciousness comprises a persistent stream of such stimulus, much of it internally generated, which the higher faculties are responsible for processing. As erratic and fleeting mental imagery, most raw impressions are highly suspect and unsuited to elevation as knowledge.

Opinions, the second category of comprehension, represent the broad spectrum of uncertain and potentially flawed concepts or beliefs bridging the space between raw impressions and certain knowledge. Judgments based on probability or incomplete information are opinions, as are beliefs shaped by education, cultural perspective, or personal biases. Unlike impressions, opinions have undergone at least some processing by the higher faculties of reason. Unlike knowledge, opinions are unverified by observable truth and therefore fall short of absolute confidence.

Knowledge, the highest category of comprehension, entails complete certainty, unchangeable by reason. Importantly, the Stoics deny true knowledge can come from internal thoughts alone. Previewing what would someday be considered *Empiricism*, Stoics hold that all comprehension originates in the senses. As opposed to their rivals, the Skeptics, Stoics insist absolute truths are discoverable only in what can be observed or otherwise physically perceived.[17]

Of course, not all sense impressions are necessarily the beginnings of knowledge. As we have said, most are erratic discharges of mental energy. On the other hand, some sensory perceptions are so clear, vivid, and irrefutable that the truth underlying them cannot be denied; it is recognized instantly and with absolute confidence. Cicero likens this involuntary comprehension to the tipping of scales: "For just as a scale must sink when weights are placed in the balance, so the mind must give way to what is self-evident. It is no more possible for a living creature to refrain from assenting to something self-evident than for it to fail to pursue what appears appropriate to its nature."[18] The Stoics reserve a special category for these kind of sensory data; they are called "cataleptic" impressions and are considered to be the "criterion of reality."[19] A cataleptic impression is "one which arises from what is

---

16 DL 7.50.
17 See Cicero, *Academics* 2.19, 2.45, and Long and Sedley, *The Hellenistic Philosophers*, 1: 249–53. Throughout their history, the Stoics consistently upheld Zeno's original thesis that it *is* possible to attain infallible knowledge of the world and every normal human possesses an innate ability to distinguish securely between discoverable truths and falsehoods. This stance faced strong opposition from other philosophical schools such as the Skeptics and the Academics. The ensuing centuries-long debate is regarded as one of the most significant and influential philosophical discussions of the Hellenistic period, contributing importantly to modern epistemological theory.
18 Ibid. 2.37–8 = LS 40O.
19 Some authors may translate these "cognitive" or "comprehending" impressions, however "cataleptic" remains the most common rendering in current literature. It is an adaptation of *katalēpsis*, an ancient Greek term for "comprehension."

and is stamped and impressed exactly in accordance with what is, of such a kind as could not arise from what is not."[20]

In other words, cataleptic impressions are clear and undeniable perceptions that accurately represent external reality. These sense data, derived directly from experience, form the foundation of knowledge. For an impression to meet this standard, five factors must align: "the sense-organ, the sense-object, the place, the manner, and the mind."[21] If the mind is in an "abnormal state," such as intoxication or insanity, the resulting impressions fall short of being cataleptic.[22] Rebuttals involving failing senses, hallucinations, or realistic deceptions miss the point, although the Stoics did address such criticisms in their time.[23] The point is that only cataleptic impressions are dependable enough to serve as a basis for certainty, unlike non-cataleptic impressions, which are unreliable and prone to error. Therefore, a critical task for the Stoics is to distinguish cataleptic from non-cataleptic impressions.

Such distinctions may initially seem like an artifact of excessive theorizing, far removed from practical concerns. It's understandable to doubt these concepts have any meaningful application in everyday life, but there is a familiar way to think about it which might be of some use. First, consider non-cataleptic impressions as encompassing the vast territory of uncertainty—not merely outright falsehoods, but the entire spectrum of estimates, assumptions, feelings, inferences, conjectures, hypotheses and innumerable other gradations of opinion that fall short of certainty. Isolated from this morass, cataleptic impressions correspond to a single concept in contemporary terms: facts. There is just one truth amid infinite variants of not-quite-truth, or to paraphrase Seneca once again, there can be a hundred kinds of crooked but nothing "straighter than the straight."

'Fact' is not a perfect term for cataleptic impressions; a more accurate description would be the 'undeniable perception of fact'. However, 'fact' conveys the essential idea and grounds this esoteric discussion in concrete reality. An individual who claims to meticulously categorize cataleptic and non-cataleptic impressions when making decisions might receive skeptical looks and could be perceived as unsuitable for positions of high responsibility. On the other hand, a commitment to separating fact from opinion is standard procedure in serious, high-stakes professions. It would seem almost anyone would benefit from a way to improve and habituate it.

---

20 Sextus Empiricus, *Against the Professors* 7.247–52 (SVF 2.65, Part I) = LS 40E. See also DL 7.46.
21 Ibid. 7.424 = LS 40L.
22 Ibid. 7.247–52 (SVF 2.65, Part I) = LS 40E.
23 For example, the king Ptolemy successfully deceived the Stoic philosopher Sphaerus with wax pomegranates to expose him for assenting to a false impression. However, Sphaerus cleverly responded he had only assented to the impression that it was reasonable to believe they were pomegranates. DL 7.177; Athenæuss 354E (SVF I.624, Part) = LS 40F.

As it happens, this imperative leads to one of the most iconic practices of the Stoic regimen: the mental exercise of *katharsis* (purification).[24] This technique involves deliberately separating sense impressions from any value judgments attached to them. It is most clearly articulated in the writings of Marcus Aurelius, in which he emphasizes the need to "always define or describe to yourself every impression that occurs to your mind, so that you can clearly see what the thing is like in its entirety, stripped to its essence, and tell yourself its proper name …"[25] Throughout his writings, Marcus attempts to analyze his impressions objectively, considering their impermanence, their dependence on value judgments, and, ultimately, their lack of power over his inner state: "How useful it is, when you're served roast meat and similar dishes, to think to yourself: this is the corpse of a fish, this is the corpse of a bird or a pig!"[26]

Marcus' austere approach to sensual pleasures has contributed to the long-standing criticism that Stoics promote a joyless worldview. He even suggests 'purifying' the notes of music to resist its emotional impact.[27] However, it is crucial to consider the context of the *Meditations* as intensely personal self-exhortations of the most powerful man in the world, who would have faced constant temptations to abandon his banal responsibilities for more pleasurable pursuits. It is clear Marcus Aurelius might have wished for a different life, one devoted entirely to the study and practice of philosophy. However, he approached his role as emperor—and the responsibilities of military leadership that came with it—as solemn and unavoidable duties.

Purification serves as a reminder that even the most fearsome beasts, once deconstructed from their threatening fur and fangs, are just flesh and bone. Such beasts might be literal physical dangers or otherwise might represent the vanities and sensual indulgences that lurk in the shadows of both peasants and emperors. By distinguishing between the cataleptic and the non-cataleptic, Stoics aim to dismantle the illusions fueling emotional turmoil, rendering false judgments powerless against them. It is not about the denial of pleasure but rather about preserving mental clarity and resisting domination by irrational desires, fears, or even other people.

---

24 *Katharsis* translates as purification, cleansing, or purgation. The modern understanding of "catharsis" likely originates with Aristotle, who, in *Poetics*, argues that theatrical tragedy functions to purge negative emotions in the audience by allowing them to experience these emotions indirectly through the performance. In contrast, Epictetus explicitly describes *katharsis* as the purgation of passions by correcting the underlying judgements. Marucs Aurelius, in turn, habitually applies this teaching. The practice might also be described as 'stripping', 'deconstruction', or *phantasia kataleptike* ("objective representation"). It is analogous to the concept of 'distancing' in modern CBT. See Epictetus, *Discourses* 4.11.5–8; Beck, *Cognitive Therapy and the Emotional Disorders*, 242–43; Robertson, *The Philosophy of Cognitive-Behavioural Therapy* (*CBT*), 12, 157–60.
25 Marcus Aurelius, *Meditations* 3.11.
26 Ibid. 6.13.
27 Marcus Aurelius, *Meditations* 11.2.

After all, there are no more deflating words to a potential extortionist than 'you have nothing I want'.

When impressions are reduced to their bare facts, even the most seemingly momentous matters can appear trivial. By introducing an element of time and considering these facts against the backdrop of an infinite universe—one with an endless past and future—Stoics encourage individuals to mentally distance themselves from their immediate concerns. This 'extended purification' effectively becomes a separate mental exercise, one of envisioning the world from a higher, broader perspective. From this vantage point, one appreciates the smallness of human affairs and the insignificance of personal anxieties in the grand scheme of things. Scholars refer to this routine as the "view from above":[28]

> You can get rid of many superfluous troubles that depend entirely on your beliefs, and you'll immediately provide yourself with plenty of mental space. Encompass the whole universe with your mind, contemplate the everlastingness of time, and consider the speed with which individual things change. How short the time is between birth and disintegration, how vast the time before your birth, and how similarly infinite the time after your disintegration![29]

The "view from above" is fundamentally about context. Consider that a mouse knows nothing more important than the affairs of a mouse: securing food, avoiding predators, finding a place to burrow and reproduce. Any disruption to these priorities feels like a catastrophe to the mouse; nothing could seem more significant. But we are not mice. The human faculty of reason affords the capacity to recognize our highest ambitions, desires, and treasures are, in the grand scheme, trivial. When one appreciates the wider context of existence, threats and problems also become trivial. This is precisely what Marcus aims to achieve through the elevated perspective. By cultivating an ability to see personal troubles against the vastness of space and time, one becomes invulnerable to their power over the mind. All we can do is accept that our time is brief and focus on doing what is right.

There is Always a Choice

Once a given impression is recognized as non-cataleptic, there is still work to do. Even with a perfect purification process, it would not be possible or desirable to simply reject all non-facts outright—after all, some opinions may turn out to be correct. Additional processing is necessary to sort them out. To envision this process, we need to follow the path of an impression through the system, moving beyond the simplistic separation of truth from uncertainty and into the complex swamp of value judgments. This brings us back into the central governing faculty of the mind, which the Stoics call the ruling center.

---

28 E.g., Hadot, *The Inner Citadel*, 171–79.
29 Marcus Aurelius, *Meditations* 9.32; cf. *Meditations* 6.36, 12.32.

Recall that the ruling center is like a military command post, whose governing operations work through the interdependent processes of assent, desire, and action. Nefarious actors can do great damage in such a sensitive space, so we would not let just anyone in. The process of assent, specifically, works like an entry processing station; factual or cataleptic impressions are given the fast-track through. The remaining opinions must be examined for their worthiness. A properly run ruling center will post a formidable sentry at the gate, whose task is to verify the credentials of all impressions as they approach. Those who do not pass the test are sent away:

> For just as Socrates used to say that we shouldn't live an unexamined life, we shouldn't accept any impression without subjecting it to examination, but should say to it, "Wait, let me see who you are, and where you've come from"—just as night watchmen say: "Show me your marks of identification"—"Do you have that mark from nature that every impression must have if it is to be accepted?"[30]

What Epictetus describes is the activity of attention. However, to meticulously sift through every impression approaching the mind is an immense cognitive burden. Without a quick and effective screening procedure, our processing station might become overwhelmed, allowing unfit opinions to spill over the gate and into the command center. Some kind of identifier is needed to quickly separate the important from the irrelevant. And what of this puzzling "mark from nature" to which Epictetus refers? Suppose that is our identifier; how are we supposed to recognize it?

Fortunately, the reasoning mind is naturally equipped with an efficient sorting mechanism. It is, once again, the ever-versatile Stoic knife. Far from just a reminder not to worry about what we can't control, the knife can be applied to matters of judgment, cutting away the incorrect and irrelevant minutia. Again, it is easily carried on the person and is always ready for use:

> As soon as you leave the house at break of day, examine everyone whom you see, everyone whom you hear, and answer as if under questioning. What did you see? A handsome man or beautiful woman? Apply the rule. Does this lie within the sphere of choice or outside it? Outside. Throw it away. What did you see? Someone grieving over the death of his child? Apply the rule. Death is something that lies outside the sphere of choice. Away with it. You met a consul? Apply the rule. What kind of thing is a consulship? One that lies outside the sphere of choice, or inside? Outside. Throw that away too, it doesn't stand the test. Away with it; it is nothing to you.[31]

The knife works swiftly and decisively, cleaving opinions to one side or the other. It tolerates no middle ground: there is nothing 'partially' or 'somewhat' within our

---

30 Epictetus, *Discourses* 3.12.15.
31 Ibid. 3.3.14.

power.[32] While we are obligated to act according to reason, we are not entitled to any specific outcome from our efforts. The correct judgment for any particular non-cataleptic impression, then, depends on whether it falls within or beyond our sphere of choice (Figure 4). If the matter is beyond our power, it holds no moral significance and therefore no significance to us whatsoever. It is indifferent, or as Epictetus would say, it is 'nothing to us':

> Practice, then, from the very beginning to say to every disagreeable impression, "you're an impression and not at all what you appear to be." Then examine it and test it by these rules that you possess, and first and foremost by this one, whether the impression relates to those things that are within our power, or those that aren't within our power and if it relates to anything that isn't within our power, be ready to reply, "that's nothing to me."[33]

As noted earlier, 'that which is not up to us is not ours'. Nonmoral matters—those external to the individual or impressions of such externals—are to be set aside. While I have compared this approach to cutting, Epictetus employs a different term that resists direct translation. In ancient Greek, he refers to it as *prohairesis*, a concept that can be interpreted as "capacity of choice" or simply "choice." *Prohairesis* literally means "pre-choice" or "choice before choice," referring to the 'separation' or 'selection' of impressions within one's power from those outside of it. In this sense, *prohairesis* can be understood as 'the choice of what can be chosen'. To Stoics, a state of attention entails the constant application of this power.

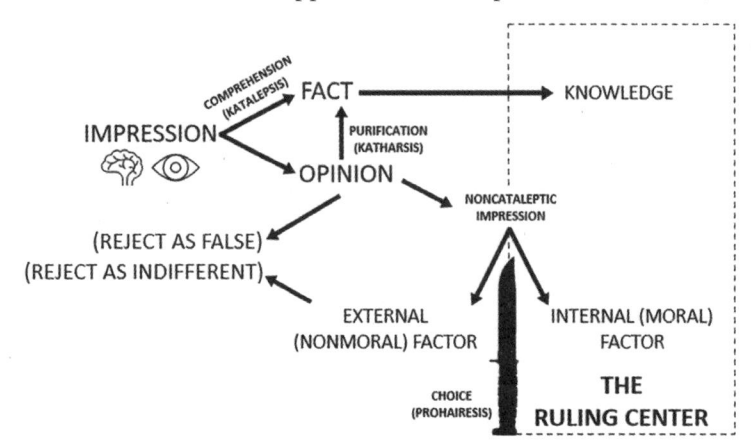

Figure 4. The discipline of Assent as a process diagram.

---

32 William B. Irvine suggests improving upon Epictetus' construct by reframing it as a "trichotomy of control," distinguishing between things over which we have complete control, limited control (such as future events like winning a tennis match), and no control at all. *Pace* Irvine, while this construct is intriguing, it has little to do with Epictetus and is incompatible with anything beyond the most superficial interpretation of his teachings. Later in this chapter, I will describe how Stoics deal with future events. See Irvine, *Guide to the Good Life*, 85–101.
33 Epictetus, *Handbook* 1.5.

Because 'choice' is obviously insufficient, *prohairesis* is sometimes represented as "will," "volition," or "agency," each of which still imperfectly captures the scope of Epictetus' key concept.[34] Among these, agency comes closest to representing choice in the sense that Epictetus deploys it. As conventionally understood, agency refers to the capacity of an individual, or agent, to act intentionally and make decisions based on their own will. It is effectively the act of being oneself: an active, self-determining consciousness capable of initiating actions and influencing the course of events. Agency involves the exercise of autonomy and the ability to take responsibility for one's actions.

Where the Stoic concept of choice looks most like agency is in light of its wider implications. Although it is tightly limited in scope to internal factors, moral choice is still all-encompassing within that internal realm, absorbing consciousness, character, judgments, goals, and desires within a single comprehensive idea.[35] It comprises the entire personal identity, abstracted as it is from the physical body that is not ours. As everything we actually own, we are morally bound to exercise it with intentionality: "For you yourself are neither flesh nor hair, but choice, and if you render that beautiful, then you yourself will be beautiful."[36]

The uncompromising logic of the Stoic knife thus evolves to incorporate the principle: "that which is not ours is not us." Developed as a syllogism, its advanced form emerges alongside its utility as a philosophical razor: "that which is not up to one is not one." Neither you nor I are anything indifferent—not even our physical bodies. Our identity is exclusively defined by our capacity of choice, and it is only within this domain that genuine freedom resides.

When Epictetus says that indifferents are "nothing to me," then, we have to bear in mind precisely what is meant by "me." To think like Epictetus is to accept that almost nothing is actually within one's power and to elevate what remains—what is actually *me*—accordingly.[37] While such a close-cropping of the self-concept may intuitively seem diminishing, what it actually achieves is to reveal a path to invulnerability, hardening the remaining identity against harm or coercion. Such is on display in Epictetus' attitude toward imprisonment: "What are you saying, man, chain *me* up?"[38] The threat is nonsensical in light of choice-as-self; a jailor might as well try to imprison one's taste in music or sense of humor.

This is what it means to elevate what remains. True good and bad lie solely in the alignment or misalignment of choice—free and invulnerable—with essential human

---

34 To align with the most-common translations of Epictetus, I will continue to render *prohairesis* as "choice," or more specifically "moral choice" as necessary to distinguish it from simple selection.
35 See Long, *Epictetus*, 28–29.
36 Epictetus, *Discourses* 3.1.40.
37 Pierre Hadot calls this practice "circumscribing [drawing a circle around] the self." See Hadot, *The Inner Citadel*, 112–25.
38 Ibid. 1.1.23, emphasis mine.

nature. Its perfection is virtue, that *sole good* which surpasses all other pursuits in importance. Choice not only defines the boundaries of a distinct personality within the greater system but also manifests that greater system, gleaming like a radiant fragment of the universal intelligence or divine *Logos* within each rational being:

> Consider who you are. First of all, a human being, that is to say, one who has no faculty more authoritative than choice, but subordinates everything else to that, keeping choice itself free from enslavement and subjection. Consider, then, what you're distinguished from through possession of reason: you're distinguished from wild beasts; you're distinguished from sheep.[39]

A state of attention, then, is not merely one of alertness. Attention is an active process, involving the testing of all incident impressions to first distinguish fact from opinion and then to cut away everything external and therefore indifferent. What remains is what matters, prompting the final task: to act appropriately with this knowledge; that is, to act with intentionality. This is not just a healthy mental exercise but a moral imperative, compelling one to treat their own capacity of choice with the respect it is due as a microcosm of universal order. Thus *agency* may be as helpful a translation of *prohairesis* as any other, but it does not quite capture the whole picture.

Where *prohairesis* looks least like agency is in that agency, as it is conventionally understood, can be denied by external actors or circumstances. For example, an authoritarian government that imprisons its political dissidents would be said to deprive them of agency. In contrast, moral choice is wholly internal and is therefore definitionally within one's power. Epictetus repeatedly demonstrates that, regardless of the situation, one must choose how to deal with it—how to think and how to act. A difficult situation, he says, is like a house filled with smoke: one should stay if it is tolerable and depart if it is not. "For one should remember this fact and keep it firmly in mind," he says, "that the door stands open."[40]

Even in the face of torture and death, succumbing to such pressures is still a choice; death is an option like any other. *If you want to quit, there's the door*, Epictetus seems to say. The point of this grim observation is not to promote or normalize death but to emphasize that coercion is impossible for one who does not fear it.[41] Because reason requires not only dismissing what is beyond one's power

---

39 Ibid. 2.10.1–3.
40 Ibid. 1.25.18.
41 Much has been written on the Stoics' permissive attitude toward suicide, but I think this reputation is somewhat overblown. In *Discourses* 1.9.16–7, Epictetus advises "you must wait for God," echoing the sentiments of Socrates in *Phaedo* 61b–2e, where Socrates suggests suicide is a crime against the divine unless a sign indicates death is necessary. Generally, the Stoics believe suicide can be justified when one's ability to live a virtuous life is compromised, but they would not countenance a selfish dismissal of its destructive consequences, nor would they excuse the abandonment of earthly responsibilities. In the passage cited above, Epictetus goes on to compare life to a military assignment from God, where "for the present, you must resign yourselves to remaining in this post in which he has stationed you."

but also taking full responsibility for what lies within it, invulnerability is achieved through—and only through—the union of these two activities. Freedom, then, is found in responsibility. As long as there is a choice, there is freedom, and there is always a choice.

Emotions

In the Stoic framework, emotions are not typically conceived as involuntary experiences but the result of judgments and beliefs about certain impressions. I say 'typically' because the Stoics do acknowledge the existence of involuntary or biological reactions to certain stimuli, which I will address shortly. Generally speaking, though, Stoics say emotions arise when external or internal impressions transform into value-laden judgments through the process of assent. For example, if we become angry at somebody's offensive remark, we should attribute the anger to our own assent to the impression that the remark was harmful. As Epictetus states, "what insults you isn't the person who abuses you or hits you, but your judgment that such people are insulting you."[42]

In essence, Stoics claim it is not the events themselves that elicit emotions, but rather our subjective interpretations and evaluations of these events. We are therefore not just responsible for what we do, but for how we feel. By recognizing that emotions stem from subjective judgments rather than objective reality, Stoics aim to align their perceptions with reason and thereby maintain a state of emotional equanimity:

> For what is weeping and groaning? A judgement. What is misfortune? A judgement. What is civil strife, dissension, fault-finding, accusation, impiety, foolishness? All of these are judgements and nothing more, and judgements that are passed, moreover, about things that lie outside the sphere of choice, under the supposition that such things are good or bad. Let someone transfer these judgements to things that lie within the sphere of choice, and I guarantee that he'll preserve his peace of mind, regardless of what his circumstances may be.[43]

Not all emotions are bad or irrational. If the underlying judgment is correct, then there is no problem and the emotion that follows will accord with nature. The resulting sentiments are what Stoics call *eupatheiai*, or "rational emotions." Joy is one such example, described by Seneca as an "elation of spirit that trusts in what is its own."[44] A Stoic might find joy in fulfillment of duties or in the company of good friends. Similar rational emotions like delight, mirth, or cheerfulness are considered species of rational joy (Table 2).

---

42 Epictetus, *Handbook* 20.
43 Epictetus, *Discourses* 3.3.18.
44 Seneca, *Letters* 59.2.

Table 2. A Stoic Taxonomy of "Rational Emotions"[45]

Joy	*Caution*	*Wishing*
Delight	Reverence	Benevolence
Mirth	Modesty [shame]	Friendliness
Cheerfulness		Respect
		Affection

Rational emotions need not be pleasant to be considered 'good'.[46] For example, the rational emotion of 'caution' is not pleasant to experience but it is still appropriate when dealing with what is rationally to be avoided. Caution is contrasted with the irrational emotion of fear, which results from an incorrect judgment that an indifferent is actually harmful. Imagine changing a tire next to a high-speed freeway. A sage, fully possessed with the virtue of courage, would not experience fear in this situation (since injury and death are not evils) but would be naturally compelled to feel a sense of caution around physical hazards. Shame (*aidōs*), a species of caution against actions or thoughts that are shameful, applies the same reasoning to moral hazards. It was discussed in the previous chapter as a Stoic version of what we call honor.

One recurring debate concerns whether the Stoics might view anger as a rational emotion, potentially serving as a motivator for appropriate actions. Examples often cited include addressing injustice, excelling in competition, or performing in military combat. However, for the Stoics, the 'rationality' of an emotion lies not in the actions it inspires—beneficial or otherwise—but in the correctness of the underlying judgment. When it comes to matters like injustice or danger, they seem to encourage appropriate action uncomplicated by the distracting features of emotion. Cicero argues, "Are we then to say that madness is useful? Study the definitions of courage and you will understand that it has no need of bad temper." He then lists numerous Stoic definitions of courage, ultimately concluding, "And once this has been uncovered, who would require anything more of the warrior, the general, or the orator, and not think them capable of performing any courageous act without rage?"[47]

Despite the Stoics' perfectionist understanding of virtue, rational emotions are not strictly limited to sages. An imperfect progressor can still make the occasional correct judgment, just as they can accurately perceive cataleptic impressions. For

---

45 DL 7.116 trans. Hicks.
46 Surprisingly, the Stoics classified anger as a pleasant, future-oriented emotion, associating it with the contemplation of revenge. Nussbaum, *Upheavals*, 160.
47 Cicero, *Tusculan Disputations* 4.53 = LS 32H.

example, although he explicitly denies being a sage, Epictetus frequently refers to his own *aidōs*—translated variously as "modesty," "shame," or "self-respect."[48]

Unfortunately, such good judgment is rare in the untrained mind and few emotions meet the standard of *eupatheiai*. Most instead are *pathe*, or "passions." These are the harmful reactions that arise from incorrect judgments about what is good or bad, or what is or is not within our power. Anger following an insult is just one such example. Cicero characterizes these flawed impressions as "morbidities" of the soul, similar to diseases in that they degrade and corrupt the body that harbors them.[49] Seneca amplifies, "I do not grasp how any halfway disease can be wholesome or helpful."[50] In essence, the Stoics view passions as byproducts of bad judgment, leading to disturbances that can negatively impact one's life.

Much of the Stoics' popular reputation for opposing all emotion stems from a general failure to distinguish between *pathe* and *eupatheiai*. When Stoics rail against passions in their works, some readers interpret this as a denunciation of emotion writ large. A correct reading is that Stoics do not seek to eradicate emotions so much as the incorrect judgments that lead to unruly and destructive passions. Once these defective judgments are properly neutralized, only lucid and healthy rational emotions remain. The resulting mental state, consistent with rational nature, is called *apatheia*. This state is characterized by total intellectual clarity and freedom from passion.

Apatheia is decidedly *not* apathy. It is sometimes wrongly translated as such, and even Seneca writes of the difficulties and risks of misunderstanding when attempting to translate it from Greek to his native Latin.[51] It is more like total serenity or equanimity, which follows from a faculty of judgment both deliberate and correct in receipt of emotional stimulus. While *apatheia* is sometimes imagined as a sort of invulnerability to emotions, Stoics do not claim emotions can be suppressed or avoided, only controlled. Seneca writes that even the ideal sage "feels his troubles, but overcomes them."[52] The sage is invulnerable in the sense that "troubles" affect neither his actions nor his ultimate happiness.

It seems paradoxical to say one can experience an emotion and yet remain unaffected by it. To make sense of this, it helps to think of an emotion as a multi-stage series of events. This process starts with the mind receiving an impression, followed by stages of processing and reaction. The Stoics refer to these phases as motions. Seneca clearly delineates three such motions when describing the sensation of anger:

> The first motion of anger is in truth involuntary, and only a kind of menacing preparation towards it. The second deliberates; as who should say, "this injury should not pass without a

---

48 E.g., Epictetus, *Fragments* 14; cf. *Discourses* 1.2.35.
49 Cicero, *On Ends* 3.10.
50 Seneca, *Letters* 116.1.
51 Ibid. 9.2.
52 Ibid. 9.3.

revenge," and there it stops. The third is impotent; and, right or wrong, resolves upon vengeance. The first motion is not to be avoided, nor indeed the second, any more than yawning for company; custom and care may lessen it, but reason itself cannot overcome it. The third, as it rises upon consideration, it must fall so too, for that motion which proceeds with judgment may be taken away with judgment.[53]

The first motion is an involuntary response any human being would experience. Epictetus illustrates this by postulating a sage startled by a loud noise or shocking news, asserting that "even the mind of a wise person is bound to be disturbed, and to shrink back and grow pale for a moment, not from any idea that something bad is going to happen, but because of certain swift and unconsidered movements which forestall the proper functioning of the mind and reason."[54] With this in mind, it would be foolish to chastise ourselves for the initial wave of anger or fear we might feel in response to some stimulus, as it is effectively a biological function over which we have no control. Reactions like blushing or shuddering, for example, are dismissible as bodily impulses when they occur involuntarily.[55]

Our responsibility begins at the second motion. This is essentially the faculty of judgment or assent, which Seneca describes above as an act of will. Judgment, in the example he describes, entails an assessment of what is good or bad, e.g., 'it is bad that I have been injured', which leads to 'it is appropriate that I should avenge myself'. Correct judgment then requires a refusal to grant assent to the false impressions, permitting the proper classification of indifferents or externals as such. Exercised with due attention, this faculty should arrest the processing of whatever defective emotion might emerge from the initial impression.

Failure to arrest a flawed impression during the second motion opens a path to the third, which necessarily involves a loss of control. At this stage, the incorrect assessment of an event transforms into a desire for a specific outcome, impervious to reason, and instead characterized by an attitude of 'come what may'. To be 'carried away' by emotion, then, is to reject the expected addendum of 'if it is appropriate' to the desired outcome. Irrational and counterproductive actions would naturally follow.[56] Described in terms of a tripartite ruling center, this would be what happens when a flawed impression is permitted to enter the facility and disrupt or co-opt the governing process of action.

The early Stoic Chrysippus describes passion as an "excess of impulse" that is like the momentum developed when running, potentially causing one to overstep their intended position.[57] In a similar analogy, Seneca compares an emotional state to standing near a precipice where, once one slips, all control can be lost. He advises,

---

53 Seneca, *On Anger* 2.4.1.
54 Epictetus, *Fragments* 9.
55 Seneca, *On Anger* 2.3.1–2.4.
56 After Sorabji, *Emotion and Peace of Mind*, 61.
57 Galen, *On Hippocrates' and Plato's Doctrines* 4.2.10–8 (SVF 3.462, part) = LS 65J.

"In so far as we are able, let us step back from slippery places; even on dry ground it is hard enough to take a sturdy stand."[58] This third motion, the loss of control and vanquishing of reason, is to be avoided with great urgency. It is what inevitably follows, though, when the second motion is not arrested by deliberate judgment. It is wholly avoidable, Stoics would say, provided assent is denied to faulty impressions.

Stoic *apatheia*, then, is cultivated at the level of sensory input through the habituation of judgment as applied to impressions. This process begins with the recognition of the emotional first motion, which should be immediately followed by correct judgment, thereby interrupting the second motion and preventing the third. Self-training methods such as Marcus' technique of purification aid in this process, encouraging individuals to dissect and analyze their impressions rationally. Ultimately, *apatheia* is conceived as freedom from incorrect judgments and the passions that follow, preventing bad decisions and leading to a state of clarity, resilience, and inner peace.

Apatheia and Sociability

An ancient critique of Stoic *apatheia* is that it fosters a sense of austerity and emotional detachment that hinders healthy social relationships. This criticism could be simply dismissed in light of the often-overlooked distinction between passions and rational emotions, which we clarified earlier. However, since it persists in contemporary commentary, let us examine the issue more closely. As a point of comparison, consider that some philosophers, such as the Stoics' ancient rivals the Epicureans, overtly promote a withdrawal from social life to focus on individual well-being. In stark contrast, the Stoics continuously emphasize the importance of social engagement, which benefits both the individual and their wider society. For example, observe Epictetus' uncharitable critique of an Epicurean:

> In God's name, I ask you, can you imagine a city of Epicureans? "I shan't marry." "Nor I, for one shouldn't marry." "Nor should one have children; nor should one perform any civic duties." So what will happen, then? Where are the citizens to come from? Who'll educate them? Who'll be superintendent of the cadets? Who'll be director of the gymnasium? And then, what will the young men be taught?[59]

Instead of loafing at the fringes of culture like Epicureans (as they are stereotyped), Stoics are expected to do their part to make society work. Epictetus proceeds to lecture his mark, "You're living in a city of the empire; you must exercise your authority, judge in accordance with what is right, keep your hands off other people's property."[60] As social creatures, it is consistent with rational nature that we should

---

58 Seneca, *Letters* 116.6.
59 Epictetus, *Discourses* 3.7.19.
60 Ibid. 3.7.21.

get along, abide the rules, cultivate relationships, and contribute to the community. This comports with the intuitive notion human excellence includes healthy social skills in the list of desirable qualities, which should reflect the virtues of prudence and justice. In modern terms, we recognize these skills as part of emotional intelligence.

No portrayal of human excellence recommends emotional incompetence. Reasonable people can disagree on what the ideal human looks like, but those who are cold, tactless, haughty, or overtly judgmental are not it in any era or social stratum. Opposing such inclinations, Seneca writes, "The first thing which philosophy undertakes to give is fellow-feeling with all men; in other words, sympathy and sociability."[61] In that same spirit, Epictetus recognizes dealing with humans involves dealing with emotions and that one's fellows will generally not be Stoics, much less sages. One can inwardly recognize the emotions of their companions as likely products of incorrect judgments without outwardly dismissing them as irrational or invalid:

> When you see someone weeping in sorrow because his child has gone away, or because he has lost his possessions, take care that you're not carried away by the impression that he is indeed in misfortune because of these external things, but be ready at once with this thought, "It isn't what has happened that so distresses this person—for someone else could suffer the same without feeling that distress—but rather the judgement that he has formed about it." As far as words go, however, don't hesitate to sympathize with him, or even, if the occasion arises, to join in his lamentations, but take care that you don't also lament deep inside.[62]

In other words, one can recognize the facts without forgetting how to act like a human. On interactions with emotional companions, Epictetus says elsewhere, "I shouldn't be unfeeling like a statue, but should preserve my natural and acquired relationships, as one who honors the gods, as a son, as a brother, as a father, as a citizen."[63] The full meaning requires context; Epictetus is speaking to a quorum of students who understand a Stoic's intellectual duty to parse facts from value judgments, but who might clumsily hazard their most precious relationships in the attempt. He is specifically clarifying the *manner* in which one should embody *apatheia*, i.e., not like a statue, but like a decent and faithful companion possessed with emotional intelligence.

Proper sociability is central to this discussion because it balances the Stoic ideal of *apatheia* with the obligations and practicalities of human relationships. For example, when Epictetus lectures his students about a philosopher's dignity, he emphasizes a would-be philosopher should never be drunk or rude, nor should he talk

---

61 Seneca, *Letters* 5.4.
62 Epictetus, *Handbook* 16. Cf. Seneca, *Letters* 99.15, 104.3. Seneca seems to say we should sometimes carefully indulge in grief for reasons of fellowship, implying certain forms of grief might qualify as rational emotions. Epictetus, on the other hand, seems to advocate for occasionally feigning grief, a stance David Hume later criticized. See Hume, *Of Moral Prejudices*.
63 Epictetus, *Discourses* 3.2.4.

overmuch, particularly about vulgar or lowbrow subjects. But he also should avoid annoying his companions by showing off with philosophical talk.[64] Furthermore, and contrary to the stereotype of stiff and dour intellectuals, Epictetus suggests mirth and merrymaking are part of the philosopher's life:

> And next, we must remember who we are, and what name we bear, and strive to direct our appropriate actions according to the demands of our social relationships, remembering what is the proper time to sing, the proper time to play, and in whose company, and what will be out of place, and how we may make sure that our companions don't despise us, and that we don't despise ourselves; when we should joke, and whom we should laugh at, and to what end we should associate with others, and with whom, and finally, how we should preserve our proper character when doing so.[65]

The takeaway from these passages is that one's appropriate acts are shaped by social relations. Emotional expressions like laughter, affection, and gestures of sympathy are all frequently part of acting appropriately. Caution is warranted, though; as Seneca, Epictetus, and Marcus Aurelius each observe, such forays onto the slippery slope of emotion can quickly plunge us into irrationality if we fail to pay attention. We cannot avoid the slope, so we must learn to navigate it competently.

Obligatory Emotions?

The Stoics' emphasis on sociability raises an intriguing question: are we not obligated to feel certain emotions in support of our social responsibilities? For example, is it not considered virtuous for citizens to feel a sense of pride in their own country or community? Further, is not a soldier expected to develop sentiments of kinship and mutual loyalty with his comrades-in-arms, such that any soldier who lacked these feelings would be deficient as such? Let us consider the question at a biological level: are not mothers and fathers obligated to love their children? Finally, aren't all of these individuals expected to feel fear and outrage toward whatever threatens the objects of their affection?

This line of inquiry strikes into the very heart of human experience, where incomplete or misunderstood answers could irretrievably poison the conversation. We should tread carefully. Let us focus on the example of a parent, specifically a father, since Epictetus illustrates several concepts in the context of paternal duty. Childrearing may be the most demanding and consequential responsibility an individual human can undertake, involving emotions of unparalleled intensity. This is probably why Epictetus employs parenthood in his teachings, despite having no biological offspring. No scenario challenges Stoic principles more directly or requires a greater leap from intuition to understanding than for a parent to identify their

---

64 E.g., Epictetus, *Handbook* 33, 46.
65 Epictetus, *Discourses* 4.12.16–17.

own child's life as neither good nor bad, but indifferent. If the logic of rational emotion holds up under the weight of parenthood, it should be understandable in other situations as well. Following Epictetus' lead, then, we will use the parent–child relationship to illustrate these challenging concepts.

To the point of our question: Stoics would not say one is obligated to *feel* or *think* anything, other than what is true or what follows from the truth. This is to say Stoics are obligated to appraise their impressions accurately. Affective emotions like familial love—let alone camaraderie or patriotism—would have to stand up to the same faculty of judgment as every other product of impressions. Passions like fear and rage would generally fail such a test, especially in the face of danger, which is exactly when one should be at their most calculating. Passions, as the byproducts of incorrect judgments, are unequivocally bad to Stoics. Recall that both Cicero and Seneca compare them to diseases.

The upside is that love doesn't have to be a passion; it can be a rational emotion, arising from correctly judged impressions. Epictetus even argues that only the wise can truly experience love.[66] *Of course* parents should love their children—what could be more consistent with nature? Likewise, generally speaking, good soldiers should share in a sense of common loyalty with their comrades-in-arms, and good citizens should acquire feelings of communal pride, but such emotions would have to be supported by correct underlying judgments to have any validity. Whether they are passions or rational emotions is contingent upon the soundness of whatever judgments produced them. In Chapter 5, we will look more deeply into community moral dynamics.

Let us consider the perspective of a Stoic sage who also happens to be the father of a small child. Such a man would necessarily judge that his child's life is neither good nor bad but indifferent, which is to say it is external to his sphere of control. At the same time, the child's well-being and happiness would be preferred by the sage, as would consist with nature. Further, the sage would recognize it is virtuous to fulfill his duties toward the child and therefore that doing so is a genuine good.[67] The sage might also take delight in his child's company, but his emotion would stop short of getting him 'carried away' to the realm of crippling passion. Perhaps most importantly, the sage would recognize his child as a transitory gift of nature that

---

[66] See Epictetus, *Discourses* 2.22.3. Epictetus suggests the unwise will invariably prioritize their (mis) perceived self-interests over those whom they purport to love. His point in this argument is really to illustrate what he sees as a mechanical and irresistible attraction to the perceived good, thus, if one misperceives indifferents like wealth to be goods, then their attraction to actual goods like properly attended familial duty will be diminished. Cf. Zeno in DL 7.124, "friendship exists only among the virtuous," and Seneca, *Letters* 35.1: "Try to perfect yourself, if for no other reason, in order that you may learn how to love."

[67] Cf. Epictetus, *Discourses* 3.3.8: "Yet if we place the good in right choice, the preservation of our relationships itself becomes a good."

could disappear at any moment, and with whom every available second should be cherished, as Epictetus says:

> So, too, in life, when you kiss your child, your brother, your friend, never let your imagination run free, or your transports carry you as far as they might wish, but hold them back, restrain them, like those who stand behind generals when they're riding in triumph and keep reminding them that they're mortal. In the same way, you should remind yourself that what you love is mortal, that what you love is not your own; it has been granted to you just for the present, not irrevocably, and not for ever …[68]

Thus, the Stoic knife returns to the conversation with its irresistible powers of separation. In the world of Epictetus, not even our children are truly ours—sooner or later, we will be parted, and it is better to accept this eventuality early on. However, our duty toward them is indeed ours and it should be embraced with a fully engaged faculty of judgment, informed as such by reason and virtue. This means there are right and wrong ways to fulfill the attendant duties. For example, familial love does not excuse injustice; we would condemn a parent who bribes school administrators to ensure their child's advantage over others more deserving. Nor does love excuse dereliction or cowardice. Despite our natural affinity, we must be willing to part company with loved ones to fulfill our societal obligations. In one of nature's great ironies, if we become 'carried away' and unable to control our emotions, we will fail those who depend on us—particularly those whom we love most.

This possibility is poignantly illustrated in a conversation between Epictetus and a father of small children. The father recalls an incident wherein his daughter had fallen ill, and his distress became so great that he could not bear to be in the same room as her. Rather than assist in her care, he instead fled his family to await news of her recovery from afar. Rebuked by Epictetus, the father justifies his behavior as natural, as if it were "what any normal father would do." Epictetus dismantles his excuse, suggesting the father conflates what is normal—to be less than perfect—with what is natural—to embody the faculty of reason. Comparing moral imperfections to tumors, Epictetus insists instead that "whatever is done in accordance with nature is rightly done."[69] While infections, parasites, obesity, and passions may be common, they are far from representing the natural state of a healthy human being.

It appears the dialogue's purpose is to clear up this common misconception about the Stoic concept of life in accordance with nature. However, the scenario described therein also serves as a case study in the third motion, whose momentum takes one over a precipice from which there is no return. The itinerant father's responsibility is self-evident, as is his abandonment of it when unrestrained passions reached such

---

[68] Ibid. 3.24.85. Cf. Seneca, *To Marcia* 1.7, 9.2, 10.3: "We should love all of our dear ones, but always with the thought that we have no promise that we may keep them forever—nay, no promise even that we may keep them for long."

[69] Epictetus, *Discourses* 1.11.5. Cf. *Discourses* 3.22.70–74 for a different angle on parental duty.

intensity he became unable to perform his most basic job. What might have been a respectable man is instead pathetic, condemnable once for his negligence and twice for his undignified self-excusing. Thus, the dialogue also serves as a warning, not unlike the anti-drug posters that adorn today's public schools. This, it implies, is your brain on passion.

Returning to our example of the sagacious father—we should acknowledge the philosophical acrobatics involved in preserving conventional notions of familial affection through hypothetical judgments no real human is likely to hold. What we can confidently state is that, even within a strictly Stoic framework, real human relationships almost always involve a mix of correct and incorrect judgments, rational emotions, and passions. As we have shown and will continue to explore, the Stoics view human sociability as essential to a well-lived life, with particular duties reserved for blood relations. While conventional wisdom might deem it inhumane to suggest the life of one's own child is a matter of indifference, it remains true that the child's life is beyond the parent's control. This is the key point. The crux of this reasoning is to place the moral value of the parent–child love within the rational agent who does the loving.

A true sage would calmly accept the death of his own child as neither a bad thing nor a good thing, but rather an indifferent event fated for all time. If we can accept this in theory, then we can see how the same logic applies to the death of a comrade, a professional calamity, a regrettable event of the past, or any other dispreferred occurrence. Such a degree of *apatheia* may not seem realistic or even desirable. However, the realism of this ideal is irrelevant to the coherence of the theory underlying it, within which the sage serves as a fictional example. Stoic virtue theory aims to show what is correct, or morally perfect, and it is up to each individual to determine what degree of perfection is realistic for them.

Amid our many shortcomings, real humans will invariably mix reason with passion and fail to make perfectly rational judgments. Just as it is normal to fall short of one's goals, it is also normal to become frustrated at such shortfalls, fostering a cycle of ambitious determination and self-disappointment for the would-be sage. But there is no value in adding the lamentation of human imperfection to one's woes, so it is perhaps in the interest of arresting such cycles that Seneca adopts a temperate tone toward self-regulation: "We may weep," he says, "but we must not wail."[70]

Acting Like You've Been There

If thinking clearly under conditions of emotional trauma is so important, then surely the Stoics must suggest some way to cultivate or train this ability. In fact, they do; it is implied in Epictetus' refrain to "remind yourself that what you love is mortal." What

---

70 Seneca, *Letters* 63.1.

he actually refers to is not just a simple reminder, but the deliberate and meditative exercise of contemplating the unthinkable. This technique, associated with Stoics going back to Chrysippus, is historically known as *premeditatio malorum*, a Latin phrase translating to "anticipation of evil." In popular literature, it is sometimes called "negative visualization."[71] Business-friendly analogs like 'fear-setting', 'pre-mortem', or 'defensive pessimism' adopt the same idea in management and performance psychology, but these sanitized adaptations do not approach the visceral cauterizing of the Stoics, who would think through the worst possible outcomes in the most vivid possible detail. For instance, Epictetus suggests, and Marcus repeats, that as we kiss our children goodnight, we should softly remind ourselves, "Tomorrow you will die."[72]

What benefit could possibly come of such self-torture? As it appears, many things. First, I should clarify that visualizing hardship is not about inducing emotional discomfort for its own sake. It is a form of *askēsis*, or "training" which, as employed by the Stoics, usually implies a kind of hardening. Physical forms of Stoic *askēsis*, for example, include fasting and the forfeiture of comfort and convenience, the aim of which is to make one familiar with the experience of poverty and accordingly unafraid of it. Seneca compares *askēsis* to the activity of a soldier in peacetime, who "performs maneuvers, throws up earthworks with no enemy in sight, and wearies himself by gratuitous toil, in order that he may be equal to unavoidable toil."[73] This process of creating adversity thus allows one to build resilience and reduce the shock of unexpected misfortunes. "If you would not have a man flinch when the crisis comes," he continues, "train him before it comes."

To visualize hardship, then, is effectively a kind of internal simulation Stoics suggest will dull the pain of emotional events when they do occur. Consider the difference between losing a healthy loved one to a tragic accident versus the moment an elderly or terminally ill relative reaches their long-foreseen conclusion. Both are painful, but there is a clear difference between the two attributable at least in part to the matter of shock and expectation. As Seneca writes, "by looking forward to the coming of our sorrows we take the sting out of them when they come."[74] If the foreseen hardship never occurs, then so much the better.

Because death is among the most innately 'dispreferred' of indifferents, it is the most common subject of this exercise in the Stoic sources. But the logic of this practice applies to any dispreferred event, such as financial loss, professional setbacks,

---

71 I prefer the straightforward phrase 'visualizing hardship' over 'negative visualization', as negative implies something inherently "bad" or "wrong" about what occurs. Hardship, however, is natural and inevitable. At times, it may even be self-imposed to constructive ends, such as through physical exercise or fasting, which can rightly be seen as forms of Stoic *askēsis*.
72 Marcus Aurelius, *Meditations* 11.34.
73 Seneca, *Letters* 18.5.
74 Seneca, *To Marcia* 9; cf. *Letters* 91.4–9.

or social rejection. By vividly imagining such scenarios, one can mentally prepare for them, blunting their emotional impact and fostering a sense of resilience. The ideal result is a kind of artificial veterancy—an air of having been there before, surprised by nothing. In this way, the dispreferred is transformed into a source of strength. There is, after all, a right and a wrong way to react to any life event, and hardships present a distinctive, if undesired, opportunity to add to the 'right' column.

Another purpose of anticipating hardship, then, is to serve as a kind of rehearsal, not just for how one should feel but for what one should do. Practical equivalents are close at hand; a good military planner, for example, considers all possible permutations of the campaign, particularly at junctures where events might not unfold as hoped. The resulting "branches and sequels" to the plan lay out the expected actions for unexpected outcomes, preventing setbacks from becoming catastrophes. Similarly, a good ship captain trains his crew in pre-planned responses for every conceivable casualty, leaving as little as possible to chance. It is especially when things go wrong that everyone should know what they are supposed to do.

Emotional hardships are not especially different. As we have said, there are right and wrong ways to react to any event; reacting poorly can make any bad situation worse. For example, when a family is struck by hardship—say, the house burns down—all members will be affected, and numerous practical tasks will require attention. It is better in these situations to be a source of strength and stability than another burden to carry. Milder setbacks happen every day, such as a rejected application to a desired program or a failure to receive an expected award or promotion. To react with bitterness or cries of foul always makes such things worse, but having thought through the dignified response makes it more likely to come about when called for.

One way to perceive potential hardships in exquisite and lifelike detail is to take note of their occurrence upon others. The unthinkable becomes real when it happens to those nearby, such that our neighbors and fellows can reveal our own vulnerabilities. Seneca vividly depicts this in the imagery of battle:

> Do you wish to know how completely exposed you are to every stroke of fate, and that the same shafts which have transfixed others are whirling around yourself? Then imagine that you are mounting without sufficient armor to assault some city wall or some strong and lofty position manned by a great host, expect a wound, and suppose that all those stones, arrows, and darts which fill the upper air are aimed at your body: whenever anyone falls at your side or behind your back, exclaim, "Fortune, you will not outwit me, or catch me confident and heedless: I know what you are preparing to do: you have struck down another, but you aimed at me."[75]

Every military leader knows how hard it is to motivate sincere efforts against dangers that seem remote or unrealistic. In contrast, it is much easier to prepare for the

---

75 Seneca, *To Marcia* 9.

proximate threat. For example, when the ship across the pier burns to the waterline, a crew will feel a sudden and reflexive impulse to prioritize fire prevention. A poor captain squanders the learning moment, scoffing, "Look at those fools; they have paid the price for their mistakes and low standards." In contrast, a good captain reflects, "There go we; let us consider our faults and take action to correct them." To judge is easy and fruitless, but to empathize is hard, yet useful.

The good captain's empathetic response recognizes a precarious condition shared with the neighboring crew. In this way, much like virtue itself, empathy is a form of knowledge. As consciousness of one's own vulnerability, it is self-knowledge. It creates a point of harmony—of *homologia*—between properties of communal solidarity and practical competence, or what reduce to the cardinal virtues of justice and prudence. To regularly anticipate hardship, especially as observed in the experiences of others, serves not only to cultivate but also to effectively apply the essential virtue of empathy.

There is still more to gain from anticipating hardship. Despite the bleak and gloomy thoughts it involves upfront, a final and surprising benefit is to yield a joyful state of mind. The basic idea is that by contemplating the possibility of loss, we enhance our appreciation of what we currently possess and prevent life's greatest pleasures from escaping notice. Practically speaking, we are surrounded by luxuries—air conditioning and tablet computers, nutrition and shelter and the freedom to move about—all of them treasures and none of them guaranteed. Even a glass of water is a luxury to one who is fully conscious of what it would be like to go without it.

So much the greater should be our appreciation of friends and family. Epictetus insists, "What you love is mortal; it has been granted to you just for the present, not irrevocably, and not forever."[76] He compares them to fruit like grapes or figs, which are only available for a season; to long for a companion who is no longer with us, then, is to long for a "fig in winter." By bearing this impermanence in mind, we permit ourselves to cherish our time with loved ones and to extract every trace of joy they can provide, without being carried away by notions of entitlement.

Such a perspective makes one not just a more joyful companion, but a better one. Imagine how many petty grievances and arguments would simply dissolve if we knew a given conversation would be our last. Epictetus suggests we train ourselves to think precisely this way, privately whispering of dear friends, "tomorrow you'll go abroad, or I will, and we'll never see each other again."[77] Such a mindset encourages one to savor the most mundane moments, transforming knowledge into happiness and improved relationships. Ultimately, it translates to a life of freedom, with full appreciation of the present and those with whom we share it.

---

76 Epictetus, *Discourses* 3.24.86.
77 Ibid. 3.24.88.

The Here and Now

As an exercise in attention, the imperative to appreciate what one has is generally categorized within the discipline of desire discussed earlier. This principle aligns with the widely recognized philosophical idea that true happiness arises not from 'getting what you want' but from 'wanting what you've got'. While this sentiment is frequently associated with Eastern traditions such as Buddhism and Taoism, it also surfaces across a broad spectrum of religious and philosophical systems, including Stoicism. However, it is important to avoid oversimplifying Epictetus' teachings by equating them with this familiar, and at times overly reductive, aphorism.

Epictetus would certainly agree with the claim true happiness is not found in getting what one wants, at least not in any conventional sense. He would probably also agree, albeit cautiously, that desiring what one has is the way to happiness. But his perspective sharply diverges from any common sensibility on the topic of 'what one has'. To Epictetus, even the simplest accommodations are still externals; a straw hut can still burn to the ground. Such things do not truly belong to us. 'Wanting what we have', then, is less about possessions or companions and more about appropriately valuing our own internal faculties. The discipline of desire, likewise, is not merely about wanting what we have but also about correctly identifying what is ours in the first place and separating the rest.

Our instrument for this task is the Stoic knife, fully developed: "that which is not up to one is not one." We have discussed it extensively throughout the chapter, showing how it cuts away all superficiality from the person, starting with trivialities like wealth and status, and continuing on to cut away friends, family, and even one's own body. Amazingly, there is still more cutting to do. What we have not yet done is lay the self-concept out over time; when we do this, we see there is still some excess. So let us get down to business: we can do nothing to affect the past; it is nothing to us. Cut it off. We also do not own the future; begone with it. What remains on the table is finally the core of who and what 'we' are, raw and exposed: moral choice, observed instantaneously.[78]

Of course, a practical emphasis on the present had been a tenet of Stoicism long before Epictetus came along to anchor everything upon moral choice. There are many reasons for this emphasis, some dispositional and some technical. Recall from Chapter 1, for example, that Stoics are early proponents of both *Materialism* and *Nominalism*. To briefly review, *Materialism* means Stoics believe everything that exists is composed of physical substance, including thoughts and impressions occurring within the body and brain. *Nominalism*, on the other hand, means abstract concepts like 'education' or 'beauty' are not independent entities but rather names we assign to describe groups of similar ideas.

---

78 Pierre Hadot calls this practice "circumscribing the present." See Hadot, *The Inner Citadel*, 131–37.

Incorporating these two principles, the Stoic view is that thoughts and impressions can only exist in the present. There are no such things as potential or dispositional thoughts, or what one might call thoughts that could exist or are held in a dormant state. Past thoughts may be remembered or recorded, and future thoughts may be postulated, but neither actually exist as anything but concepts. Instead, thoughts exist when and only when they are actively being conceived within the physical substance of the being that conceives them.

Although we don't have evidence of a tripartite ruling center within Stoicism before Epictetus, we can see how these effects manifest within its distinct governing processes. Assent, or the capacity to judge and accept or reject impressions, is concerned with the impressions we perceive in the present moment. Desire, as discussed earlier, pertains to the attractions and repulsions we feel at the very instant we experience them. Action, the third governing process of the ruling center, refers to what we are doing in the present, not what we have done in the past or what we may do in the future.

Thus, whether viewed from an early or late Stoic vantage point, there is a technical basis for an undercurrent of *Presentism* within Stoic teachings. We should note it is not accurate to call Stoics presentists in the formal sense, because the formal theory of *Presentism*—which did not crystallize until centuries after the Stoics—denies the past and future are real. In contrast, the past and future are real enough to Stoics, but they do not matter nor do they contain 'us' in any meaningful sense. In academic language, then, Stoics could be properly called 'soft' presentists. The important point is, for the Stoics, the essence of our existence and moral agency reside firmly in the present moment, where our thoughts, desires, and actions intersect to form our lived experience.

It is not even clear the Stoics agree on how the present should be defined. The problem is not quite as simple as bounding the past and the future, since both are infinite and it is not necessarily a given anything lies between them. Chrysippus even argues the past and the future, being infinitely divisible, leave nothing behind that can be considered "wholly present."[79] This would make the present like a transition period involving some mixture of past or future, but indistinguishable as a discrete timeframe. The middle Stoic Posidonius seems to agree with this framing, describing it as "a part of the past and a part of the future, encompassing the actual division," itself described as "point-like."[80] Seneca captures the issue poetically: "Infinitely swift is the flight of time, as those see more clearly who are looking backwards. For when we are intent on the present, we do not notice it, so gentle is the passage of time's headlong flight."[81]

---

79 Stobaeus I.106,5–23 (SVF 2.509) = LS 51B.
80 Ibid. I.105,17–106,4 (Posidonius fragment 98) = LS 51E.
81 Seneca, *Letters* 49.10.6.

Intriguingly, despite his claim that no time is "wholly present," Chrysippus also asserts that "only the present belongs; the past and the future subsist, but belong in no way."[82] He illustrates this idea with the example of walking. This action, he explains, "belongs" to one only when one is actually walking. When lying down or sitting, although it may be true that one has walked or will walk, those activities do not "belong" at any moment when they are not occurring; they merely "subsist." In this context, "subsist" means past or future walks are conceivable only as states of potential or memory, not as existing realities, which aligns with the Stoics' materialist and nominalist inclinations.

Compared to the obscurity of early and middle Stoics, the Epictetan take is mercifully intuitive. Viewed through the framework of moral choice, we can at least confirm what the present, as that which "belongs," is not. The past, for one thing, is clearly beyond us, and that we cannot control it is not an especially challenging claim. The past should not be dismissed outright, as we can extract great value from it as a learning asset, especially when considering what mistakes we might otherwise repeat. Seneca, for example, describes a nightly routine of rigorous self-examination and atonement, as if standing before a self-presided court.[83] But to dwell on the past, to ruminate on it, or to carry it as emotional baggage is useless. It is not ours, as Epictetus would say, and therefore it has no moral significance.

That we cannot control the future is more controversial. Do we not influence the future when we study for a test, plant crops, or build a house? This is a common area of confusion that points to a deeper misconception about *Determinism* and free will. It is famously put to Chrysippus in the form of a critique known as "the lazy argument" (*argos logos*), which proposes a Stoic beset by illness should not even bother with a doctor, since their recovery or demise is already decided by fate. It is thereby suggested Stoicism promotes a fatalistic outlook indistinguishable from laziness or passivity, wherein all efforts are abandoned to the results of chance.

As Cicero describes the rebuttal, Chrysippus points out that a visit to the doctor, which would be a plainly appropriate action, might also be fated for the ill Stoic. Whether recovery or death is fated, either fate would follow from some set of antecedent causes. The doctor's visit, which Chrysippus would call 'co-fated', would be a perfectly normal preceding cause of recovery. When we consider that actions and their outcomes are intertwined in a web of causality, the lazy argument falls apart. "If we gave in to it," says Cicero, "we would do nothing whatever in life."[84]

Chrysippus' reply to the lazy argument encapsulates a Stoic attitude toward what would later become a pressing question for philosophers: whether a predetermined universe would make free will an illusion. According to one tradition, called "hard"

---

82 Stobaeus I.106,5–23 (SVF 2.509) = LS 51B.
83 Seneca, *On Anger* 3.36.
84 Cicero, *On Fate*, 28–30 = LS 55S.

determinism, if all human actions are the inevitable results of prior events, then humans are effectively 'locked in' to a particular set of choices with no hope of acting otherwise.[85] Moral responsibility is thus undermined, as individuals are merely conduits for deterministic processes. In some circles, people with this view are called 'incompatibilists', because they hold that *Determinism* is incompatible with free will.[86]

The Stoics, for their part, do not entertain any such conflict between *Determinism* and free will or, perhaps more pertinently, between *Determinism* and moral responsibility. Stoics maintain that while the universe operates according to a web of causality and fate, human beings still possess a form of agency, making them early 'compatibilists'. Although whatever actions we might undertake to influence the future are already part of the causal chain and are therefore already 'baked in' to the cosmic plan, the causal chain is effectively imperceptible in the moment we make choices.[87] All we have to work with is the present moment because that is the only timeframe in which a faculty of moral choice exists. From 'our' perspective, as creatures of the present, we are entirely free.

Determinism, then, does not absolve us of any degree of responsibility to act appropriately, such as it might be appropriate to plan, study, or train for some future event (we will deal more with appropriate action in the next chapter). The crucial distinction between passivity and accepting fate is that, regardless of our (appropriate) efforts to influence the future, we still must not suffer any emotional attachment to their outcomes. We should study for the test and yet the schoolhouse might burn down with us inside it. Whatever happens has always been fated to happen and we will have the tools to deal with it when it comes. Epictetus expands, "Now doesn't the future lie outside the sphere of choice? Yes. And doesn't the nature of the good and the bad lie within the sphere of choice? Yes indeed. So whatever may happen, isn't it possible for you to make use of it in accordance with nature?"[88]

A serene focus on the present has long been a feature of the philosopher stereotype, alongside gray beards and simple clothing. For the Stoics, though, this is not just a practical affectation, but the necessary endpoint of two interrelated but distinct logical paths. One is a product of physics, as described in the arcane theorizing of

---

85 The most influential 'hard' determinist is probably Baruch Spinoza, whose *Ethics Demonstrated in Geometrical Order* (1677) systematically argues for a deterministic worldview and the denial of free will. Spinoza is deeply influenced by the Stoics, particularly their pantheistic view of the universe, which aligns with his own view of 'God or Nature' as a single, all-encompassing substance.
86 See Caruso, "Skepticism About Moral Responsibility," *The Stanford Encyclopedia of Philosophy* (Summer 2021).
87 This is a simplified explanation. For a thorough breakdown of Crysippean causal-fate determinism, and how Epictetus differs from Chrysippus on what is "up to us," see Bobzien, "Stoic Conceptions of Freedom."
88 Epictetus, *Discourses* 4.10.8.

Chrysippus and his ilk. The other is borne of ethics, coming to fruition in the practical teachings of Epictetus. When the knife is taken out to its logical conclusions, we see Stoics cannot help but attend exclusively to the present because alternatives are beyond the reach of moral choice.

Despite this multi-point foundation in Stoic theory, a predisposition to focus on the present also confers numerous practical benefits, which explains its popularity in a variety of philosophical traditions. I can address three of them here. The first I have already covered in the previous section on anticipating hardship, which is the effect of joyfully recognizing what one 'has'. In the context of visualizing hardship, whatever lies outside of moral choice is effectively borrowed and temporary, and thus can be best appreciated with full sensitivity to what it would be like to do without it. This leads naturally to the focus on the present, which comprises everything that merits this joyful recognition. Anticipating hardship and focusing on the present are thus two sides of the same coin.

The second benefit coincides with the development of personal discipline, specifically as represented in the disciplines of assent and action. To focus on the present is to pull what is currently being thought or being done to the forefront of mind, making both thoughts and actions more accessible to a faculty of judgment. Both begin as impressions and, as Epictetus says, "the most important task of a philosopher, and his first task, is to test out impressions and distinguish between them."[89] Exposed to scrutiny, irrational thoughts and impulses can be identified and interrupted in the moment they occur. Through this mechanism, attention, discipline, and *Presentism* all work together in a mutually reinforcing cycle.

The third benefit is to cultivate emotional resilience, achieved by transforming seemingly insurmountable challenges into individual tasks. By focusing solely on the immediate next steps—what needs to be done in the present—big problems are broken into smaller, more manageable segments. This technique is well-established in modern performance psychology, where determined individuals overcome long-term endeavors, such as authoring a book or completing a doctoral program, by focusing on the immediate actions in front of them. Endurance athletes, in a similar fashion, are trained to disregard the vast distance ahead and instead to meditatively concentrate on putting one foot ahead of the other. As recognized by the Stoics, the same approach reveals a path through long-term emotional hardships such as grief, depression, or chronic illness. As Marcus Aurelius frames it:

> Beware of the disquiet that can follow from picturing your life as a whole. Don't dwell on all the various kind of troubles that have happened and are likely to happen in the future as well. No, focus on the present, and ask yourself whether there's anything about the task before you that's unbearable and insupportable, because it would be shameful to admit that there is. And

---

89 Ibid. 1.20.7.

then remind yourself that neither the future nor the past can weigh on you, but only the present, and that the present becomes easier to bear if you take it on its own.[90]

By focusing on the present, Stoics live out the key tenets of their philosophy while also cultivating emotional resilience, personal discipline, and appreciation for life's blessings. Stoics recognize the present as the temporal seat of moral choice and the only timeframe in which one can exercise agency and reason. Two lines of reasoning converge on this orientation: the technical principles of physics laid down by early Stoics, and the ethical doctrine of moral choice put forward by late Stoic Epictetus. Both emphasize the present moment as the only thing that truly belongs and the only thing we can control. By internalizing this and directing their attention accordingly, Stoics aim to live in harmony with nature, exercising total dominion over what is within their power while calmly accepting what is not.

A Responsibility Heuristic

When first encountering the ideas in this chapter, a reader might protest that the Stoics promote an unrealistic standard of self-control. This concern is particularly salient in light of neuroses like addiction or depression, which, in the absence of modern medical science, the Stoics might have regarded as mere flaws of character. However, it would not be entirely accurate to say the Stoics believed any human could consistently maintain perfect self-control. This question reduces to whether Stoics genuinely believed in the existence of sages, which, as I have suggested, might depend on which Stoic you ask. Nonetheless, the point of the sage is not so much to show what is achievable as it is to show what human perfection would look like, were it achieved. As I demonstrated in the previous chapter, Epictetus acknowledges human fallibility, including his own fallibility, but brushes off the matter as irrelevant to his wider point. For him, what matters is not so much the attainability of perfection but the imperative to strive for it earnestly.

The Stoics' general dismissal of human fallibility resembles a phenomenon observable in all areas of human responsibility: outcomes generally improve when one acts *as if* they were in control of everything for which they are responsible. This should be familiar to anyone with experience in a military organization. Consider, for example, the obligations of a typical aircraft squadron commander. Within her cognizance are countless materials, people, and events whose conditions and behaviors are not fully within her control. However, if the commander bemoans such limitations or cites them as the reason things do not go as planned, then more unsatisfactory results are likely to follow. Conversely, if the commander rejects such talk and

---

90 Marcus Aurelius, *Meditations* 8.36. Cf. *Meditations* 6.32. According to Gretchen Reydams-Schils, Marcus' conception of a bound present is incompatible with that of the early Stoics. See Reydams-Schils, *The Roman Stoics*, 30.

focuses on what she actually can control, effectively behaving *as if* everything within her responsibility were also within her power, then that commander will naturally wield her finite influence more effectively and will tend to generate better results.

This is not to say the commander should internally harbor illusions about her own influence, that she should claim credit for unearned success, or that she should neurotically micromanage every detail within her cognizance. It does mean, though, that the commander understands those details are ultimately her own responsibility, regardless of the limits to her influence, as are whatever events or results follow from those details.

An effective commander will therefore establish conditions conducive to optimal outcomes by whatever means she has available, including prudent risk-taking and delegation. It rarely matters that the specifics of one event or another might have been beyond her ability to control. What matters, in the aggregate, is her overall performance, the assessment of which will be informed by her propensity to assume responsibility. Seniors instinctively recognize this in the behaviors and reports of their subordinate commanders, and they tend to have more confidence in those commanders who naturally behave *as if* they had full control of events that, examined realistically, are subject to the vagaries of chance.

If we were to put a name to this phenomenon, we might call it a 'responsibility heuristic'. A heuristic is a practical, experience-based technique or rule of thumb used to solve problems and make decisions quickly. It is, in effect, a mental shortcut. A responsibility heuristic, then, refers to the specific behavioral strategy where individuals act *as if* they were in control of everything they identify as falling within their responsibility, regardless of whether they truly believe they have that degree of control. It is the logical extension of an Epictetan dismissal of everything that is beyond one's power. It is not an absolute rule or a guarantor of outcomes, but it reflects a general disposition that encourages useful behaviors and discourages fruitless agonizing and self-victimization.

There is a well-established concept in modern psychology that should be distinguished from a responsibility heuristic. It is called the *locus of control* and it describes an individual's belief about the extent to which they have control over the events in their lives.[91] According to the underlying theory, individuals exist on a spectrum between two tendencies. At one end is an internal locus of control, where people believe they have significant control over their life events and outcomes, attributing success and failure to their own actions and decisions. At the opposite end is an external locus of control, where individuals believe external factors—such as luck, fate, or other people—have more control over their life events, attributing outcomes to forces outside their control. In pejorative terms, an external locus of control might be called a 'victim mentality'. Although an extreme internal locus of

---

91 Rotter, "Generalized Expectancies for Internal versus External Control of Reinforcement," 1–28.

control can introduce some unique problems, a moderate internal locus of control is associated with healthy attitudes and positive outcomes, making its cultivation a common aim in training and education.

A responsibility heuristic and an internal locus of control are therefore adjacent, but separate ideas. The key difference between them lies in the distinction between belief and behavior. Both concepts reflect the practical wisdom that life is like a game of cards, where the outcome depends not on the cards one is dealt but on how one plays the hand. However, they differ in their appraisal of matters beyond one's control. An extreme internal locus of control would have one literally believe the game's outcome is not affected by the hand one is dealt. In contrast, the responsibility heuristic would have one behave *as if* luck is not a factor, even while understanding the hand one is dealt does influence the outcome. It is therefore a kind of practical accommodation to the statistical fact the cards do influence the likelihood of winning or losing. Its result is to effectively 'force' the benefits of an internal locus of control, regardless of the individual's literal belief in their capacity to affect their situation.

I broach these ideas in this chapter because I think they are important to the way Stoics think about their own limitations or, rather, do not think about them. For Stoics, a responsibility heuristic does not just appear in practical behaviors and a dismissive attitude toward worldly fortune, although it certainly manifests in these ways.[92] It also reveals itself in their approach to internal human fallibility and the possibility of sagacity. As we saw with Epictetus, whether or not perfect discipline is attainable is beside the point of what one should do. Like an effective commander, a person is obligated to exercise whatever influence they can over their internal command center and, more importantly, to take full responsibility for it.

From Attention to Discipline

Throughout this chapter, I have explored the workings of the human mind as conceived by the Stoics, tracing a path from the activity of attention to the virtue of discipline. I have shown how these two ideas are inextricably related, creating a mutually reinforcing relationship that is essential for achieving one's potential as conceived in the Stoic ideal of life in accordance with nature.

To review, the Stoic theory of mind is centered upon the *hegemonikon*, or ruling center, which governs an individual's thoughts, emotions, and actions through the

---

92 We should not mistake this to suggest that Stoics would claim credit for worldly successes; on the contrary, such trifles are indifferents, and where fate has any role to play in their attainment, it must be given full credit: "Even though they are in our possession, they are to be reckoned as things subordinate and poor, the possession of which gives no man a right to plume himself. For what is more foolish than being self-complacent about something which one has not accomplished by one's own efforts?" Seneca, *Letters* 74.17. Cf. Epictetus, *Discourses* 3.14.11–4; *Fragments* 18.

interdependent processes of assent, desire, and action. What these processes actually *do* is to sort and manage impressions, which include sense data, thoughts, appetites, and behavioral impulses. Establishing dominion over these processes, or achieving the respective 'disciplines' of assent, desire, and action, entails a state of constant attention to what is happening in thought and deed.

Central to the sorting and filtering of impressions is the concept of *prohairesis*, or moral choice. Uniquely among the Stoics, Epictetus places this concept at the heart of his philosophy. By distinguishing between what is within our power and what is not, and elevating the former to supreme importance, Epictetus creates a powerful framework for navigating life's challenges. Far from just a reminder not to worry about what one cannot control, this framework allows one to sort impressions effectively, akin to an incredibly sharp knife that cuts away everything external and indifferent. This has profound implications for the meanings of personal identity and freedom.

Our journey through the ruling center also led us into the Stoic theory of emotions, which are described as the result of judgments about impressions. Passions, or the products of bad judgments, are eliminated not by suppression but by correcting the judgments that produce them. An active and effective mechanism for filtering impressions does not only benefit decision-making, but also emotional resilience. Crucially, emotions are not all bad to Stoics, and the proper management of *eupatheiai* or "rational emotions" is important to human sociability. The desired state of *apatheia*, or emotional clarity, describes a healthy and domesticated emotional condition completely free of passions.

Finally, I explored the Stoic emphasis on the present moment, which emerges as the logical culmination and point of convergence for their ideas on time, causality, and moral choice. As a form of self-training to encourage the presentist mentality, I explained how visualizing loss and adversity can serve to place the blessings of the present in perspective. Furthermore, although a tendency to focus on the present follows naturally from fundamental Stoic beliefs, I also showed how it delivers practical benefits toward the cultivation of emotional resilience, personal discipline, and the accurate appraisal of life's bountiful joys.

We have now reached a critical point of transition. Earlier in the chapter, I distilled the Stoic value system into three primary aims: to think what is true, to desire what is one's own, and to do what is right. I devoted much of the discussion to the first two aims, leaving the third relatively unexplored. How, then, are we to do what is right? Moreover, how can we even discern what the right thing to do is? A life in accordance with nature does not end with the refinement of one's internal faculties; it must extend outward to manifest reason as ethical action and the fulfillment of moral obligations. The next logical step, then, is to examine how Stoics propose to identify and perform appropriate actions—those that align with reason, virtue, and the natural order.

CHAPTER 4

Duty

> Tell yourself first what kind of person you want to be,
> then act accordingly in all that you do.
>
> EPICTETUS, *DISCOURSES* 3.23.1.

In the previous chapter, I introduced the concept of a mind governed by three interlinked psychological processes: assent, desire, and action. Together, these processes comprise a kind of 'command center' of the soul. Mastery, or 'discipline', over each of these processes is the path to fulfilling one's rational nature: to think what is true, to desire what is truly one's own, and to do what is right. Throughout the chapter, we examined the control of one's internal thoughts, known as the discipline of assent, illustrating how it enables the dismissal of unhelpful impressions. This practice engenders a reflexive gratitude for one's present circumstances, setting aside anything beyond the current moment as external and irrelevant—along with any desires for things beyond one's own control. This is the essence of the discipline of desire. Now, I shift attention to the third process: action.

I will begin by revisiting an important yet puzzling distinction between the perfectly virtuous actions of the sage, known as "right actions," and the behaviors of imperfect individuals who still manage to do what they ought to do, referred to as "appropriate actions." From there, I will dive deeper into the concept of "appropriate action," isolating the key criteria Stoics use to determine whether an action is appropriate or inappropriate. Additionally, I will establish a distinction between appropriate actions and duties, demonstrating these terms are not interchangeable.

These ideas will set the stage for a specific approach to appropriate action unique to the teachings of Epictetus. Known as "role ethics," his method frames moral obligations through the lens of one's various roles—whether personal or professional—offering a practical structure for understanding and fulfilling one's responsibilities. As I unpack this framework, I will confront important questions that arise when striving to do what one ought: What does it mean to act in accordance with nature? How can one resolve moral conflicts while staying true to virtues like prudence, courage, moderation, and justice? And, finally, when is it appropriate to diligently fulfill one's role-based duties and when is principled nonconformity warranted?

Through this investigation, I will show that, for the Stoics, the discipline of action is not about rigid adherence to a set of rules, but rather about rational and context-sensitive discernment following from an accurate understanding of the facts. This approach shapes the Stoic view of moral obligations. It is important to recognize Stoics do not have a word for duty in the way it is often understood today, as seen in more formalized ethical systems like Kantian ethics. However, they offer a rich and nuanced framework for addressing moral responsibility, showing, for human beings, our shared rational nature is expressed and fulfilled through the actions we choose to undertake.

What Virtue Compels

In Chapter 2, I established that right actions and appropriate actions are distinct, with the difference hinging on the internal qualities of the actor. To recap, right actions, translated from the Greek term *katorthōma*, are morally perfect behaviors. Such actions would be performed by a fully wise and virtuous person—a sage. What makes an action 'right' is not merely the outward behavior, but the inner disposition from which it arises. A right action must be motivated by pure intentions and carried out with a sense of tranquility and contentment. It naturally flows from a character in perfect harmony with reason and nature.

In contrast, appropriate actions, or *kathēkonta*, are those activities that resemble right actions in their external appearance and consequence but do not originate from a perfect internal disposition. They are the actions ordinary, non-sage humans can perform when they are making progress toward wisdom and virtue. An appropriate action is one that accords with nature and is suitable for a given situation, and yet it may be compromised by ulterior motives. For example, repaying a debt is normally an appropriate action, but we might only do so with an eye to our narrow self-interest, for example, to preserve an ability to secure future loans. Still, even if the specific action is performed with pure motives as an isolated action, it is still not a right action if it originates from a non-sage.

This idea connects with the Stoic concept of virtue as a unified construct. Unlike right actions, appropriate actions can follow from particular discrete virtues. Cicero explains, "Though these four virtues are bound up and interconnected with each other, certain types of obligation arise from each of them individually."[1] I might repay the debt because and only because I am prudent, or because and only because I am just. In contrast, truly right action—the action of the sage—manifests virtue in its entirety. A sage would not only repay the debt but would be sincerely happy to do it; indeed, it would not occur to him to act in any other way. Perfection in one virtue entails perfection in all virtues, just as deficiency in one virtue entails

---

1   Cicero, *On Duties* 1.15.

deficiency in all. The sage's right action, then, reflects not just outward correctness, but a harmonious inner state where all virtues cohere in effortless expression.

An ordinary non-sage—a progressor—performs appropriate actions through conscious effort and discipline but may still experience internal conflict or struggle. This distinction from the perfect equanimity of a sage describes the transition into sagacity. As Chrysippus explains, "The man who progresses to the furthest point performs all proper functions without exception and omits none. Yet his life ... is not yet happy, but happiness supervenes on it when these intermediate actions acquire the additional properties of firmness and tenor and their own particular fixity."[2] Beneath the jargon is a critical insight: when I am on the cusp of sagacity I may outwardly perform *nothing but* appropriate actions, such that I am externally indistinguishable from a sage. However, I will not experience the inner tranquility and joy of the sage until my actions become habitual and instinctive.

There are two other points we should clarify regarding the difference between right action and appropriate action. The first is that all right actions are technically a special kind of appropriate action; we might call them 'perfected appropriate actions'.[3] This detail is important because a complete separation between right and appropriate actions could imply the existence of two distinct moral systems—one for sages and another for everyone else. Some scholars have even suggested what is effectively a practical, 'second-best' morality of appropriate actions for non-sages, whereas sages would be bound by different moral standards.[4] However, progressors and sages are not evaluated differently; they are simply at different points along the same continuum of moral development. Furthermore, the question of whether perfection is truly achievable is irrelevant to this evaluation.

The second outstanding point is that, in the Stoic view, it is impossible to do anything other than what one perceives to be the appropriate action, while virtue lies in clarifying what that is. In effect, this is a facet of Stoic *egoism*, the principle we introduced in the previous chapter. It describes the theory individuals must be irresistibly attracted to the perceived good. Consistent with the Socratic principle that virtue is knowledge, Stoics leave no room for the idea we might do something knowingly improper or against our own interest, which is equivalent to our natural purposes. As Epictetus says, "When someone acts badly towards you, or speaks badly of you, remember that he is acting or speaking in that way because he regards that as being the proper thing for him to do."[5]

---

2   Stobaeus 5.906,18–907,5 (SVF 3.510) = LS 59I.
3   Ibid. 2.93,14–8 (SVF 3.500) = LS 59K. See also Brennan, *The Stoic Life*, 170ff.
4   E.g., Schmekel, *Die Philosophie der mittleren Stoa*, 358–66. For refutations of the two-tiered view of morality, see Inwood, "Rules and Reasoning in Stoic Ethics," 99–100; Visnjic, *Invention of Duty*, 60–61; Long and Sedley, *The Hellenistic Philosophers*, 1: 364–68.
5   Epictetus, *Handbook* 42.

For example, a cigarette smoker in the act of smoking must believe, at some level, that smoking is the 'thing to do', otherwise they would not engage in it. Their action reflects assent to the 'impulsive impression' that smoking is appropriate, which drives their body to act.[6] This belief subsists—must subsist, based on the smoker's behavior—regardless of any knowledge they may possess about the health risks or social consequences. This doesn't imply the smoker is consciously weighing all these factors; rather, it illustrates the Stoic view that every action begins as an impression. Even someone committing an objectively unjust act, such as burglary or murder, is motivated by the belief their actions are the thing to do within the context of their specific situation.[7]

An important consequence of this point, for many scholars, is to preclude a direct equivalence between appropriate action and duty. In earlier scholarship, *kathêkon* was frequently translated as "duty," and some of the sources referenced in this book maintain that translation. However, this practice has largely fallen out of favor, with "appropriate action" becoming the most common rendering.[8] Some scholars still remain unsatisfied with "appropriate action," arguing it fails to fully capture the naturalistic aspects of *kathêkon* as employed by the Stoics. Alternatives such as "befitting actions," "prescribed actions," or "proper functions" have been proposed and appear in some of the quoted sources. Nevertheless, to preserve compatibility with the majority of literature, I use appropriate action throughout this book. This does not, however, preclude appropriate actions from also being considered duties.

To clarify, let's consider some of the issues scholars have with translating *kathêkon* as "duty." One major concern is that not every action can be meaningfully considered a duty. However, based on Stoic psychological theory, every action is viewed as appropriate by the actor at the moment they perform it. For example, when a robber snatches a purse, they necessarily believe this is *kathêkon*. But if we say they think this is their duty, we are not using the term in any recognizable sense. At the same time, alternatives like 'appropriate', 'proper', or 'prescribed' would not be any better. The issue here isn't with how we interpret *kathêkon*, but rather how the hypothetical robber interprets it—that is, wrongly.

Admittedly, if all actions are perceived as duties, it becomes difficult to pinpoint where the Stoics would draw a line between a moral obligation (what we typically mean by duty) and a morally indifferent action that is still appropriate to one's nature, like Epictetus' example of choosing to bend or extend a finger. But why must there be such a line? There's no reason to believe the Stoics think all duties are

---

6 Stobaeus 2.86,17–87,6 (SVF 3.169, part) = LS 53Q. Note the addictive properties of nicotine would be understood as 'upstream' of the impulsive impression that smoking is the 'thing to do'. Insofar as the ancient Stoics would comprehend the neurosis of addiction at all, it would be viewed as a flaw of character, specifically a lack of self-control.
7 After Brennan, *The Stoic Life*, 175.
8 Visnjic, *Invention of Duty*, 9.

equally compelling.⁹ My duty to extinguish a fire clearly outweighs my duty to hose down an aircraft. If we accept there are greater and lesser duties, then we can also accept some otherwise arbitrary actions may become minor moral obligations simply because we prefer them. Since virtue is expressed through the rational selection of preferred and dispreferred indifferents, bending or extending a finger would indeed become the 'thing to do' the moment one preferred to do so—provided there is no overriding moral obligation at play.

A second issue for scholars in translating *kathêkon* as duty is that Stoics consider the natural life processes of infants, animals, and even plants as appropriate actions for those organisms. What defines an action as *kathêkon* is simply its alignment with nature. However, since moral obligation cannot apply to beings that lack moral agency, some argue *kathêkon* cannot mean the same thing as duty.[10] I suggest, however, that a concept of duty does not necessarily imply moral obligation. Duty can simply refer to fulfilling one's *telos*—purpose—or performing one's role within a given context.

For instance, an infant's first purpose is to preserve itself.[11] Similarly, a houseplant's purpose is to maintain a pleasing appearance when provided with adequate water and light. For the Stoics, the actions of these nonmoral agents are functionally similar to the actions of a human who fulfills their nature as a rational and virtuous being. While the Stoic concept of duty may not always require moral agency, this is hardly a reason to deny Stoics employ a concept of duty. The trouble is not that the ancient Greeks are lacking a word for duty in the strictly moralistic sense that we normally use. It is that *we* do not have a word that adequately captures the Greeks' simultaneously naturalistic and moralistic sense of appropriateness.[12]

Rather than avoid the term, we should clearly establish a meaning for it when employed in reference to Stoic ethics. One possible resolution would be to translate *kathêkon* differently based on context; in this sense, we could use something like 'appropriate actions' when speaking in the naturalistic sense, while reserving 'duty'

---

9   Tad Brennan argues that "bending one's finger in the right way, or walking and talking in the right way, are no less central expressions of the agent's nature than returning deposits and keeping promises," a claim Jack Visnjic disputes (See Brennan, *The Stoic Life*, 174; and Visnjic, *Invention of Duty*, 20). Although this is not Brennan's argument, one reason someone might conclude all duties are equal is by viewing the issue through the binary lens of Stoic moral perfectionism. If we accept people are either virtuous (perfect) or vicious (imperfect), then by extension it seems all vicious acts must be equally vicious. In this light, neglecting to hose down an aircraft could be considered equally vicious as neglecting to put out a fire. However, in any given instant (the present, where we exist as deciding moral agents), there is only one truly appropriate action—and in this case, it is clearly to put out the fire. In this way, some duties can override others while presenting no conflict with Stoic moral perfectionism.
10 Jack Visnjic cites Manuel Lorenz as an example. Visnjic, *Invention of Duty*, 20.
11 Cicero, *On Ends* 3.17, 20–2 = LS 59D; DL 7.85.
12 Visnjic, *Invention of Duty*, 10–13.

for more moralistic contexts.[13] However, I think this would be a step backward from apprehending that following nature is itself a moral obligation. In other words, when properly understood, the moralistic and the naturalistic contexts of *kathêkon* are inseparable.

In the following pages, I will outline a method for employing the term 'duty' in discussions of the Stoic moral system. Although it is not a direct translation of any specific Greek term, it serves as a context-sensitive bridge between ancient Greek concepts and modern English diction. As previously stated, I will follow the convention wherein *kathêkon* is translated as "appropriate action." However, I hold the view that, just as all right actions are a specific type of appropriate action, all appropriate actions are, in a broader sense, duties—things one ought to do. Conversely, not all duties are necessarily appropriate actions; I will clarify this distinction shortly. For now, the key takeaway is that an appropriate action, whether performed by a human adult or a house plant, is one that aligns with the actor's nature. Vice, on the other hand, stems from confusion or ignorance about what that is. Moral agency, then, is not a prerequisite to duty—appropriate or otherwise—but it is a prerequisite to vice.

Consequentiality and Reasonableness

We have established appropriate action refers to behavior that aligns with nature, but this hardly constitutes a satisfactory definition. What does it even mean to 'align with nature'? Is this truly the best we can do? As usual, our inquiry is confounded by the fragmentary and often muddled nature of the primary sources. The most granular definition on record comes from a critical commentator, who describes appropriate action as that which possesses "consequentiality in life" and "admits of a reasonable justification" when performed.[14] From such meager provisions, scholars have attempted to distill the necessary and sufficient conditions of appropriate action. As it stands, these are captured in the nebulous terms 'consequentiality' and 'reasonableness'.

Let us first consider consequentiality. Without further information, one might assume it refers to an action's impact or the importance of its outcomes—essentially equating consequentiality with 'significance'. However, this is actually the reverse of its intended meaning. In the context of an appropriate action, consequentiality refers to the action occurring *as a consequence* of something else, specifically indicating conformity with nature's plan for the actor.[15] The climbing and light-seeking behaviors of a vine have consequentiality, as do the courtship rituals of gregarious birds.

---

13 This is effectively what Jack Visnjic recommends, using his preferred term of "prescribed actions." See Visnjic, *Invention of Duty*, 19–21.
14 Stobaeus 2.85,13–86,4 (SVF 3.494) = LS 59B.
15 Long and Sedley, *The Hellenistic Philosophers*, 1: 365.

In essence, an action is consequential insofar as it arises from, or is in harmony with, nature. In this sense, plants and animals perform appropriate actions by acting in ways that are natural and fitting for their species.

Alongside consequentiality is the linguistically awkward criterion of reasonableness. As deployed by the Stoics, reasonableness implies legitimacy or justifiability in a legal sense, suggesting wider reference to moral defensibility—hence the phrase "admits of a reasonable justification." It is distinguished from consequentiality in that the latter implies an obligation to perform the act (as a natural 'consequence' of one's situation) whereas reasonableness does not. An arbitrary action with no discernable moral valence—bending or extending one's finger, for example—would be reasonable, but not consequent.

Just as consequentiality does not necessarily refer to importance or significance, reasonableness does not imply human reasoning must directly contribute to every action. For instance, reasoning has no part to play in the appropriate actions of infants, animals, or plants. Such actions merely need to align with, or be defensible through, reason. That said, for mature human beings, reasonableness does imply a well-reasoned state of intentionality. The ultimate model for this is the sage, whose perfect and infallible virtue sets the standard for what is considered reasonable.[16] Thus, an appropriate action for a human is one that could be justified by the sage's flawless reasoning or is an action the sage would perform under similar circumstances.

Within these nebulous terms, a Stoic concept of duty emerges. I propose that Stoics would understand duty as any action that is possessed with consequentiality. If an action naturally follows from a set of conditions—such as a debt, promise, or social norm—then that action possesses consequentiality and thus qualifies as a duty. However, if the action cannot be justified when all factors are considered, it will lack reasonableness, even though it remains consequential. In such cases, while it may still be considered a duty in some sense, it is not morally 'binding' and holds no legitimate claim on one's actions.

For instance, suppose I have borrowed a shotgun from my uncle for skeet shooting and now he requests its return. However, I learn he intends to use it as a murder weapon against his neighbor. While my duty to return the shotgun is overridden by my duty to preserve life, an obligation to return the borrowed item still subsists at some level. It is a consequence of borrowing the shotgun that I should return it, however, returning it in this case would not be defensible by reason. The act of returning the shotgun has consequentiality, but not reasonableness. It remains a duty—an obligation within a specific and isolated context—but it is not an appropriate action, all things considered.

---

16 Brennan, *The Stoic Life*, 170.

Because consequentiality is a necessary feature of an appropriate action, all appropriate actions must be duties under these criteria. However, not all duties qualify as appropriate actions, as some duties may be overridden by higher duties or other specific circumstances, and they will therefore lack reasonableness. The association of duty with consequentiality—what we might call a naturalistic concept of duty—thus affords a language to discuss competing duties within Stoic ethics. While many duties may simultaneously weigh upon an individual, only one action can be performed at any given moment and, thus, only one action can be deemed appropriate. In this way, all appropriate actions are duties, but not all duties are appropriate actions.

An important takeaway is that Stoic ethics do not prescribe or prohibit any particular behaviors in all circumstances. Again, there are no "thou shalt" commandments in Stoicism; I need not always return borrowed items nor must I always refrain from killing. Just as with preferred and dispreferred indifferents, Stoics acknowledge even actions typically seen as contrary to nature (i.e., prima facie wrongs) might be "conditioned by the circumstances."[17] In fact, the same principle that compels me to select preferred indifferents and avoid dispreferred ones is what compels me to perform appropriate acts: these all refer to behaviors that accord with nature. The relevant question in any moral dilemma thus becomes: "Considering all aspects of the situation, what action would a perfectly wise sage perform?"[18]

If we put these pieces together, we can say an appropriate action for a human is one that follows from rational human nature, and therefore it could be justified or defended against the standard of a sage's perfect reason. It is an action that is natural, fitting, and well-reasoned, even if it does not arise from the perfectly virtuous disposition of the sage. Within an isolated context, an action can be consequential but not reasonable, for example, if it is overridden by another course of action that is even more importantly consequential. On the other hand, an action can be reasonable but not consequential, such as the case of arbitrary actions of indifferent moral valence.

There is still more to say about consequentiality and reasonableness, and I will return to them at the end of this chapter. First, though, I need to introduce a unique perspective on appropriate action that arises specifically from the lessons of Epictetus. This will not only further clarify the conditions for appropriate action, but it will also flesh out our understanding of moral obligation as perceived by the Stoics. However, to place the indomitable former slave in the correct context,

---

17 DL 7.109. I adopt the expression prima facie, or "at first glance," from W. D. Ross, who describes normally binding obligations such as telling the truth or helping those in need as "prima facie duties" which, under specific circumstances, might be overridden by more urgent competing duties. See Ross, *Foundations of Ethics*, 84–85; *The Right and the Good*, 20.
18 As an agent-based species of virtue ethics, Stoicism is thus afforded the flexibility to avoid the perverse scenarios that challenge action-based frameworks like deontology or consequentialism.

I must approach him from a location far removed and several centuries earlier than his time. These are his intellectual origins of pre-Socratic Greece.

Role Ethics

Despite the well-earned stereotype of philosophers as overly loquacious windbags, they occasionally produce gems: compact, pithy statements of insight with boundless potential for interpretation, analysis, and extrapolation. Examples include René Descartes' "I think, therefore I am," Siddhartha Gautama's "All of life is suffering," or Jean-Paul Sartre's "Existence precedes essence." If we were to compile a list of such expressions from the entire history of human thought and rank them by their significance to intellectual tradition, at the very top would be an innocuous pair of Greek words: *gnothi seauton*. Originally inscribed at the Temple of Apollo in Delphi, they translate to "know thyself."

The author of this "Delphic Maxim," as it has come to be called, is lost to history. Predating even Socrates by several centuries, the words were likely a bit of conventional wisdom among the early Greeks who built the structure, accompanied by other temple inscriptions like the sensible "nothing in excess" and the inelegant "give a pledge and destruction is near." Legends attribute the inscriptions to Apollo himself. The specific call for self-knowledge has been adopted and reinterpreted by influential thinkers across history, with Socrates being the most famous among them. Reportedly inspired by a religious experience at Delphi, Socrates made self-knowledge a cornerstone of his philosophy, dedicating the rest of his life to teaching the value of introspection and intellectual humility to any who would listen.

For Epictetus, who idolized Socrates, the Delphic-turned-Socratic imperative for self-knowledge is embedded within a wider framework that describes all appropriate action from the perspective of individual purpose. He asks rhetorically, "For how can someone be good if he doesn't know who he is?"[19] The question can be understood literally: if virtue means fulfilling what we are meant to be, then we must begin by understanding exactly what that is. Rather than a general exercise in self-improvement, introspection is an essential prerequisite for virtue. For Epictetus, then, ethical reasoning is anchored upon our reasons for being, or what we would call 'roles'.

In practice, this means that when Epictetus addresses appropriate action, he consistently points to 'what' or 'who' someone is as a basis for determining 'why' a particular behavior is appropriate or inappropriate. If we want to understand what we should do, we must begin by examining our roles. His approach downplays the direct pursuit of sagacity as an end in itself, an ideal often criticized by the Stoics' detractors as unattainable. Instead, he frames moral excellence in terms of a human's

---

19 Epictetus, *Discourses* 3.24.20.

purpose properly met, fixing an axis of vice and virtue squarely within the center of the individual. Once fate assigns a particular role, it must be accepted without complaint:

> Remember that you're an actor in a play, which will be as the author chooses, short if he wants it to be short, and long if he wants it to be long. If he wants you to play the part of a beggar, act even that part with all your skill and likewise if you're playing a cripple, an official, or a private citizen. For that is your business, to act the role that is assigned to you as well as you can; but it is another's part to select that role.[20]

The result of this framing is that roles become a surrogate origin point for moral obligations, which begin in nature, are discerned through reason, and are fulfilled through personal action. This approach is so distinctive and central to Epictetus' teaching it warrants distinction as a unique system of 'role ethics' within the broader philosophy of Stoicism. As with Epictetus' other innovations, we do not have a clear, systematic outline of this framework in the historical record. Instead, we must deduce it through careful analysis of the available sources.[21]

We should note Epictetus was not the first to emphasize roles as an orienting concept in Stoic ethics. Roughly a century earlier, Cicero presented a basic scheme of four "personae," or social roles, to develop a broader account of "decorum." Although it is comparatively simplistic and limited in scope, Cicero's framework is laid out more logically than anything found in Epictetus' *Discourses*, and the two are often (and some say inappropriately) analyzed in concert.[22] Further, it seems both Cicero and Epictetus inherited these ideas from Panaetius, an influential leader of the transitional "middle Stoa" from which almost no original sources remain.[23] Despite the contributions of these earlier thinkers, Epictetus' approach to role ethics is uniquely versatile in application and is especially relevant to my aims in this book, thus it will enjoy the lion's share of my attention.

It is also important to clarify Epictetus' innovations do not represent a break from early Stoic orthodoxy, to the extent that such an orthodoxy can be said to exist. Rather, he generally follows the doctrines of Chrysippus, deviating mainly in his framing and presentation, while frequently highlighting Socrates as his intellectual forebear. Epictetus' role ethics are therefore best seen as an advancement of the Stoic conversation uniquely tailored to communicate what he finds most important. They effectively repackage Stoic ethics in a way optimized for efficiency of uptake, making the core ideas more accessible and relevant to his audience.

---

20 Epictetus, *Handbook* 17.
21 This section relies heavily on the insights of Brian E. Johnson, whose comprehensive examination of Epictetan role ethics is unmatched. See Johnson, *The Role Ethics of Epictetus*.
22 For a thorough comparison of Cicero's role ethics with those of Epictetus, see Johnson, *The Role Ethics of Epictetus*, 135–85.
23 Dyck, *A Commentary on Cicero, "De Officiis,"* 285–86.

The First Role

In Chapter 1, we investigated Stoic teleology: the belief the universe is rationally ordered and purposeful, with everything in nature—including human actions—progressing toward the fulfillment of a rational, cosmic plan. Recall that, as a general philosophical concept, teleology involves the investigation and contemplation of mission, or purpose. If we accept virtue means being what one is supposed to be, then Stoic teleology concerns the designs that determine this 'what'. It is inherently theistic, as the notion of a plan implies the existence of a planner. To live in accordance with this natural order is, therefore, to embody divine reason in both thought and action, aligning individual purpose with a greater cosmic intelligence.

Epictetus' signature method is to refrain from dwelling on such dense theoretical principles, not ignoring them but instead encapsulating them within practical imperatives that are easily digested and habituated. For instance, concepts like *telos*, or natural purposes, are framed in terms of one's role—the who or what someone is supposed to be. The various roles one might occupy are further categorized into two distinct tiers, each with its own set of attendant duties. The first tier, which encompasses *telos* in its broadest sense, refers to a single role played by all mature humans: that of a reasoning being. We might call it the 'universal' or 'fundamental' role. Reflecting my participation in the universal community of rational beings, this role requires I live in accordance with nature—essentially, that I consistently demonstrate reason in thought and action.

When Epictetus reminds his students of this assignment, he effectively forces them into an elevated perspective externalized from the worldly self and its petty concerns—the "view from above" discussed in the previous chapter. He often employs this technique at the start of a lesson, using it as a deliberate method of pedagogical slate clearing. It functions like the orientation sticker on an airport map, where instead of 'you are here' the message is 'you are human', with all that this status implies. For those who grasp the significance of reason and its accompanying powers of moral choice—the Stoic knife—it implies a great deal. Let us revisit a passage of Epictetus from the previous chapter:

> Consider who you are. First of all, a human being, that is to say, one who has no faculty more authoritative than choice, but subordinates everything else to that, keeping choice itself free from enslavement and subjection. Consider, then, what you're distinguished from through possession of reason: you're distinguished from wild beasts; you're distinguished from sheep. What is more, you're a citizen of the world and a part of it, and moreover no subordinate part, but one of the leading parts in so far as you're capable of understanding the divine governing order of the world, and of reflecting about all that follows from it.[24]

The role of a human is no 'bit part' in the cosmic production. Considering the vastness of the universe and how few of its dynamic systems are actually invested with

---

24 Epictetus, *Discourses* 2.10.1–3.

life—let alone capable of reason—the human role is, indeed, a leading one. With this distinction comes immense responsibility. It is incumbent upon the individual, for example, to recognize their own significance, to regard it as a high office, and to perform the appropriate actions that follow (i.e., that have consequentiality) with the sincerity and determination the role demands.

Underneath this fundamental role is a second tier of specific roles arising from our unique capacities and relationships, such as parent, teacher, soldier, or senator. These roles can be chosen, as by pursuing a profession, or they may simply be assigned by our circumstances, such as familial relationships are. Specific roles, like the fundamental role, imply specific sets of attendant duties, which I will address shortly. And although the principal focus is on Epictetus, this dualistic distinction between fundamental and specific roles also appears in Cicero's writing, suggesting a shared middle Stoic origin:

> We must also grasp that nature has endowed us with what we may call a dual role in life. The first is that which all of us share by virtue of our participation in that reason and superiority by which we rise above the brute beasts; from this the honorable and fitting elements wholly derive, and from it too the way in which we assess our obligation. The other is that which is assigned uniquely to each individual, for just as there are great variations in physical attributes (for we see that some can run faster and others wrestle more strongly, or again, one has an imposing appearance, while another's features are graceful), so our mental make-up likewise displays variations greater still.[25]

If the fundamental role is one that is played by every human, then what purpose could there be in identifying it as a distinct role at all? It might seem to introduce an unnecessary layer between the dictates of reason and an individual's actions. However, as Epictetus employs it, this separation of roles into distinct tiers explicitly serves to establish a rule: the fundamental role of a reasoning human *always takes precedence* over specific roles, ensuring rationality and virtue have the final say over what is appropriate. While specific roles come with their own set of duties, these can never override or compromise the fundamental role.

The immediate practical effect of this hierarchy is that 'evil' or 'villain' roles are categorically eliminated, as these would involve behavior contrary to nature. Epictetus does not even address them. Further, it shuts down innumerable excuses for unvirtuous behavior. Although I am obligated to be a husband to my wife and a father to my children, this does not justify cowardice on my part when it comes time to perform a dangerous job. Finally, it has a way of clarifying appropriate actions attendant to specific roles. When faced with a difficult decision within a specific role, 'zooming out' to the perspective of a virtuous human often illuminates a path that honors both the fundamental and specific roles optimally.[26]

---

25 Cicero, *On Duties* 1.107.
26 In my own experience as a naval officer, when I have felt torn between the obligations of office and those attendant to my humanity, I have never regretted acting as a good man does. In retrospect, I have consistently found the obligations of office to be best served that way.

Regarding relationships, Epictetus asserts, "if we place the good in right choice, the preservation of our relationships itself becomes a good."[27] What he is saying is that relationships must be understood in the context of what we are, which is what is in our power. My friends and loved ones are external; what they do and whether they live or die is not up to me. But my responsibilities toward them are fully up to me, as such, they are properly included in the circumscribed self. My attendance to those duties is a moral good. As Epictetus says, "if I am where my moral choice is, in that case alone will I be the friend, the son, the father that I ought to be."[28]

Managing Specific Roles

As they are described by Epictetus, our specific roles encompass the various details of our lives that can generate moral obligations, such as our relationships, our occupations, or our positions in the socioeconomic pecking order. Although we have certain degrees of freedom in selecting roles like occupations, most specific roles are bestowed by the universe—by God. To communicate the correct attitude we should have toward these responsibilities, Epictetus employs the analogy of a playwright or a general doling out assignments. Rather than complaining about our assignments, we are encouraged to dutifully attend to them. But how, specifically, can we determine what roles we have been assigned?

Through a careful examination of the *Discourses*, we can identify four general criteria by which Epictetus seems to think specific roles are identified. First, I shall address the least common among them, which is assignment through religious revelation. This appears to be a special category reserved for exceptional individuals who answered a philosopher's calling: Zeno, Diogenes the Cynic, and Socrates.[29] Each of them is reported to have received a kind of calling through revelation in the presence of an oracle. It does not necessarily appear that just anyone might receive a similar "vocation from God," as Epictetus puts it, but rather that one should remain ready to answer the call if it comes.[30]

The remaining criteria are more familiar. The most common is social relation, which encompasses both blood relationships like mother or son, as well as non-blood connections like friend, comrade, or coworker. The next criterion is specific nature, which refers to one's innate capacities and talents. These should inform the final criterion, which is personal choice, such as that expressed when one joins an organization or selects an occupation. What all of these criteria have in common is that they imply responsibilities involving fellow humans. Epictetus' approach is clever in its centering of moral obligation on the perspective of the performing agent,

---

27 Epictetus, *Discourses* 3.3.8.
28 Ibid. 2.22.20.
29 See Epictetus, *Discourses* 3.21.17–20; cf. DL 6.20, 7.2–3; Plato, *Apology* 20e–1a; and Xenophon, *Apology* 14–7.
30 Johnson, *The Role Ethics of Epictetus*, 34–36.

but we cannot forget the context from which this axis of right and wrong has been relocated, which is every human's inescapable connection to others. While we may contrive a role of isolation such as 'shipwreck survivor on a deserted island', humans do not naturally subsist in a vacuum, nor do their moral obligations. Humans live for one another:

> Now what is the calling of a citizen? Never to approach anything with a view to personal advantage, never to deliberate about anything as though detached from the whole, but to act as one's hand or foot would act if it had the power of reason and could understand the order of nature, and so would never exercise any desire or motive other than by reference to the whole.[31]

For those roles within one's capacity to decide, Epictetus unsurprisingly has something to say about appropriate choice. After the slate-clearing argument that one must first consider what they are—human—the next thing one should do is honestly assess what *kind* of human they hope to be; that is, what they hope to achieve. Epictetus advises, "Tell yourself first what kind of person you want to be, then act accordingly in all that you do."[32] This call to introspection—to *know thyself*—emphasizes the importance of personal agency in aligning actions to values. If one cannot muster the discipline to "act accordingly," then one cannot fulfill the associated role.

Thus, one must critically assess their own capabilities and potential when choosing a role. Self-honesty is essential to this assessment, establishing a clear partition between what one actually is and what one might wish they were. Innate capacities would ideally inform one's wishes, "for in so far as beings have different constitutions, their works and their ends will differ too."[33] Although a faulty self-assessment might lead to failure in some specifically ill-conceived endeavor, what is worse is the lost opportunity to be useful. If nature grants one a particular capability that may be of value to their fellows, then it is their duty to develop it and deploy it to productive ends. Epictetus lectures:

> As for you, you're a calf: when a lion appears, act as is proper for you, or else you'll rue the day. But you, you're a bull, come forward and fight, because that is your part in life; it befits you and lies within your power. And you, you're capable of leading the army against Troy: be Agamemnon. And you, you're capable of fighting against Hector in single combat: be Achilles.[34]

What happens when we have chosen poorly? Epictetus warns, "If you take on a role that is beyond your power, you'll not only disgrace yourself in that role, but you'll also neglect to take on that which you might have been capable of filling."[35] However, we must be cautious with this advice, lest we talk ourselves into the very disgrace we seek to avoid. For instance, when faced with the difficulties of a new role, individuals

---

31 Epictetus, *Discourses* 2.10.3–4.
32 Ibid. 3.23.1.
33 Ibid. 1.6.16; cf. *Discourses* 3.15.8–10.
34 Ibid. 3.22.6–7.
35 Epictetus, *Handbook* 37.

may feel ill-suited to the position and consider quitting, rationalizing their lack of perseverance as personal incompatibility.[36] A guardrail against such rationalizations is found in the oaths and commitments that often accompany the formal assignment of roles, serving as reminders of the responsibilities we have accepted.

A thorough self-assessment should also involve an honest evaluation of one's environment, particularly to recognize and embrace where one's abilities can be most effectively applied. This can help address the dilemma faced by highly capable individuals who might ably pursue a variety of roles. As distinguished from the fundamental role, everyone cannot do the same job; as Epictetus says, "One man must keep guard, another go out on reconnaissance, and another go into battle. It isn't possible for all to remain in the same place, nor would it be better that they should."[37] This principle applies across the wide spectrum of competitive fields and professions, where roles of high prestige or desirability often attract hundreds of aspirants for only a few key positions. Rejected applicants will inevitably find their capabilities needed elsewhere; fighter pilots cannot exist without aircraft maintainers. Stoic acceptance involves recognizing so-called undesirable roles are essential and that perceptions of prestige or desirability are mere vanities, indifferent in themselves.

This brings us to a final imperative for role selection, which is that one must honestly consider their reasons for selecting a given role. Of course, perks like admiration, wealth, and power will tend to weigh upon the calculus; a well-developed Stoic would dismiss these immediately as mere indifferents. Epictetus asks his students, "Do you want to do good or merely be praised?"[38] The question is not rhetorical; it is not a mere appeal to pure motivations. The students, who all ostensibly want to become philosophers, are directed to literally examine what it is they are really after. So, too, should anyone who aspires to a specific occupation, relationship, or position. Not only does this kind of introspection serve to clarify priorities, but it also steers behavior toward the achievement of purpose, compelling one to either "act accordingly in all that you do" or otherwise to seek a more fitting purpose.

Epictetus insists that, when contemplating one's station, it's crucial to mentally separate duties from the indifferents that accompany them. He compares those who confuse their identity with the cosmetic trappings of specific roles to deluded stage actors who "think that their masks, and high boots, and robes are their very selves."[39] The Stoic knife would make short work of such trifles. We have all observed the

---

36 The military offers a paradigmatic example. When new recruits inevitably chafe at the hardship of military service, some entertain the idea they are not temperamentally suited to it and seek an escape. Most eventually outgrow this impulse, but the occasional few will latch onto it as moral justification to default upon their commitments, such as through willful drug use or abuse of the medical system.
37 Epictetus, *Discourses* 3.24.31–5.
38 Ibid. 3.23.7.
39 Ibid. 1.29.41.

familiar trope of an individual who develops an inflated sense of self-importance when assigned to a station of prestige, for example, but there are other, less-obvious implications of this principle.

A desirable reputation, for example, can be an especially alluring perk of certain roles. Individuals naturally tend to cultivate reputations that reinforce the roles they might wish to occupy. Examples might include that of a charismatic leader, a sophisticated intellectual, a tactical innovator, or a fearless maverick. Marcus Aurelius laments the impulse to place so much stock in the opinions of others: "Everyone loves himself more than anyone else, and yet attaches less importance to his own opinion of himself than he does to what others think of him."[40] In the end, external opinions are just facsimiles that only capture a trace of reality. Looking outside for validation will inevitably bring turmoil when others' opinions inevitably do not reflect one's own opinions or desires. One so confused might forget what they are supposed to do, neurotically clamoring for reputation instead of dutifully focusing on the tasks in front of them.

Stoics insist upon separating the person from their symbols, adornments, companions, or anything external. Seneca captures the sentiment pointedly: "As he is a fool who, when purchasing a horse, does not consider the animal's points, but merely his saddle and bridle; so he is doubly a fool who values a man from his clothes or from his rank, which indeed is only a robe that clothes us."[41] Epictetus, likewise, observes an instrument does not make a musician, nor does a cap and apron make a blacksmith. "No, the costume is adapted to the art, and they take their name from their art and not from their gear."[42] No role is fulfilled by merely wearing its costume, nor is the costume what defines the person who wears it. Naturally, this bears upon the proper conduct of rulers and commanders, whose privileges of office are not just secondary to their duties but exist solely to facilitate them.[43]

Considerations like these should always be held alongside the Delphic injunction to know thyself, which, as we recall, is not merely wise counsel but a moral imperative. Looking to the wrong sources for information about one's roles can lead one to even doubt or confuse their identity outright. Again, one cannot do what one is supposed to do if one does not know what one is. Such a predicament can manifest as malfeasance within a specific role or forfeiture of one's all-important humanity, which Epictetus reminds his students when he calls them "wretches" and "slaves." Attendance to the fundamental role—that is, to virtue—can thus clarify which specific roles truly apply.

---

40 Marcus Aurelius, *Meditations* 12.4.
41 Seneca, *Letters* 47.16.
42 Epictetus, *Discourses* 4.8.16.
43 E.g., Cicero, *On the Laws* 3.8.

For all their importance as a source of responsibility, specific roles should never be regarded as a source of self-worth. These roles are, ultimately, external—they can be given and taken away. One may be assigned a position of high prestige and responsibility, but one can just as easily be stripped of it in disgrace. However, no one can be relieved of their humanity or the fundamental responsibilities that come with it. Consider, for example, the reflections of James Stockdale regarding his capture by enemy forces:

> I'm going right now from being the leader of a hundred-plus pilots and a thousand men and, goodness knows, all sorts of symbolic status and goodwill, to being an *object of contempt*. I'll be known as a "criminal." But that's not *half* the revelation that is the realization of your own *fragility*—that you can be reduced by wind and rain and ice and seawater or *men* to a helpless, sobbing wreck—unable to control even your own bowels—in a matter of *minutes*.[44]

Stockdale's moral survival, and indeed the physical survival of many of his compatriots, can be attributed to his appropriate rejection of designations chosen by the enemy, such as "criminal" and "traitor," in favor of his correct role as "commanding officer of the American prisoners of war." This is a key distinction between accepting one's situation and giving up.

Role Conflict

Let us briefly visit one of the Stoics' many philosophical successors. During the German occupation of France in World War II, long after Stoics had become a historical footnote, a young man approached the existentialist philosopher Jean-Paul Sartre with a profound moral dilemma. On one side, he felt the pull of duty toward his country, yearning to join the Free French Forces and aid in the liberation of his people from a foreign oppressor. On the other side, he bore a responsibility to care for his mother, who was estranged from her husband and whose only other son had already been lost to the war.

Although Sartre did not articulate this account as such, we can recognize the young man's situation as a conflict in specific roles. As a patriot, the young man feels compelled by his duty to country and moral principle, driven to join the resistance and contribute to the shared struggle for freedom. In doing so, his individual efforts would contribute to a virtuous and historically significant cause. Yet, as a son, his obligation to his mother holds immeasurable weight for one person; leaving her would mean consigning her to isolation and emotional suffering.

While the young man came to Sartre in hopes of a simple answer, Sartre refused to tell him what to do. Instead, he emphasized the young man's freedom to choose and the necessity of taking responsibility for his decision. He argued no

---

44 Stockdale, *Courage Under Fire*, 8–9, emphasis Stockdale's.

external framework—whether patriotic duty or filial obligation—could dictate the 'right' course of action. It was up to the young man to define his priorities and give meaning to his choice, fully accepting the consequences of whichever role he decided to honor.[45]

Were it Epictetus the young man had consulted, we can be confident he would have reacted much the same way as Sartre. He would probably remind the youth to consider what he is. First, a human being, with all the moral imperatives this entails. After that, a son, a brother, a citizen, and a patriot. Epictetus would likely advise him to consider what he wants to be, but would firmly refuse to prescribe a role for the young man. "You're the one who knows yourself," he would likely say to the youth, just as he says to a student of his own who is conflicted about roles.[46] Epictetus means the words literally; even if he were willing to identify the correct decision, he could not know what that is. What is reasonable for one person can be unreasonable for another, and in the coming pages I will explain how this is so.

The redirection to self-scrutiny is a classic philosopher's answer to the young and searching, a motif that transcends cultures and eras. Philosophers, much like today's psychotherapists, can frame a problem in ways that reveal self-evident wisdom, but it is ultimately up to the individual to identify their own path. Although this method of counsel falls short of the desired direct answer, we see Epictetus employ it masterfully to deliver a more valuable lesson. He compels his students to recognize they already have the equipment to determine appropriate action and only need to learn how to use it.

When it comes to conflict between specific roles, Epictetus acknowledges such conflicts may occur but he does not explicitly lay out a method to resolve them. As is often the case with virtue ethics, individuals must draw their own conclusions based on personal circumstances and their understanding of what best aligns with virtue. The first step in resolving role conflicts, then, is an appeal to moral coherency: any legitimate specific role must align with the universal human imperative toward virtue—the fundamental role. If a specific role imposes vicious or unethical demands on an individual, then either the role is not legitimate, or the obligations it imposes are misunderstood.

It remains possible some specific roles may pose no conflict with the fundamental role and yet still contradict one another. To explore how Epictetus might approach such dilemmas, we can consult key examples of role conflict from within the *Discourses*, each of which evaluates a tension between specific roles from a different angle.[47] From these cases, we can extract a few proven approaches to navigating

---

45 Sartre, *Existentialism Is a Humanism*, 30–33.
46 Epictetus, *Discourses* 1.2.11.
47 For a more thorough explanation of these three approaches, see Johnson, "Resolving Role Conflicts," in *The Role Ethics of Epictetus*, 123–33.

tensions between specific roles. While these strategies cannot resolve every conflict, they provide valuable insights to inform decision making when faced with such difficult choices.

The first approach applies to those who might suppose they fulfill a role of extraordinary distinction. We can call the resulting approach 'confirming exceptionality'. It pertains to situations in which an individual's distinctive abilities or circumstances seem to justify an assignment that requires bending or even breaking common conventions or expectations. Such individuals might include a noble contrarian (whom I will discuss in greater detail shortly), a misunderstood genius, or a creative prodigy whose extraordinary talents necessitate a departure from traditional paths. The relevant case from Epictetus' *Discourses* involves a prideful slave who contemplates refusing to handle his master's chamber pot, a task he deems beneath him.[48] Implicitly perceiving some exceptional status that sets himself apart from ordinary slaves, this situation represents a conflict between the role of an ordinary slave and an individual of extraordinary dignity.

We might expect Epictetus to scoff at the slave's self-importance and emphasize the moral indifference of an allegedly undignified task. However, Epictetus surprises by acknowledging the complexity of the situation, noting only the individual truly understands their own nature. It is to this prideful slave that he replies, "You're the one who knows yourself," presaging Sartre. Again, what is reasonable for one person may be unreasonable for another. Just as a typical individual lacks the capacity to perform the responsibilities of an exceptional person, an extraordinary individual might be considered unfit to hold the chamber pot. Either way, it is essential the individual figure that out on their own, rather than look to another to tell them.

The key to this approach to role conflict lies in an honest assessment of whether or not one is truly endowed (or, as the case may be, burdened) with an exceptional role. Epictetus insists such individuals cannot help but be conscious of their unique status, asking, "Isn't it clear that the possession of such power is accompanied at the same time by an awareness of that power?"[49] Critical self-reflection can help one to navigate role conflicts of this sort, with an important caveat: Identification with an exceptional role entails a commitment to that role and all the responsibility it confers. One does not rightly slip into and out of an exceptional role when it seems emotionally satisfying or expedient.

The second approach involves resolving role conflicts by modifying one's specific circumstances to accommodate competing roles. It is derived from a discussion in which Epictetus argues it is impossible to reconcile the demands of a Cynic lifestyle with the responsibilities of having a family. Recall that the Cynics were seen as monk-like radicals who pursued philosophical purity through a lifestyle of deliberate poverty,

---

48 Epictetus, *Discourses* 1.2.8–11.
49 Ibid. 1.2.30.

rejecting all material encumbrance. Epictetus' presentation of the conflict frames a family as so much baggage, irreconcilable with the activity of a Cynic philosopher:

> For consider, there would be some duties that he would have to fulfill towards his father-in-law, some that he would have to fulfill towards other relations of his wife, or towards his wife herself, so that he would finally be shut out from his calling to act as a sick-nurse and provider. Not to mention all the rest: he would need a kettle to heat water for his baby, so that it could be washed in the bath-tub, and some wool for his wife when she has had a child, along with some oil, a cot, and a cup (see how the gear is mounting up), leaving aside all the other things that would take up his time and distract him.[50]

Epictetus acknowledges such a combination of roles might be conceivable in an ideal "city of wise men," where the Cynic's calling would be recognized and shared, but he observes no such city exists.[51] To his frustration, Epictetus is challenged by students who point to the example of Crates, a renowned Cynic philosopher who married Hipparchia of Maroneia, *also* a Cynic philosopher. Epictetus acknowledges the challenge as a niche example still irrelevant to the circumstances of ordinary people. The marriage of Crates and Hipparchia was unconventional, based on personal affinity rather than the economic arrangements typical of the time; Hipparchia, being an extraordinary woman, and their unconventional marriage, did not impose any responsibilities on Crates that would conflict with his role as a Cynic. Epictetus' acknowledgment of Crates and Hipparchia as an exception emphasizes that roles and whatever conflicts arise between them must be addressed in terms of individual circumstances.

Thus, to "marry Hipparchia," so to speak, is to resolve a perceived conflict in roles by adjusting the specific circumstances of a given role so that its obligations do not interfere with competing responsibilities. Importantly, it is not necessarily the case that Crates chose Hipparchia for marriage solely because of her compatibility with his philosophical views (nor that she chose him for the same reasons, for that matter). If Crates had married another woman for more conventional reasons, it is possible we might never have known him as a philosopher. However, given his legendary commitment to Cynicism, this seems unlikely. More plausibly, finding Hipparchia did not enable Crates to pursue his philosophy so much as it allowed him to marry. As an approach to role conflict, "marrying Hipparchia" does not resolve the conflict by eliminating or prioritizing one role over another; instead, it qualifies the obligations in such a way the conflict is avoided altogether.

The third approach intriguingly involves the subordination or 'nesting' of some specific roles underneath the umbrella of a higher and yet still-specific role. It is demonstrated in an analogy wherein Epictetus compares specific roles to the individual responsibilities of soldiers and sailors. What distinguishes this example is

---

50 Ibid. 3.22.70–72.
51 This was likely a reference to the utopian *Republic* proposed by Zeno, which I discuss in the next chapter.

the delineation of subordinate specific assignments within the overarching role of a soldier or sailor, which supports the arrangement of specific roles into a hierarchical structure. This perspective facilitates an appeal to a higher role to clarify priorities between subordinate roles. The relevant excerpt should be appreciated in its entirety:

> Don't you know that this life is like a campaign? One man must keep guard, another go out on reconnaissance, and another go into battle. It isn't possible for all to remain in the same place, nor would it be better that they should. But you neglect to perform the duties assigned to you by your general, and complain when you're given an order that's at all hard, and fail to realize to what state you're reducing the army, so far as you can; because if everyone follows your example, no one will dig a trench, or build a palisade, or keep watch at night, or expose himself to danger, but everyone will show himself useless as a soldier. Again, if you embark on a ship as a sailor, settle down in a single spot and never leave it. If it should be necessary for you to climb the mast, refuse to do so; if you have to run along to the bow, refuse again. And what captain will put up with you? Won't he throw you overboard as a useless piece of tackle, a mere obstruction, and a bad example to the other sailors? So likewise in the present case, the life of every one of us is a campaign, and a long one subject to varying circumstances. You must fulfill the role of a soldier and carry out every deed as your general bids, divining his will so far as is possible. For there is no comparison between this general and an ordinary one, with regard either to his power or to the superiority of his character.[52]

We should note it does not appear Epictetus presents this analogy to address matters of role conflict. Instead, he deploys it to convey how one should approach hardships; specifically that one should receive their situation in life as a series of tasks set before them. Implicitly, the superior general to which he refers is the personified universe: God, fate, or universal causality, one and all. Rather than balk or complain about my assignment, I am expected to salute and get to work.[53]

Even if it is not expressly meant to address role conflict, the analogy is powerful in that it accommodates roles within roles. Underneath the overarching role of a soldier, for example, there exist the mutually exclusive roles of trench digger and watch stander. Again, "it isn't possible for all to remain in the same place," as Epictetus says, "nor would it be better that they should." A conflicted individual might seek a resolution by appealing to their higher role, such as that of a soldier, which would entail aligning their actions with the general's intent, "divining his will so far as is possible." This hierarchical organization permits an evaluation of priorities from a higher perspective than whatever roles might come into conflict.[54]

Of course, this approach does not necessarily provide a cipher with which to decode the will of the universe. Instead, it offers an additional lens through which one can contemplate their position within it. An intriguing aspect of Epictetus' analogy of soldiers and sailors is the emphasis on one's contribution to a moral system.

---

52 Epictetus, *Discourses* 3.24.31–35.
53 Cf. Seneca, *Letters* 120.12.
54 Johnson refers to this as a "meta-level" from which some insoluble role conflicts can be prioritized. See Johnson, *The Role Ethics of Epictetus*, 131.

Through phrases like "if everyone follows your example," "to what state you're reducing the army," and "a bad example for the other sailors," he reiterates in cadence the significance of one's impact upon the harmony and moral trajectory of a collective—a concept we will revisit in later chapters. To discern what is desired by the superior general, then, one should ask what is right for the greater system.

In summary, the capacity to take on multiple distinct roles ensures conflicts between them are virtually unavoidable. Epictetus' *Discourses* provide several examples of these tensions, from which three fundamental approaches to resolving such conflicts can be identified. The first is to engage in careful self-evaluation, particularly if one believes they occupy a role of exceptional distinction. The second is to "marry Hipparchia," or, in other words, to tailor the circumstances of one role to avoid clashes with another. The third approach is to evaluate specific roles hierarchically, nesting some beneath others, so that insoluble conflicts can be resolved by appealing to a higher priority or authority. Since Epictetus avoids laying down systematic theory, we shouldn't assume these approaches are all-encompassing, nor that they can resolve every conflict. However, they are still useful tools for navigating role tensions. Ultimately, the first step in resolving any perceived conflict between specific roles is usually sufficient; that is, to weigh one's situation against the fundamental role of a rational human being.

Roles and Duties

Returning to the idea of the *kathêkon*, or what we call appropriate action, we can gain additional insight into its constituent elements of consequentiality and reasonableness through the lens of Epictetan role ethics. Recall that consequentiality refers to the degree to which a given action follows from a particular set of circumstances. As previously suggested, when an action possesses consequentiality, it qualifies as an obligation—a duty—within the context in which it arises. In other words, if an action logically follows from certain conditions—such as a debt, a promise, or a social norm—then it is imbued with consequentiality, establishing it as a duty. This is not to say it is morally binding as such, only that it is one duty that must be weighed among many. For the context-dependent duty to be an appropriate action, it must also "admit of a reasonable justification" in light of all competing duties.

In Epictetus' framework, roles represent the most significant conditions that give rise to consequentiality, inherently generating their own attendant duties. This is presumably why roles hold such a central place in his teachings. An individual can simultaneously occupy multiple roles, each imposing its own set of obligations, and these must always be subordinate to the duties arising from one's fundamental role as a rational human being. However, conflicts between specific roles can occur, and appropriate action in such cases may require prioritizing one role over another. This decision, made with reasonable justification, ultimately hinges on which choice best aligns with the individual's fundamental role. This, then, would constitute the conflict-resolution method of appealing to an authority higher than whatever governs the role in question. The upshot of this reasoning is that when I am feeling conflicted in my duties, attendant to roles or some other set of circumstances, I am morally bound to do whatever a perfectly wise sage would do.

Epictetus offers further insights into consequentiality and reasonableness. Regarding consequentiality, he likens the logic of moral obligation to that of a hypothetical argument, asserting it is a "law" that one must accept what logically follows from a substantiated hypothesis. Far more important, he says, is "the law of life that states that we must do what follows from nature," referring to the fundamental role.[55] In this formulation, an individual's role—whether fundamental or specific—is like a hypothesis that must be supported or nullified by the result of an inquiry. In other words, my claim to a given role is a proposition that must be confirmed through appropriate actions. If I fail to do what follows (what is 'consequent') from my role, I create a contradiction, meaning the role is forfeit—just as a hypothesis is nullified if it does not hold up under scrutiny. In effect, this is a clever transposition from Stoic logic onto Stoic ethics.[56]

We don't have to look far to find this idea in everyday relationships. Leaders, managers, spouses, and parents often encounter situations where a formerly trusted individual has failed to meet their obligations, perhaps even choosing to cover their shortfalls with dishonesty. The typical reprimand might sound like, 'I'm not upset that you made a mistake; I'm upset that I can no longer trust you'. This loss of confidence directly undermines the assumption the individual is capable of fulfilling their role, presenting a real dilemma for the person in authority. What should be done with the discredited individual, and who will take on their responsibilities moving forward? We can imagine how Epictetus might handle such situations as an authority figure, as we are given an example in his rebuke of a philanderer who has forfeited his roles as both a philosopher and a human:

> How am I to treat you, man? As a neighbor, as a friend? And of what kind? As a fellow citizen? How am I to place any trust in you? If you were an old pot that was so cracked as to be good for nothing, you would be thrown out on a dung-heap, and no one would bother to pick you up again. But if, as a human being, you're unable to fulfil any human function, what are we to do with you? Well then, since you can't hold the position of friend, can you hold that of a slave? And who will trust you? Aren't you willing, then, to be thrown out in your turn onto a dung-heap somewhere, like a useless pot, like a piece of shit?[57]

It is perhaps for the best that Epictetus did not fulfill a formal leadership role. He certainly does not shy from name-calling; "wretches," "slaves," and "worms" are

---

55 Epictetus, *Discourses* 1.26.1.
56 Johnson, *The Role Ethics of Epictetus*, 51–53.
57 Epictetus, *Discourses* 2.4.3–5.

frequently featured in his assaults.[58] But Epictetus is not cruel or hateful; he is a *trainer*. His attacks are invariably purposeful, indicating the roles his targets have chosen on their own. Epictetus aims not to reduce, but to show his students where they reduce themselves by squandering their finest natural abilities. For so-called rational beings, acts of indiscretion or self-disobedience amount to the forfeiture of reason, or, in other words, a forfeiture of humanity.

Epictetus also adds to our understanding of reasonableness. As he uses the term *reasonable*, it exhibits a certain fluidity—at times aligning with the conventional Stoic standard of moral defensibility, and at other times diverging from this. For instance, in the conventional sense, Epictetus rebukes the itinerant father, saying, "I imagine that you won't deny that to abandon a child when it is ill and go off is an unreasonable thing to do."[59] Unlike an appropriate act, which "admits of a reasonable justification," the father's desertion is wholly indefensible. But in other passages, Epictetus deploys the terms "reasonable" or "unreasonable" in reference to an individual's experiences or perceptions, suggesting a meaning something like "that which should be endured."

An important instance of this latter usage appears in the same discussion where Epictetus contemplates appropriate action for the prideful slave. At the outset, he connects reasonableness to nature in the claim that "for a rational being, only what is contrary to nature is unendurable, while anything that is reasonable can be endured."[60] As the discussion evolves, he associates reasonableness with individual roles, asserting that "concepts of the reasonable and unreasonable mean different things to different people, as do those of good and bad, and the profitable and unprofitable."[61] As it refers to that which should be endured, then, reasonableness seems to capture the moral defensibility of enduring or declining to endure, which can only be judged in the context of all the contributing circumstances.

In summary, Epictetus generally invokes what is consequent to describe what observably follows from a role, while he uses what is reasonable to capture what can be accepted and understood from the perspective of the individual actor.[62] From this approach, an additional distinction between consequentiality and reasonableness arises, one that considers the imagined perspective of a third-party. Consequentiality is essentially a calculation, akin to the confirmation or nullification of a hypothesis, and it can be recognized independently by an outside observer. It implies context-specific duties—the obligations that naturally follow from the conditions of a given role. In contrast, reasonableness is perceptible only from within the actor's internal faculties,

---

58 Ibid. 1.4.14, 1.6.30, 2.20.9–10, 3.2.9, 4.1.142–143.
59 Ibid. 1.11.20.
60 Ibid. 1.2.1.
61 Ibid. 1.2.5.
62 Johnson, *The Role Ethics of Epictetus*, 55.

factoring in their understanding of the situation and the competing obligations they face. It implies appropriate action—what can be morally justified based on the totality of one's circumstances. This distinction emphasizes the interaction between external expectations and internal deliberation in shaping one's actions.

Contrarian Roles

References to external expectations and dutiful attendance to involuntarily assigned roles seem to support a common criticism of Epictetus: that his philosophy is fundamentally one for conformists. This reflects a broader stereotype of Stoicism as a whole—that it leaves little room for principled rebellion, as the acceptance of one's situation appears to stifle impulses to 'act out' when moral circumstances call for it. Such critiques cast doubt on the compatibility of Stoicism with the acts of courage and defiance that have historically fueled social and scientific progress. However, I intend to challenge this perspective, proposing that a concept of 'contrarian' roles offers a logical space for rational nonconformity within the Stoic framework.

We should imagine a Stoic's response to the challenges faced by some of history's influential nonconformists—figures who engaged in profound metaphorical battles against entrenched injustice and ignorance. Consider Rosa Parks, whose quiet yet defiant stand against racial segregation sparked a pivotal acceleration in the American civil-rights movement. Reflect on Aleksandr Solzhenitsyn, the Russian soldier turned dissident, who endured the horrors of the Soviet gulag and later weaponized his pen to expose its brutal realities. Recall Galileo Galilei, who, armed with evidence and reason, defied the dogma of religious authority to champion a heliocentric view of the cosmos. And perhaps, most iconically, think of Socrates, who fearlessly challenged the prideful ignorance of Athenian citizens, provoking them to silence him with a death sentence.

Would Stoics, in the face of such corrosive injustices, have done anything more than quietly accept and endure these realities? Would their emphasis on inner tranquility and acceptance have left them complicit, while the great cost of inaction fell upon their wider societies?

A more fitting example for this project might be that of William "Billy" Mitchell, the maverick American soldier and aviator. A pioneering air commander and tactical innovator of the First World War, Mitchell was an early advocate for military airpower. He passionately argued for the development of a strong, independent air force, even as the top brass of the Army and Navy remained hostile to his views. Frustrated by the military establishment's resistance to change, Mitchell took his case directly to the public through personal writings and congressional testimony. He did not hesitate to criticize his superiors when he felt they were putting lives at risk by neglecting aviation, leading to his court-martial for insubordination in 1925. Though the trial effectively ended his military career, Mitchell's beliefs were ultimately vindicated.

Many of the airpower applications he envisioned, such as the use of aircraft carriers and strategic bombing, became key aspects of American military power in World War II and beyond. Today, he is widely regarded as a father of the U.S. Air Force.

The question, then, is this: if any of these individuals had been Stoics, is it at all plausible they would have accomplished the important things they did? It is not just a question of whether they *could*, but if they *would*. For any philosophy to discourage or deny the appropriateness of such acts would certainly undermine its moral credibility. To be a viable and universal ethic, Stoicism must be shown to conceptually accommodate or even encourage contrarian behaviors in service of the communal good, particularly when social conventions and authorities are irrational or corrupt.

I will answer this challenge, but first, let us clarify what is so objectionable about conformity. Most people would bristle to be called conformists, and yet we are all conformists in some fashion. As every rebellious youth is bound to recognize, even self-proclaimed nonconformists still adhere to selected norms—some within the wider community, others within their tailored peer groups. Nonconformity thus devolves to hypocrisy when it is treated as an end in itself, and total nonconformity is dysfunction. Knowing this, why do we treat the descriptor "conformist" as an insult? There are several logical reasons; by parsing these out we can better evaluate whether a charge of conformism is actually a negative statement about the Stoics.

The first is that conformity can imply a kind of stupidity. A propensity to fall in line with social norms or expectations can be interpreted as a lack of independent thought or conviction. If someone simply goes along with what everyone else is doing or thinking, it suggests they may not have the capability or the will to think through the issues, form their own opinions, and defend them. In some cases, independent thoughts do actually occur but are kept secret. Conformity then takes on an element of duplicity, where one's true colors are substituted with a chameleon-like exterior. It is to this point that Seneca observes:

> It takes trickery to win popular approval; and you must need make yourself like unto them; they will withhold their approval if they do not recognize you as one of themselves. However, what you think of yourself is much more to the point than what others think of you. The favor of ignoble men can be won only by ignoble means.[63]

Second, conformity can be viewed as a form of weakness or capitulation. When we emulate others, we are, in a sense, yielding to them, allowing their judgments and expectations to replace our own in shaping our behavior. It is a submission without a fight. At the very least, this can suggest a lack of self-assurance or self-determination and a willingness to subordinate one's own desires and beliefs to those of the group. At its worst, this kind of conformity descends into cowardice and sycophancy.

---

63 Seneca, *Letters* 29.11.

Third and most significant, conformity can indicate amorality, as seen in an unwillingness to stand up for principles in the face of opposition or adversity. When we conform to unjust or unethical norms out of a desire to fit in or avoid conflict, we reveal a certain moral turpitude that abets either a lack of belief in what is right or an unwillingness to do anything about it. It is easy to see how Stoicism, which encourages acceptance of what cannot be controlled, could be misapplied in this way. One might imagine a Stoic who happens to live under a manifestly unjust regime such as Nazi Germany or Maoist China. Critics could posit that a Stoic would do nothing to resist or change the system, but would dutifully play their assigned role within a machine of cruelty and oppression.

Conformity, then, is like many other virtues: it requires moderation and, in concert with virtues like independence or creativity, it *provides* moderation. Some of it is not just good but essential. But if unchecked by higher virtues, too much of it devolves into stupidity, duplicity, cowardice, and moral depravity.

We should immediately dispense with the most severe of charges—the idea Stoicism promotes a kind of amoral quietism is unambiguously demolished by the writings of the Stoics themselves. Examples abound in the ancient sources where the appropriateness of drastic action, even death, is contemplated as a means of preventing acquiescence to injustice. As I have well-established, there is always a choice. Thus, Stoic acceptance of external circumstances is not at all the same thing as compliance with authority. Some scholars have even characterized the early Stoics as proto-anarchists, a perspective I will explore in the next chapter. Moreover, as already shown, no specific social role can override the fundamental human imperative to pursue virtue. Again, there are no 'villain roles' in Stoicism.

However, when it comes to the accusation Stoics promote a philosophy for conformists, they are indeed guilty as charged. As already noted, all functioning humans are conformists to some degree. At its very core, Stoicism is conformity to facts as they are; this bears distinction from the morally perilous area of social conformity. But that, too, is a jungle to be deftly navigated, not avoided. Epictetus acknowledges this reality, arguing, "if one told a chorus singer to know himself, wouldn't he respond to that instruction by paying attention to the other singers in the chorus so as to sing in harmony with them?"[64] In this sense, Stoicism does not so much promote conformity as it provides guidelines for doing it rightly.

As a case in point, the ancient sources are filled with exhortations to act in ways that should be expected of someone who is wise and temperate: to avoid showing off, drunkenness, gluttony, and excessive or vulgar talk. Seneca, Epictetus, and Marcus Aurelius all provide numerous examples of such admonitions.[65] Considered

---

64 Epictetus, *Fragments* 1.
65 E.g., Epictetus, *Discourses* 3.12, 4.12.16–17; *Handbook* 33, 46, 48; Marcus Aurelius, *Meditations* 8.9, 11.15, 11.18, 12.27; Seneca, *Letters* 105.3, 92.11, 47.17, 28.10.

in isolation, these injunctions might be interpreted as encouraging a kind of timid preoccupation with the opinions of others. Cicero even suggests social reactions can provide valuable information, observing:

> ... a glance of the eyes, a raising or knitting of the eyebrows, a sad or a cheerful look, a smile, a remark or its suppression, the raising or lowering of the voice—these and the like will enable us to readily assess which of them is an apt reaction, and which of them is at odds with obligation and with nature.[66]

However, this is very different from saying external opinions *matter*. On the contrary, the Stoics repeatedly indicate one should not care one iota for the opinions of others. This is not the flippant, faux-contrarian rejection of social convention often seen in teens or misfits. Rather, it is a technical claim grounded in the mechanics of Stoic virtue theory. Opinion and reputation are clearly indifferents, ready to be severed by the ever-reliable Stoic knife. Furthermore, there is little reason to heed the judgments of those unqualified to judge. "Why worry about them?" scoffs Epictetus, "any more than a craftsman worries about people who have no knowledge of his craft?"[67]

So how can we reconcile these seemingly contradictory messages—the social injunctions to act a certain way on the one hand, and the dismissal of external opinions on the other? One way to understand this apparent tension is to consider the specific contexts in which the social exhortations were made. In the case of Epictetus, for example, he was often speaking to an audience of would-be philosophers. His advice on proper conduct can thus be seen as an attempt to reinforce the unique role and responsibilities of a philosopher within society. As someone dedicated to the pursuit of wisdom and virtue, a philosopher should embody these qualities in his actions and serve as an example to others. Likewise, when Marcus tells himself "Don't let anyone, even you yourself, ever again hear you finding fault with palace life," such self-admonitions should be understood in the context of official responsibility.[68]

More broadly, however, the Stoics emphasize acting rightly because it is right, rather than out of any particular concern for external opinion. Many of their social injunctions might be understood as heuristics or rules of thumb to align one's behavior with virtues such as self-control, wisdom, and justice. It happens that one invested with such virtues would tend to behave in ways that do not annoy their fellows—consistent with a healthy communitarian ethic. But the opinions of such fellows are beside the point, or, more precisely, they can only serve as a means to an end. Consider, for example, Seneca's portrayal of the Stoic sage:

> Who is there who knows not that none of those things which are thought to be good or evil are looked upon by the wise man and by mankind in general in the same manner? He does not

---

66 Cicero, *On Duties* 1.146.
67 Epictetus, *Discourses* 4.5.22. Cf. *Handbook* 35.
68 Marcus Aurelius, *Meditations* 8.9.

regard what all men think low or wretched; he does not follow the people's track, but as the stars move in a path opposite to that of the earth, so he proceeds contrary to the prejudices of all.[69]

Having properly clarified the Stoic position on conformity, I can now return to the topic of role ethics and the broader subject of this chapter: duty. Specifically, we should explore whether a form of purposeful, virtue-regulated nonconformity could contribute to one's fulfillment of moral duty, thereby creating a contrarian role with its own set of responsibilities. I propose this must indeed be the case from a Stoic perspective and, furthermore, that this concept of virtuous nonconformity should occupy a more central place in the popular understanding of Stoicism than it currently does.

Epictetus, in particular, openly endorses well-reasoned nonconformity throughout his *Discourses*. He often expresses admiration for the Cynics, who were a notoriously contrarian fringe element of Athenian society. Epictetus himself embodied this nonconformist spirit, adopting a simple and austere lifestyle to fully dedicate himself to his role as an educator. His teachings not only permit contrarian roles but actively engage with the idea of principled resistance to authority, even when such resistance might appear futile from a conventional standpoint.

For example, in one important discussion, he employs an analogy of the single purple stripe that adorns the otherwise plain tunics of senators, which "makes all the rest appear splendid and beautiful." This discussion point was set against a series of anecdotes about then-popular figures who went against the grain of their circumstances to stand up for principle: statesmen who would fearlessly confront the ambitious Caesar, and an athlete who accepted death over forced castration. Epictetus denies such courage is futile, asking rhetorically, "And what does the purple achieve for the tunic? What else than standing out in it as purple, and setting a fine example for all the rest?"[70]

In the same discussion, Epictetus suggests he would personally accept beheading rather than be forced to shave his beard—at the time, a symbol of the philosopher—as might happen if philosophers were banished.[71] Whatever one may think of such bravado, it certainly does not support the image of Stoics meekly falling in line with unjust authority. However, this stance is tempered by the essential point that prudence requires discernment. Stoics respond to authority and social pressure with neither reflexive contrarianism nor blind compliance. There are times when it is right and proper to align with societal norms and expectations, just as there are times when it is appropriate to resist them. The key is to act in accordance with reason and virtue, rather than out of fear, pride, or inertia.

---

69 Seneca, *On the Firmness of the Wise Person* 14.3–4, trans. Stewart.
70 Epictetus, *Discourses* 1.2.12–2.
71 Before the *Discourses* were recorded, Epictetus would have been among the philosophers exiled from Rome by Emperor Domitian in 89 CE.

Perhaps, then, a final example of the noble contrarian would be fitting to illustrate a balanced and discerning approach. Cato the Younger, a famous Stoic politician of the late Roman Republic, is remembered for his unwavering integrity and his willingness to stand up for his values. His strict adherence to Roman political tradition brought him into conflict with powerful and ambitious opponents, particularly the authoritarian populist Julius Caesar. At the same time, Cato was no reckless or futile dissident. He worked within the system, competently holding various high offices and acting through legal and official means to oppose corruption and the consolidation of dictatorial power. He conformed to the norms and institutions of his society in ways that were materially important, if ultimately unsuccessful, but never at the expense of his moral convictions.

After Caesar defeated the republican forces at the Battle of Thapsus in 46 BCE, Cato refused to live under what he saw as tyrannical rule. Rather than submit to Caesar, who might have pardoned him to create a reputation for comity, Cato took his own life in a final act of defiance. He has since been regarded as a historical moral exemplar, particularly highlighting both the significance and the fragility of individual political liberty. Recognizing the historical relevance of these lessons, George Washington even arranged the performance of a play about Cato for his troops at Valley Forge.

In light of such examples, I suggest this is the Stoic stance on conformity and nonconformity: it is not an all-or-nothing proposition, but a matter of context and judgment. The Stoics would agree some nonconformist, contrarian roles are appropriate and necessary. Stoics would further insist nonconformity is a means to an end and that it is pointless and incoherent when treated as an end itself. They would agree both contrarian and conformist impulses must be tempered by reason and guided by an overarching commitment to virtue. Stoicism, as always, is less a rigid code of conduct than a framework for navigating the moral complexities of life with wisdom and integrity.

Toward a Common Duty

In this chapter, I examined the Stoic understanding of appropriate action and its connection to rational nature. I began by differentiating between the perfect right actions of the sage and the appropriate actions of those still progressing toward wisdom. Appropriate action was defined as behavior characterized by consequentiality and reasonableness, even when it does not originate in a morally perfect disposition. Within this framework, I established a Stoic concept of duty, identifying it with any action that possesses consequentiality. This approach allows us to discuss the management of competing duties, where the correct course of action is that which enjoys reasonableness in addition to consequentiality. Notably, this naturalistic concept of duty does not require moral agency, a seemingly innocuous detail that will have significant implications in the next chapter.

I then turned to Epictetus' use of role ethics, which anchors moral obligations upon the various roles and relationships one may hold. I discussed strategies for identifying, prioritizing, and navigating conflicts between these roles. I also grappled with the tension between conformity and moral independence that arises from contemplating one's obligations to others, recognizing that neither conformism nor contrarianism serves as a moral end in itself.

Moral tension was a recurring theme throughout this discussion. In Chapter 2, I said discrete virtues may individually drift into extremes and that the sage finds harmony in balance and moderation. Now I am saying moral obligations can also act at cross purposes, as can the roles that generate them, and, here again, I must defer to moderation as prudence in what is chosen. One can hold many beliefs, values, and responsibilities but can only do one thing at a time. When duties come into conflict, some must win out as the appropriate thing to do, while others must take a back seat.

Another emergent theme of this chapter is that no individual exists in isolation. Moral roles extend beyond personal or professional spheres and close relationships, reaching into broader societal contexts. As members of communities and nations, individuals inherit responsibilities that profoundly shape the lives and behaviors of others. In the next chapter, the Stoic perspective on these extended roles will be explored, particularly in the interactions of social morality, patriotism, and *Cosmopolitanism*. The discussion will consider ways in which Stoic ethics inform one's duties to others, including their communities and political institutions. It will examine how a rational and virtuous person navigates the complexities of civic life while staying true to fundamental moral principles.

CHAPTER 5

Country

> After speaking of the Gods, it is most reasonable to show, in the next place, how we should conduct ourselves towards our country. For, by Jupiter, our country is as it were a certain secondary God, and our first and greatest parent.
>
> HIEROCLES THE STOIC, ETHICAL FRAGMENTS,
> "HOW WE OUGHT TO CONDUCT OURSELVES TOWARDS OUR COUNTRY."

If we were to name the most-celebrated single work of ancient philosophy, it would probably have to be Plato's *Republic*. It is a Socratic dialogue that explores the nature of justice through the framework of an idealized state, which would be governed by philosopher-kings endowed with wisdom and virtue. Plato envisions a hierarchical society where each class—rulers, warriors, and producers—fulfills its specific role for the benefit of the whole. These three classes analogize to parts of a human soul—the rational, the spirited, and the appetitive, respectively—where the supreme virtue of justice is presumed to reside in harmonic concord between them. Through allegory and metaphor, Plato deploys Socrates to illustrate the journey of humankind from ignorance to knowledge, advocating for a life guided by reason and the pursuit of moral virtue. It is an undeniable masterpiece, but it is not a Stoic work, as it preceded the Stoics' founding by about a century.

In what now might appear as a regrettable bit of imitation, early Stoics Zeno and Chrysippus wrote their own *Republics*, as did their forebear Diogenes the Cynic. Evidently never reaching the acclaim of Plato's text, today these works exist only in fragments and critical commentary, most of it hostile.[1] It does seem as if they generated more than the usual degrees of controversy and ridicule and they might have been somewhat of an embarrassment to later Stoics.[2]

Unlike Plato's hierarchical society governed by philosopher-kings, early Stoics imagine a purely egalitarian community based on principles of reason, equality, and shared virtue. For example, Zeno envisions "that we should regard all men as our fellow citizens and local residents, and there should be one way of life and order, like

---

1 E.g., DL 7.32–3 and 7.187–9. Following Curt Wachsmuth and Jaap Mansfeld, Malcom Schofield suggests these passages likely reflect different aspects of a single critique directed at Zeno and Chrysippus by the ancient Sceptic commentator Cassius. See Schofield, *The Stoic Idea of the City*, 1–8; Wachsmuth, "Stichometrisches," 39–42; Mansfeld, "Diogenes Laertius," 344–46.
2 Schofield, *The Stoic Idea of the City*, 94; Clement, *Miscellanies* 5.9.58.2 (SVF I.43) = LS 67E.

that of a herd grazing together and nurtured by a common law."[3] Zeno's emphasis on universal equality lays the groundwork for later Stoic ideas about the inherent moral reasoning of every human being, which is agnostic of social or economic status. More radically, he denies the authority of any earthly government to compel or coerce, earning him later recognition as a forerunner of anarchism.[4] Specifically, he argues qualities like freedom, sovereignty (e.g., kingship or political authority), and even friendship are attainable only by the sage, making these designations contradictory and false when applied to ordinary non-sages.[5]

A central theme of these early Stoic ideas is the dissolution of conventional institutions. Zeno proposes to eliminate traditional structures such as temples, law courts, money, and even marriage, believing, in a society governed by reason, such institutions would become irrelevant.[6] Private property would be replaced with the shared custody of land and goods. Polyamory would be the norm, with the resulting children being raised by a collective community. In an apparent swipe at the convention of modesty, people would wear the minimum necessary clothing, taking no great care to cover up any body part. Scandalously, taboos like incest and the consumption of human flesh could be entertained from a utilitarian standpoint.[7] If it is useful, it might as well be allowed, or so it would appear. The dead, even family, were to be discarded like trash.[8]

By today's standards, it sounds like the first Stoics envision some kind of nightmarish, collectivist sex cult. If we judge by the tone of their critics, it seems their grand vision sounded much the same to ancient ears as well. But if we are charitable in our interpretations, which by all philosophical norms we should be, there is a reasonable explanation for these views. There is little convincing evidence Zeno and Chrysippus actually believe their ideal society is practically achievable, much less that its distinguishing features are genuinely intended as policy prescriptions. Instead, it is probable their aim was expressly to describe what society might look like if everyone were a sage, specifically as it compares to the sordid reality. Early Stoic political theory, such that it exists at all, makes a lot more sense in this light. Everything the early Stoics would abolish, or that they would at least cease to enforce or to encourage, is something they see as an affectation or accommodation of human irrationality. Such crutches would not be necessary in a city of the wise.

---

3 Plutarch, *On the Fortune of Alexander* 329A–B (SVF I.262, part) = LS 67A.
4 See Kropotkin, *Anarchism*, 288, and Konstantakos, "Stoicism and Just War Theory," 60–61.
5 See DL 7.32–3, 7.121–2, 7.124; Plutarch, *On Listening to Poetry* 33D (SVF I.219) = LS 67O.
6 See DL 7.32–3 and Plutarch, *On Stoic Self-contradictions* 1034B (SVF 1.264, part) = LS 67C. The 'defacing of coinage', in particular, seems to be a trademark of Zeno's predecessor Diogenes and a metaphor for dismantling social institutions. See DL 6.20–1, DL 6.71, and Schofield, *The Stoic Idea of the City*, 12–3.
7 See Plutarch, *On Stoic Self-contradictions* 1044F–5A (SVF 3.753, part) = LS 67F; Sextus Empiricus, *Outlines of Pyrrhonism* 3.247–8 = LS 67G.
8 Sextus Empiricus, *Outlines of Pyrrhonism* 3.247–8 = LS 67G.

Ultimately, the early Stoics' idealized society and Zeno's *Republic*, in particular, is a message about moral autonomy and virtue. As Zeno sees it, individuals should be morally independent, guided by their reasoning faculties rather than relying on external institutions. The salacious details of this message, I suggest, are less about describing the perfect human society and more about describing a society of perfect humans. His successors predictably tempered these views, particularly as Stoicism transitioned from a small Hellenistic clique to a mainstream framework for ethical thinking.[9]

To appreciate the magnitude of this evolution, consider the contrast between Zeno's anarchism and the patriotism coursing through this chapter's epigraph. The passage belongs to Hierocles, a lesser-known late Stoic whose introduction I have reserved for this chapter. Hierocles lived around the same time as Marcus Aurelius, just before Stoicism began to decline as a mainstream social force. Together, Zeno and Hierocles effectively bookend the Stoics' existence as a recognizable tradition of ancient philosophy.

Did the Stoics really change so much over the course of their run? Zeno, the first Stoic, envisions a radical dissolution of boundaries between people, shedding the deadweight of conventions designed to accommodate human flaws. His successors would refine these ideas, reimagining this dissolution as a natural process of moral expansion with widespread implications. This chapter will explore these developments, seeking to uncover a common thread that ties the disparate Stoic visions into a shared understanding of social relationships. I will examine how the Stoics conceived of their communities within the broader framework of the universe, and how they balanced their communitarian and cosmopolitan impulses.

I will start the chapter by exploring the natural process of moral expansion, as briefly mentioned in the first chapter. This time, I will investigate it more thoroughly by drawing on the writings of Hierocles, who introduces an innovative model of concentric circles that represent our various social relationships. Hierocles argues that, as we advance morally, we should attempt to bring these circles closer to the center, thereby reducing (but not eliminating) the moral distance between ourselves and others.

I will also revisit the balance between an individual's relationship with their earthly community and their connection to the greater cosmic reality. This can be thought of as similar to dual citizenship, prompting us to consider the tensions that arise between local and cosmic allegiances. To address these tensions, I will turn to the virtue of moderation, a form of prudence that guides the expansion of moral concern from the self to all of humanity. As I will demonstrate, Stoic cosmopolitanism does not demand we treat all people equally but rather encourages a dutiful concern for those closest to us, *balanced* alongside our empathy and obligations toward all human beings.

---

9 See Long and Sedley, *The Hellenistic Philosophers*, 1: 436.

Building on Hierocles' ideas, I infer a Stoic theory of collective duty, through which communities themselves bear moral responsibilities. I explore how this framework can support our understanding of the obligations between individuals and their countries, and I will consider how the Stoics themselves thought through these questions. Ultimately, I argue for a philosophically-informed Stoic patriotism that rejects chauvinistic tribalism while still recognizing special duties to one's country and fellow citizens. The ideal Stoic patriot, I propose, seeks to support their country in the harmonious fulfillment of its natural purposes, both toward its own citizens and toward the global community.

Back to the Center

As discussed in Chapter 1, Stoic social morality begins with obedience to reason in individual affairs and then extends the moral horizon outward to include the immediate community. The resulting communitarian ethic is extremely important to Stoics, but their sense of social morality does not stop at the local level. Instead, it continues to expand, radiating from the local to the global, and ultimately to the cosmic level. In this way, Stoic communitarianism is balanced by a cosmopolitan ethic, where everyone is a citizen of the same universe. Stoics believe all humans are connected by a shared rational nature, which imposes certain moral obligations on each of us, extending beyond our immediate community to all of humanity.

The idea is put forward in broad strokes by Seneca when he writes, "It is of course required of a man that he should benefit his fellow men—many if he can; if not, a few; if not a few, those who are nearest; if not these, himself. For when he renders himself useful to others, he engages in public affairs."[10] As with much of Seneca's advice, it requires no support from Stoic doctrine, nor does it constitute any sort of uniquely Stoic claim. Instead, it reflects a kind of universal wisdom, accessible to anyone who has progressed beyond the most rudimentary stages of moral development. However, the elegant simplicity of his formulation conceals a complex theory of moral growth. Once again, there is much going on under the hood.

The pertinent concept, which was touched upon earlier, is an intriguingly named process called *oikeiōsis*. If judging only by its foreignness, then this term should be no more peculiar than those other Greek words we normally translate in writing, like *hêgemonikon* or *kathēkon* ("ruling center" and "appropriate action" respectively). Rather, the strangeness of *oikeiōsis* is in its utter defiance of translation. Taken literally, it means something like "appropriation" or "taking for one's household," however the process described involves far more than the meaning of these words. Other unsuccessful candidates that have been tried in scholarly literature include "affinity," "familiarization," and "attachment," but none have caught on in regular

---

10 Seneca, *On Leisure* 3.5.

usage. As a result, it is most commonly expressed simply as the transliterated Greek term, as we employ it here.

The word comes from *oikos*, or "household," and *oikeiōn*, or "having to do with the household," as in family or kin. *Oikeiōsis* is essentially the aspect of moral progress that encompasses the recognition of oneself and one's kin as objects of material interest, as well as the extension of said interest to ever-larger communities as one matures. *Oikeiōsis* can be imagined as encompassing the twin moral functions of self-preservation and sociability, but it would be inaccurate to describe these as two separate processes. Instead, they are more like different activities or phases of the same *oikeiotic* impulse. In *oikeiōsis*, sociability is an advanced form of self-preservation.[11]

It seems only natural to discuss the concept of *oikeiōn* in terms of "ownership" or "what belongs to one." However, we must be careful not to create contradictions in the search for linguistic simplicity. Recall that in the Stoic view, particularly as put forward by Epictetus, all that I am and all that I own is my faculty of choice—that which is *up to me*. The Stoic knife cuts everything else away. It would be incoherent, then, to say *oikeiōsis* constitutes an extension of what *belongs* to me or likewise that my *identity* expands with my moral horizon. A better way to describe it would be to say that what is *oikeiōn*, that is, what belongs in my figurative "household," is *that for which I bear responsibility*. When something is *oikeiōn*, its welfare gives me reasons to act.[12] I do not grow, then, by accumulating things; I grow by accumulating responsibilities.

The general theory of *oikeiōsis* is derived from observations of animal behavior. Animals, which occupy a position between plants and humans in the hierarchy of life forms, are driven by an innate impulse that manifests as observable acts of self-preservation. This impulse, present from birth, represents the initial stage of *oikeiōsis*—an instinctual concern for one's own well-being. Although lengthy, the following passage from an ancient commentator is worth reviewing in full, as it both effectively illustrates this concept and employs it to shed light on other important ideas:

> They say that an animal's first impulse is to preserve itself, because nature from the start makes the animal attached [*oikeiōn*] to itself ... for in this way it repels what is harmful and pursues what is appropriate. What some people say, namely that the primary impulse of animals has pleasure as its object, the Stoics' claim is false. For they say that pleasure, if it is actually felt, is a by-product that arises only after nature, by itself, has sought and found what is suitable to

---

11 I believe this is consistent with the account of *oikeiōsis* put forward by Tad Brennan, who offers an alternative to a "near consensus among critics that there are two separate kinds of *oikeiōsis*, to oneself and to others." On account of its explanatory power, I think Brennan's "unitary" interpretation is more coherent with the wider Stoic system than the "dualistic" take even if the latter is more common. See Brennan, *The Stoic Life*, 154–67.

12 Brennan, *The Stoic Life*, 158.

the animal's constitution; it is in this way that animals frolic and plants bloom. They say that nature made no distinction between plants and animals, since she regulates the latter as well as the former without impulse and sensation; and even in us certain processes are plantlike. When, in the case of animals, impulse is added, by means of which they pursue what is appropriate [is *oikeiōn*] for them, then for them what is natural is to be governed by impulse. And when reason, as a more perfect authority, has been bestowed on rational beings, then for them what is natural and proper is to be governed by reason. For reason, like a craftsman, overrides impulse.[13]

I shall highlight three key points from the passage. First, there is a reference to those who claim pleasure is the primary impulse of animals—an allusion to the Epicureans, whose philosophy the Stoics traditionally oppose.[14] Second, the passage offers perhaps the clearest available articulation of the idea that living in accordance with nature does not mean living like an animal, but rather living as a human, *as distinguished from animals*, because, for humans, "what is natural and proper is to be governed by reason." Although I have emphasized this point before, it remains both crucial and counterintuitive; thus, it bears repeating. The final point, more pertinent to our current discussion, is the progression from simple to advanced beings as indicated by the properties of nature, impulse, and, finally, reason. Plants and human embryos possess a 'nature', but animals and human infants are driven by 'impulse', where *oikeiōsis* begins. Finally, humans alone develop reason as we mature. The most critical juncture in human *oikeiōsis* is this transition from a pre-rational phase to the emergence of reason.[15]

It may be tempting to think of *oikeiōsis* as simply another term for moral progress, but the two are not identical. What *oikeiōsis* describes is a critical *aspect* of moral progress that encompasses the natural development of self-awareness and affiliation, beginning with oneself and expanding to include others. This process underlies the development of moral reasoning and prosocial behavior. It can be seen as the initial framework or starting point upon which moral progress is built. *Oikeiotic* morality is therefore reflected in the progression from animalistic self-preservation to sociability. Even in animals there is an observable self-awareness and adaptive set of behaviors which include actions that benefit others. Examples include care for one's young, defense of one's group, and symbiosis between species for mutual benefit. Marcus observes:

> At any rate, from the very beginning, among irrational creatures there existed swarms, flocks, the feeding of young, and something like love, because there were, after all, souls involved, and at this higher level there is a tendency to unity of an intensity not to be found in plants or stones or logs. In rational creatures, this same tendency manifests as communities, friendships, households, assemblies, and treaties and truces at times of war. And among still higher beings there exists a kind of unity consisting of discrete things, such as one finds among the heavenly

---

13 DL 7.85–6.
14 A notable exception to this is Seneca, who often quotes Epicurus approvingly.
15 Reydams-Schils, "Human Bonding and Oikeiōsis in Roman Stoicism," 223.

bodies. Thus the higher up the scale one goes, the greater the possibility there is of an interactive connection being forged among discrete things.[16]

Importantly, unlike in animals, self-preservation in rational beings involves preserving the rational, or virtuous, self. This perspective explains how, in line with the *oikeiotic* principle, an advanced being might sacrifice oneself in defense of one's country, or, in extreme cases, commit suicide to serve a higher purpose. As Chrysippus puts it, "What am I to begin from, and what am I to take as the proper function and the material of virtue if I pass over nature and what accords with nature?"[17] To act in a way that contradicts one's virtuous nature is to annihilate the rational self. Stated in terms of Epictetan consequentiality, it is to contradict the hypothesis that one is a rational being.

From Self to Community

The ancients left us no complete treatises on *oikeiōsis*. Instead, as with many significant topics, we rely on a brief summary by Diogenes Laertius, scattered references in the writings of Cicero and Seneca, and a few fragments from Chrysippus and his contemporaries. While Epictetus and Marcus Aurelius occasionally touch on the subject when discussing moral progress, they offer little direct insight into the *oikeiōsis* process itself. Our most illustrative source is a fragment from a relatively obscure late Stoic, Hierocles, whom I mentioned in this chapter's introduction. Were it not for his contributions to this topic, his name might have faded from the record. However, the model of expanding social morality he outlines has emerged as one of the more versatile ideas to come from the Stoics, and it bridges several critical gaps in our understanding of their worldview.

Hierocles' major innovation is to represent the various scales of community as concentric circles. At the center of his model is the individual self, which he takes care to describe as comprising both the mind and the physical body as separate elements. This is surrounded by a circle of immediate family, which is itself inside a larger circle including distant relatives, and a yet larger one that includes fellow members of one's own tribe. The series of ever-greater circles continues, encompassing one's fellow citizens, nearby cities, surrounding regions and countryside, and, finally, all of humankind (Figure 5).

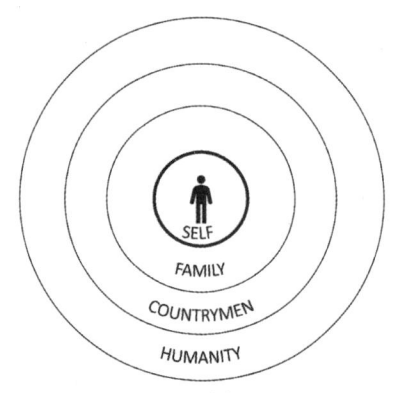

Figure 5. A simplified diagram of Hierocles' circles.

---

16 Marcus Aurelius, *Meditations* 9.9.
17 Plutarch, *On Common Conceptions* 1069E (SVF 3.491) = LS 59A.

Hierocles is not content to merely describe human sociability; he aims to improve it by laying out a moral imperative:

> Once these have all been surveyed, it is the task of a well-tempered man, in his proper treatment of each group, to draw the circles together somehow towards the center, and to keep zealously transferring those from the enclosing circles into the enclosed ones ... It is incumbent on us to respect people from the third circle as if they were those from the second, and again to respect our other relatives as if they were those from the third circle. For although the greater distance in blood will remove some affection, we must still try hard to assimilate them. The right point will be reached if, through our own initiative, we reduce the distance of the relationship with each person.[18]

As an exercise to help draw the circles together, Hierocles suggests we address members of each outer circle as if they belonged to the next inner circle. For instance, he encourages us to refer to aunts and uncles as parents and to address our neighbors as if they were part of our family. The "right point," as he puts it, involves reducing the perceived distance between ourselves and *all others* by some unspecified degree. In effect, then, our moral horizon, encompassing that for which we bear responsibility, expands as we draw the far circles inward. Interestingly, Hierocles limits this contraction to a certain extent; he never implies we should collapse all the circles entirely inward. I will consider the implications of this moderated approach shortly.

What, then, does it mean to reduce the moral distance to another? We can begin to answer this question by considering the basic habits that promote coordination, cooperation, and conflict resolution among individuals. As an individual's reasoning develops, these habits gradually evolve into an awareness of one's role within a broader community, along with the responsibilities attendant to that role. A transition to fully human moral agency occurs when the individual comes to recognize the welfare of others can provide valid reasons for action. When the interests of a wider circle become indistinguishable from self-interests, that circle becomes *oikeiōn*.

Other-interest, then, is advanced self-interest, and to perceive these as one and the same marks a key development in moral progress. Virtues like justice and prudence emerge to optimize behavior within both physical and social contexts. *Oikeiōsis* continues the process, capturing progressively larger communities within a growing concept of self-interest. When a community is *oikeiōn*, or "one's own," then its welfare gives one reasons to act; its harm is self-harm and its destruction is self-destruction. Hierocles explains:

> Just as someone who prefers one finger over the five is senseless, but one who prefers the five over the one is reasonable—for the former dishonors even his preferred finger, while the latter saves the one in saving the five—in this way too someone who wishes to save himself more than his country, in addition to doing what is unlawful, is also senseless, desiring what is impossible,

---

18 Hierocles in Stobaeus 4.671–3 = LS 57G.

while the one who honors his country above himself is both dear to the gods and equipped with rational arguments.[19]

Hierocles thus depicts an inextricable unity between the common interest and the individual interest. Just as severing the hand would make the survival of its individual fingers impossible, the destruction of a city renders the preservation of its citizens (*as* citizens) impossible. The gory analogy echoes the Chrysippean comparison of an isolated individual to a severed foot, which is "no longer a foot" when it is separated from the whole.[20] Both early and late Stoics recognize community interest as manifesting the shared human faculty of reason that connects its members like parts of a body.[21]

Recall the principle of Stoic egoism, first discussed in Chapter 2, wherein a human always behaves *egoistically*, or selfishly, in their inexorable pursuit of the perceived good. Virtue is developed, then, by clarifying what is or is not actually good. The same *egoistic* behavior appears in *oikeiotic* social morality: a morally advanced individual comes to see members of their community as *oikeiōn* and, by perceiving the community welfare as their own self-interest, their necessarily self-interested behaviors will manifest as moral actions beneficial to the community.

Therefore, it makes no sense to harm another in pursuit of so-called self-interest. We should recognize this as a repackaging of the Socratic idea that vice is a kind of ignorance, where one who has proper understanding can only see injustice as a kind of self-harm. Whatever one may acquire through injustice to another, a good it is not. Cicero elaborates upon this point to suggest injustice harms not just the perpetrator but the greater community as a whole:

> If a person deprives his neighbor of something, and furthers his own advantage by another's loss, such behavior flies in the face of nature more than death or poverty or pain or anything which can affect our persons or our external possessions; for first and foremost, it undermines the fellowship and alliance between members of the human race … for though nature does not object to our opting to obtain for ourselves individually rather than for another what is needed for life's necessities, she does not permit us to increase our own resources, wealth, and possessions by plundering those of other people.[22]

He goes on to draw a parallel between written human law and 'natural law', both of which are understood to serve the common good. Probably echoing the middle Stoic Panaetius, Cicero describes natural law as a universal standard governing

---

19 Hierocles, (51,5–10), from Wedgwood, "Hierocles' Concentric Circles," 293–332.
20 Epictetus, *Discourses* 2.5.26.
21 Cf. Marcus in Marcus Aurelius, *Meditations* 7.13: "Rational beings, in their separate bodies, have the same relationship to one another as limbs do in unified organisms, since they were made for a single cooperative purpose." See also Cicero, *On Duties* 3.22: "If each of our bodily limbs took the notion that it could flourish by appropriating the strength of the adjacent limb, then the whole of our body would inevitably be weakened, and would die."
22 Cicero, *On Duties* 3.21–22.

human behavior, rooted in the rational order of the universe. In his view, this is "a force of nature; this is the mind and reason of the prudent man; this is the rule of right and wrong."[23]

In light of modern sensibilities, one might quibble with such moralizing from a man as rich and powerful as Cicero. A highly successful statesman whose career culminated in the consulship of Rome, he would have owned numerous estates with countless slaves at the peak of his wealth. The same is true for elites like Seneca and Marcus Aurelius. Modern concepts of social and economic justice would be several degrees removed from anything these men would understand as practical or realistic, and we can comprehend this without excusing it. What is pertinent to our discussion is the reasoning behind Stoic social morality, which Cicero endeavors to identify with nature.[24] While the Stoics did endorse the pursuit of preferred indifferents, Cicero, echoing Chrysippus, emphasizes the vital caveat that this pursuit must not come at the expense of others:

> Each of us should safeguard any personal interest which does not cause injustice to another. Chrysippus as usual put it neatly when he said: "A runner on the racetrack must strain and compete with all his might to come first, but on no account must he trip or hand off a fellow-competitor; and likewise in life, there is nothing wrong in an individual's seeking what is in his own interest, but it is unjust to deprive another."[25]

We should emphasize that Stoic social morality does not require the adoption of any particular ideology or set of political beliefs. For example, there is plenty of room for disagreement about foreign policy, education, liberty, equality, or what truly constitutes injustice. At the same time, to be properly Stoic, whatever policy preferences result would have to be based upon convictions about what is genuinely best for everybody; any unabashedly selfish motivations would be rejected. This sentiment is evident in the words of Musonius Rufus, a renowned Stoic philosopher of his era and mentor to Epictetus: "evil consists in injustice and cruelty and indifference to a neighbor's trouble, while virtue is brotherly love and goodness and justice and beneficence and concern for the welfare of one's neighbor."[26]

The Problem of Other Peoples' Indifferents

While altruism toward others certainly seems right and just on its face, an interesting question arises when considering it in light of key Stoic doctrines. Specifically, there

---

23 Cicero, *On the Laws* 1.19. Cf. *On Duties* 3.23. Although Cicero does not explicitly describe his theory of natural law as Stoic in origin, Malcolm Schofield argues it is "clearly a reworking of basically Stoic material." See Schofield, *The Stoic Idea of the City*, 67–69.
24 For a more thorough analysis of Stoic social morality, particularly as understood through these passages from Cicero, see Brennan, *The Stoic Life*, 182–230.
25 Cicero, *On Duties* 3.42.
26 Lutz, *Disdain Hardships*, 68–69.

is the belief virtue is the sole good, such that all matters external to virtue (effectively, everything beyond one's power) are not truly good nor bad but indifferent. This claim, if it is to be fully embraced, seems to dissolve any rationale for caring about the less fortunate or, for that matter, anyone at all other than one's own moral self. If the health and comfort of our neighbors are indifferent, then why should it matter how we act toward them? Deprived of its ostensible reasons for existing, Stoic social morality would seem to collapse.

And yet, the Stoics seem not to notice the apparent contradiction, continuously emphasizing social imperatives while only indirectly addressing why one should care about what is supposedly indifferent. The issue isn't whether the Stoics endorse social morality—they clearly do—but whether they do so inconsistently with their purported principles. Considering the emphasis on technical defensibility that defined the debates among early philosophical schools, it is surprising this question does not receive more explicit attention in the surviving texts. At least some modern scholars have tackled the problem, and although I will not try to reproduce their full arguments here, I can provide a simplified account.[27]

The question, "If a malicious act does not cause harm, why is it considered wrong?" presumes malice is only morally wrong when it results in some harm or evil. However, from the Stoic perspective, virtue or vice resides in the internal disposition of the actor. Consider Seneca's thoughts on assaulting a sage: "We declare that a wise man cannot receive an injury; yet, if a man hits him with his fist, that man will be found guilty of doing him an injury."[28] The wrongness of the act is inherent, regardless of its outcome.

Suppose, for example, I intentionally aim a rifle at an innocent person and pull the trigger. My act does not become less wrong if I miss. Similarly, if I am standing next to a pool that contains a drowning child and I do nothing to save the child, my inaction is no less negligent if the child ultimately makes it to the shallow end and survives. Things might be different if the pool is far away, if there is a lifeguard or other adults nearer to the child, or if other such circumstances are altered. But the appropriateness of my action or inaction is not determined by what harm, illusory or otherwise, actually comes to another. My intentions are what matters, and just as I should select preferred indifferents over the dispreferred when given the choice, I should also select preferred indifferents for my neighbors, who are *oikeiōn* to me, when given the choice.

That a Stoic should make selections based upon not just their own preferences, but also the preferences of others, is a challenging claim, so I shall elaborate further. Recall that what is *oikeiōn*, which should include my neighbors and more distant

---

27 For example, criticism of this apparent incompatibility can be found in Card, *The Atrocity Paradigm*, 245–53. For a thorough response, see Seregin, "Stoicism and the Impossibility of Social Morality," 58–77.
28 Seneca, *On Benefits* 2.35, trans. Stewart.

communities, is *that for which I bear responsibility*. Their welfare gives me reasons to act. Recall also that virtue, or what constitutes the fulfillment of my natural purposes, is expressed in the appropriate selection of preferred over dispreferred indifferents. The cardinal virtue of justice is expressed when my selections affect the indifferents available to my neighbors. Just as my neighbors pursue their own natural purposes by correctly selecting among indifferents, if I perceive them as *oikeiōn*, then I will actively consider what they *should* prefer at all times. Regarding altruism, for example, Seneca argues we should "divine every man's wishes," such that we may bestow upon them what is needed without subjecting them to the indignity of asking.[29]

Thus arises a natural mandate to empathize with my neighbor.[30] This does not imply I am always required to forfeit my own preferences in favor of theirs; I do not have to give away my cake simply because another guest at the party might prefer it. In considering my *oikeiōn* neighbor's wishes, I should respond to what is appropriate, or to what they *would* prefer if they were a sage. Seneca wisely tempers generosity with prudence: "When we are about to lend money, we first make a careful inquiry into the means and habits of life of our debtor, and avoid sowing seed in worn-out or unfruitful soil; yet, without any judgment, we scatter our benefits at random rather than bestow them."[31] In Seneca's view, unregulated generosity deteriorates into profligacy, but when kept on target by prudence, the virtue of justice shines through.

As a duty, assisting my neighbors to achieve their preferred indifferents or to avoid the dispreferred is not an absolute; it must be considered in light of all the other duties that weigh upon me, role-based or otherwise. But it must be considered. Furthermore, this consideration does not constitute any sort of belief in the intrinsic or moral importance of what comes about, but rather it is about aligning my actions to the presumed will of universal nature.[32] To promote the welfare of my neighbors is consistent with nature; to neglect their welfare would be contrary to nature. These claims align mercifully with our fundamental, dare I say natural, moral intuitions.

The Problem of Partiality

As a concept of moral development, the Stoic theory of *oikeiōsis* warrants criticism on several fronts, both in its general description by earlier Stoics and specifically as it is presented in Hierocles' more detailed account. For instance, the idea *oikeiōsis*

---

29 Ibid. 2.2.
30 Cf. Marcus Aurelius, *Meditations* 6.53: "Get into the habit of listening attentively to anything that anyone says, and enter, as much as you can, into the mind of the speaker"; and Epictetus, *Discourses* 3.24.23: "Someone else's grief is not my own concern, but my own grief is. It is thus my responsibility to put an end to it at all cost, because that is within my power; as to the grief of another, I'll strive to put an end to it so far as I am able, but won't strive to do so at all costs."
31 Seneca, *On Benefits* 1.1, trans. Stewart.
32 This is a simplification of the argument put forward by Andrei Seregin.

must always proceed from the center outward seems overly simplistic. Even if this notion aligns with earlier teachings, it appears restricted to only the most normative of circumstances. In reality, it is entirely plausible for someone to feel a stronger connection to their country than to their hometown or family. Alternatively, an individual might identify more deeply with humanity as a whole or with a specific community, such as a particular race or ethnic diaspora, while simultaneously feeling indifferent or even hostile toward their country of origin.

A Stoic apologist might argue these unconventional scenarios would indicate an irrational outlook, whereas the theory of *oikeiōsis* presupposes a wise (i.e., perfectly virtuous) disposition. But that cannot be right; what *oikeiōsis* itself describes is moral progress, which should be irrelevant to a sage, whose journey is presumed complete. Because it involves progress, it must necessarily occur within a progressor, that is, an irrational human. Even if the apologist's explanation were tempered to only deal in *appropriate* (if not necessarily *right*) perceptions of what is *oikeiōn*, it would still represent an implausible position.[33] It would deny that someone could *appropriately* accept a more distant circle before a nearer one, even in cases such as being brought up in an abusive family or a manifestly unjust society, for instance.

Another issue with *oikeiōsis* as it is presented is we do not see any acknowledgment of a transition in status of what is or is not *oikeiōn*; that is to say, *oikeiōsis* appears to be a process of instantaneous and incremental expansion. In addition to occurring in only one direction, the expansion of responsibility seems to proceed in a linear, stepwise fashion. Something is not *oikeiōn* to me until one day it is—a binary, either/or status—and only when it is *oikeiōn* do we contemplate something beyond it becoming *oikeiōn*. In reality, the connection and sense of duty I perceive toward a distant circle, for example, my country, might begin at an early age but continue to crystallize over the course of a lifetime.

It is plausible early Stoics did consider these details, but their reflections on these matters are simply lost to history. We really do have very little to work with when reconstructing their ideas—mere secondhand reports and fragments of decayed papyrus. Further, while it would be incorrect to claim the critiques above lack significant moral implications, it's fair to say they are somewhat peripheral to the valuable insights the Stoics offer us today. We might as well criticize their early scientific theories. The more serious issue, which has a substantive impact on our understanding of Stoic social morality, is that we are not provided with a clear vision of what the circles of concern should look like for a sage.

For example, it is unclear whether Hierocles restricts his naming exercise—such as treating aunts and uncles as parents—to a single "degree" of contraction solely

---

33 I refer to the Stoic distinction between right actions, or those undertaken from a perfectly virtuous disposition, and appropriate actions, or those that resemble right actions but are undertaken from a flawed disposition. The idea was introduced in Chapter 2 and further developed in Chapter 4.

for pragmatic reasons, or whether he views this as representing a full and perfected expression of sociability, as would be seen in a sage. Additionally, as we noted earlier, Hierocles suggests the right point is achieved when all of one's circles are drawn inward to some degree, but he does not suggest one should draw them all the way in. The interesting question is, why not?

This question highlights a broader issue that extends far beyond the Stoic tradition and has challenged philosophers for centuries. We may call it the problem of partiality. Whether one is a father, a daughter, a laborer, or an emperor, specific roles obligate one to prioritize certain groups or individuals over others. In other words, some roles rightfully ask for our loyalty, which Seneca extols as "the holiest good in the human heart."[34] But how can we prioritize those who are close to us and still claim to be cosmopolitans? Alternatively, does not *Cosmopolitanism* inevitably reduce the notion of loyalty? Consider Marcus Aurelius: how could he claim to be a citizen of the world without compromising his citizenship, much less his *emperorship*, of Rome?

As a classic moral dilemma, the problem of partiality asks whether I am justified in treating those closest to me, such as my own family or countrymen, with greater care and concern than those distant from me, such as impoverished children on another continent. On one hand, it seems I owe a certain degree of preferential attention and affection to those in my immediate circle, such as those specific duties toward blood relatives that Epictetus frequently emphasizes. On the other hand, it seems wrong to disregard someone based on arbitrary standards like birthplace or geographic distance. As Cicero says, "the mere fact that someone is a man makes it incumbent on another man not to regard him as alien."[35] And yet, to treat all humans the same would require the rejection of any institution or custom that assigns special value to certain individuals, even the traditional family. This, it would seem, is what Zeno is getting at in his collectivist society of the wise.

Excepting Marcus' curious and regular return to the topic, the Stoics do not seem to betray any particular anxiety or moral conflict on this point. Stoics clearly do not override the needs of the local community with cosmopolitan ideals, nor do they deny the responsibilities of membership in an earthly nation-state. Rather, they approach the balance as one would approach dual citizenship within two great civilizations. Seneca captures it with characteristic eloquence: "There are two communities—the one, which is great and truly common, embracing gods and men, in which we look neither to this corner nor to that, but measure the boundaries of our state by the sun; the other, the one to which we have been assigned by the accident of our birth."[36]

One way to interpret this concept of dual citizenship is to consider it an effect of Self-Similarity, a principle we introduced in the first chapter. The local community

---

34 Seneca, *Letters* 88.29.
35 Cicero, *On Ends* 3.62–8 = LS 57F.
36 Seneca, *On Leisure* 4.1 = LS 67K.

is properly understood as "a microcosm of the universal city," a metaphor implying the dynamics, relationships, and ethical responsibilities present in an earthly city reflect those at the universal level.[37] In other words, the way individuals interact with their neighbors, govern local affairs, and contribute to communal well-being serves as a scaled-down model of how they should engage with the "cosmopolis," or the city "of gods and men." The local is therefore not merely subordinate to the global but is a part of it and a reflection of it, embodying similar fundamental principles and moral imperatives.

As with any occasion of divided loyalties, one must navigate potential conflicts of interest carefully. Marcus Aurelius, echoing Epictetus, asserts it is indeed possible to serve both cities: "As Antonius, my social community and my country is Rome, but as a human being it's the universe. So it's only things that benefit these communities that are good for me."[38] This suggests that moral reasoning must operate on multiple levels, with the moral good residing in the alignment and consistency between them. For Marcus, the recognition of a shared human community would serve as a necessary check on the destructive potential of imperial military power. His reflection that "anything which isn't good for the hive isn't good for the bee either" encapsulates a commitment to serving both the local and universal communities.[39]

By prioritizing harmony between principles, Marcus avoids subordinating the local to the universal, and he also points out a way to navigate most occasions of competing interests. However, his approach does not clearly acknowledge the possibility of irreconcilable conflicts between communitarian and cosmopolitan ideals, nor does it suggest a solution for times of crisis. Moreover, several key passages in his writings do seem to suggest we are called to transcend the local community and its specific concerns. These exist in an unresolved tension with familial and communitarian duties.

While it is always hazardous to put words into the mouths of our forebears, we can probably do better than this. If we aim to draw out a common thread between the anarchism of Zeno and the patriotism of Hierocles, or between the benevolent humanism evident in all Stoic writings and the imperial warfare of Marcus Aurelius, we will need to engage in some careful inference and speculation. To that end, I propose that two major misconceptions contribute to the perceived conflict between Stoic communitarian principles, which necessitate partiality, and Stoic cosmopolitanism. The first misconception is the belief moral progress should ideally culminate in an equal moral regard for all the world's people. I will argue such an outlook is not only far from the Stoic ideal but also profoundly unjust. The second misconception is that *Cosmopolitanism* serves as the foundational perspective

---

37 Epictetus, *Discourses* 2.5.26.
38 Marcus Aurelius, *Meditations* 6.44. Consistent with Roman custom, Marcus calls himself "Antonius" to honor his adoptive father Antonius Pius.
39 Ibid. 6.54.

from which all concepts of justice must flow, a view seemingly supported by the subordination of specific roles to the fundamental role imposed by reason. I will argue this is essentially backward from the way it should be understood. I will then suggest a way of thinking about our special obligations to others that describes what the circles of concern might look like for a sage.

Extreme Cosmopolitanism

We have repeatedly witnessed the importance Stoics place on social morality, which is practically observed as traditional communitarian values, including partiality toward family, tribe, and local community. Emerging from the earliest stages of moral development, such values are simply intuitive. At the same time, we can also plainly see the dangers of an unchecked communitarian impulse. Benign tribal affinities can easily degenerate into racism or sectarianism, and healthy patriotism requires only a hint of contempt to become chauvinistic nationalism. From this precipice, destructive ideologies like jingoism and fascism are only a stumble away. Exercises to draw distant circles of concern inward appear as deliberate countermeasures against such tendencies. So, if *Cosmopolitanism* is what follows from moral progress, then is not more of it always better?

Suppose the moral horizon for a sage really does expand to encompass all of humanity, with no discrimination between things distant and nearby—*oikeiōn* is *oikeiōn*, in this view. Or in the Hieroclean model, suppose the sage's circles of concern really do collapse upon the center with no boundary or space remaining between them. We might call such a state "extreme cosmopolitanism."[40] It is characterized by an equally positive disposition toward all of the world's people, prohibiting harm and promoting obligations to assist all people equally, recognizing no preference or specific duties toward members of any group, including one's own family or countrymen. Although it is a radical theory, extreme cosmopolitanism does find its proponents in the modern day, who argue arbitrary differences should not influence the scope or limit of our moral obligations. They believe every person should be treated with equal consideration, regardless of geographical, cultural, or genetic distance, and that discrimination based on parochial values such as national citizenship is a severe moral failing.[41]

As a modern idea, extreme cosmopolitanism emerges from various schools of moral theory, but most notably consequentialism, which holds the morally correct act is that which provides the greatest happiness to the greatest number. "Hard" consequentialists believe there is no justification for prioritizing the happiness of

---

40 The term is credited to Stephen Nathanson. See Nathanson, "Is Cosmopolitan Anti-Patriotism a Virtue?" 69–82.
41 E.g., Gomberg, "Patriotism Is Like Racism," 144–50.

those with whom I am familiar over anyone else; net happiness is what matters.[42] This degree of impartiality is decidedly not what the Stoics promoted in their ideal of a world citizen, even for a sage. This is not just because it is impractical outside of theory, but also because it would be profoundly unjust to those who are rightfully deserving of our special attentions.

Epictetus insists I should "preserve my natural and acquired relationships, as one who honors the gods, as a son, as a brother, as a father, as a citizen."[43] Within my moral horizon, discrete relationships exist between myself and certain individuals but not others. If such relationships have any meaning, then I will feel certain responsibilities toward these specific individuals: to provide them with certain benefits, to protect them from harm, and to generally give them attention I do not give to others. This belief forms a significant part of my everyday morality. If *oikeiōsis*—as natural affection and sense of belonging—is truly observed in animal behavior, then such prioritization of close relationships should be a fundamental aspect of it. Reason, then, would be expressed in *correct* prioritization, not the elimination of prioritization.

For example, up to some limit, I would be justified in protecting my own child from harm even if it meant some stranger suffered a somewhat greater harm. Anything less would render me a sorry parent. At the same time, I would be wrong to prioritize saving my own child from a minor cut or bruise over saving a stranger's life.[44] In this scenario, there is a trade-space between the somewhat lesser degree of harm I can prevent for my child while justifiably permitting a somewhat greater harm to some stranger. It is conceivable two wise and just people might reach different conclusions as to what difference in harm for each party can be justified.

However, no reasonable person can deny that, for a society to function, people have to depend on one another. We must build relationships and trust to form communities, which naturally involves assigning various forms of preference to some individuals and groups over others. A parent cannot give equal attention to all the world's children, nor can a child give equal attention to all the world's parents. Likewise, I cannot be a friend, a mate, or a protector to all the world's people. If I spread my loyalty too thin, I effectively abstract it into meaninglessness. Such an ethos might provide me with a vague feeling of moral superiority, but it does nothing for any of the people who depend on me.

---

42 William Godwin, the 18th-century consequentialist, provides the archetypal example of this thinking, positing one should prefer to save Archbishop Fénelon (presumably a more valuable contributor to society) from a burning building over their own father. While Godwin was serious in making this argument, it is most widely cited as a *reductio ad absurdum* of consequentialist thinking. See Godwin, *An Enquiry Concerning Political Justice*, Vol. I, 82.
43 Epictetus, *Discourses* 3.2.4.
44 I borrow this thought experiment from Derek Parfit. See Parfit, *Reasons and Persons*, 95.

If we want to imagine what the Stoics might have looked like without a communitarian ethic to counterbalance their *Cosmopolitanism*, we can get a good idea from the Cynics, from whom the Stoics inherited many of their fundamental claims. It was specifically Diogenes the Cynic who coined the phrase "citizen of the world."[45] Although Epictetus looks back on them with admiration, the Cynics were a critically flawed prototype of what would become the Stoics. One of the Stoics' most significant improvements over their philosophy was to embrace the social conventions Cynics rejected. Cynics could not participate productively in society while remaining true to their philosophy; instead, they lived as vagrants, relying on the charity of patrons for survival while simultaneously mocking all social norms.

The Cynic experiment predictably failed because its denial of basic human nature could never be sustained at scale. In comparison, the Stoics thrived in no small part because they recognized social conventions as a vital element of human flourishing. In a pattern we see repeated into our present day, history tends to reward those systems that leverage human nature while it punishes those that seek to re-engineer it. It is most vividly illustrated by the 20th century's disastrous experiments in forced collectivism, which are perhaps the closest humanity has ever come to realizing Zeno's *Republic*—except, of course, the part about its members being perfectly wise and just.[46]

History repeatedly indicates utopian ideologies are dangerous in the hands of power, particularly because nearly any means can be rationalized in light of an effectively unlimited promise of greater good. We should hope, then, that extreme cosmopolitanism remains a curiosity of fringe theorists. Those yearning for a world that transcends national allegiance, borders, and the dangers of war must articulate a path to achieve it. For such a plan to be more than idle conjecture, it has to be informed by political and economic realities. It especially must address what is intended for those parties who disagree with the plan. If our aspirations require the quashing of human nature, then we should say who does the quashing and how it is to be done.

The Expanded Horizon

One attractive resolution to the problem of partiality is to suggest that a universal perspective facilitates the local perspective. All mothers of mammals preferentially care

---

45 DL 6.63.
46 Steven Pinker writes, "To hope that the human empathy gradient can be flattened so much that strangers would mean as much to us as family and friends is utopian in the worst 20th-century sense, requiring an unattainable and dubiously desirable quashing of human nature." Pinker, *The Better Angels of Our Nature*, 591. Cf. Michael Walzer: "The crimes of the twentieth century have been committed alternately, as it were, by perverted patriots and perverted cosmopolitans. If fascism represents the first of these perversions, communism, in its Leninist and Maoist versions, represents the second." Walzer, "Spheres of Affection," 125–27.

for their offspring, and this behavior facilitates the survival of the species; likewise in this view all of our individual roles in the cosmic system require we prioritize local systems. Specific duties are therefore effectively folded into universal duties, and the reasons one should attend to them are situated within one's place in the greater universe.

This view would essentially establish two tiers of reasoning: the everyday attention to specific duties, which constitutes the world in which most of us operate; and, separate from that, a higher tier of reflection on one's place in the universe. It is on this elevated plane of thought we would presumably discover the true reasons behind our actions. One appealing feature of this perspective is it aligns with the mental exercise of focusing on one's situation from an elevated perspective, discussed in Chapter 3 as the "view from above." Through this lens, we might observe ourselves attending to our own minor concerns and desires, recognizing these behaviors as consistent with nature.

Such reasoning is awfully convenient. If my specific duties are merely extensions of universal duties, then I can never encounter a conflict between the two. I can act without a single thought toward anyone beyond my immediate sphere and remain satisfied I am doing what the universe requires of me. Therein lies a problem with this view: moral concern for those more distant is effectively abstracted into impotence. I can ignore it completely at no cost to my identity as a cosmopolitan.

The more proximate problem with this reasoning is nobody actually thinks like this. When I take my sick child to the doctor, I do it for the child, not for some nebulous principle that has something to do with my place in the cosmos. Right or wrong, I tend not to think much about the world's other sick children until mine is well. Furthermore, such an abstract tier of reasoning would only be accessible to those with both the time and the intellectual proclivity for moral theorizing. Nothing in Stoicism works this way; it is more likely a modern idea masquerading as an ancient one.[47] As it is presented in the ancient sources, Stoicism encourages individuals to fulfill their everyday roles—be it as a parent, sibling, or community member—through the lens of moral principles. The idea is to embody virtue within these roles, living life from various perspectives informed by both social norms and reason, while ultimately striving to align one's local duties with a broader cosmopolitan outlook.

Even when we make moral progress, our circles—representing our priorities—remain distinct. We still naturally prioritize those closer to us, such as family, over those further removed, like distant acquaintances or strangers. The idea of "drawing the circles together" emphasizes reducing, but not eliminating, the natural distance between these social bonds, ensuring we balance our moral obligations with a

---

47 See Annas, "My Station and its Duties," 113.

realistic sense of proximity and connection.[48] In other words, our sociability toward those more distant from us is not absolute, and the sequence of *oikeiotic* progress matters. Rather than transcend our partiality toward those we consider our own, we are expected to fulfill the duties it imposes, and then gradually extend that sense of belonging onto others.[49] The process is not instantaneous.[50]

In some ways, the process seems paradoxical. One might wonder, for example, "Where should I draw the line?"—as if there exists an invisible threshold that, once our expanding moral horizon crosses it, would lead us to neglect our local duties and transform us into extreme cosmopolitans. But this cannot be correct; we are clearly meant to accept the entire universe as *oikeiōn*. We must, therefore, still be able to discriminate and set priorities among things that are *oikeiōn*. Yet, if we are still allowed to prioritize those closest to us, what is the practical effect of an extended moral horizon?

Much of the answer, I propose, lies in the "special perspective" of moderation, discussed in Chapter 2. At a theoretical level, *Cosmopolitanism* is an extension of the communitarian ethic that expands the boundary of community to capture all of humanity. In practical terms, however, *Cosmopolitanism* and *Communitarianism* exist in balance, regulating one another in the same way virtues like prudence and courage maintain a similar equilibrium. Moderation in this sense does not dilute or weaken any principle; rather, it involves prudence in evaluating the duties imposed by one principle *in light of* the competing duties imposed by another. To better understand this balance, we can contrast an unmoderated individual, who might be overwhelmed by conflicting duties, with a moderated individual, who navigates them with clarity and equanimity.

For example, lacking moderation, an early progressor might become captured by an unhinged communitarian or cosmopolitan ideology—the particular flavor does not matter. Alternately, they might struggle with an incoherent mishmash of both communitarian and cosmopolitan sentiments. In either event, they would be unable to navigate conflicting priorities, blind to some duties while blindly pursuing others, potentially incurring emotions of guilt, doubt, and regret in the course of their moral travels. In contrast is the Stoic sage; just as they would perfectly balance the virtues of prudence and courage, they would also flawlessly integrate both communitarian and cosmopolitan principles to recognize a specific appropriate action in every event. Where the progressor's circles would be blurry and loose, the sage's would be defined and firm. The sage would resemble a well-calibrated machine of moral clarity, seamlessly negotiating local and global responsibilities, and making hard

---

48 See Wedgwood, "Hierocles' Concentric Circles," 293–332.
49 See Brennan, *The Stoic Life*, 163.
50 Citing Seneca, *Letters* 12.6 and 49.3, Gretchen Reydams-Schils credits Seneca with contributing a time dimension to moral expansion, which she intriguingly maps onto Hierocles' circles to describe an "inverted cone." See Reydams-Schils, *The Roman Stoics*, 30–31.

choices swiftly while fully accounting for all relevant moral factors. Without a fully expanded moral horizon, some of those factors would be left out of the calculus.

A sage, then, would be someone who appreciates the moral equality of all persons and yet still attends to their duties with equanimity, accepting only those responsibilities that consist with reason. This seems intuitive when the duty performed is something agreeable like preferentially caring for an elderly parent or ushering one's child through their education. It becomes less intuitive when the duty is one of those grim necessities of a complex social reality, such as evicting a nonpaying tenant, jailing a drug offender, or terminating an unproductive employee. I may not want to do this thing, but it may be my job nonetheless, and I can do it without notions my subject is somehow any less important or less human than me. But it is not clear this supposed moral equality actually does any good for my subject. The question is especially pertinent to the role of a warrior, who may be required to harm or kill their ostensible moral equals. I'll talk more about the implications of a cosmopolitan ethic within warriors in the next chapter.

One remaining issue with the center-out extension of the moral horizon we must address is its apparent conflict with Epictetus' principle of subordinating specific roles to the fundamental role. As discussed in the previous chapter, I must navigate two "tiers" of moral obligation: those tied to my specific roles and occupations, and those linked to my identity as a rational human being. However, we should be cautious not to conflate the fundamental role with *Cosmopolitanism*. When Epictetus reminds me I am "first of all, a human,"[51] he is not using humanity to as a surrogate for *Cosmopolitanism*, but for virtue writ large. This includes the impulses to act with wisdom, courage, moderation, and justice—including the just treatment of those closest to me, who are, by necessity, fellow citizens of the universal city. Epictetus' point in framing my humanity as the fundamental role is that, as a rational being, I should never entertain the idea a specific role could compel me to act against the dictates of reason.

Communities Within Communities

The matter of national loyalty remains a sticking point, where key passages suggest a hard rejection of certain communitarian values. For example, following a rich tradition of philosophers before him, Epictetus seems to say one should deny allegiance to any earthly city or kingdom. Let us revisit his point at length:

> If there is any truth in what the philosophers say about the kinship between God and humanity, what course is left for human beings than to follow the example of Socrates, and when one is asked where one is from, never to reply, "I'm an Athenian" or "I'm a Corinthian," but rather, "I'm a citizen of the universe"? For why say, in fact, that you're an Athenian rather

---

51 Epictetus, *Discourses* 2.10.1–3.

than just a citizen of that corner in which your poor body was thrown down at the time of your birth? Isn't it obvious that you choose the place that is more sovereign, and not merely that little corner, but also your whole household, and, in a word, the source that your entire race of ancestors has come down to you, and on that basis you call yourself an "Athenian" or a "Corinthian"?[52]

Here, Epictetus is sometimes read to present an antipatriotic position, reminiscent of Zeno's proto-anarchism, despite a repeated insistence—often in the same breath as he promotes familial duty—on fulfilling one's obligations "as a citizen": obeying the law, exercising authority justly, respecting others' property, building relationships, and contributing to the community.[53] Furthermore, in a different passage, he practically fawns over the patriotic military service of Socrates:

And so that you may not think that I'm offering you as an example a man who lived on his own, having neither wife, nor children, nor country, nor friends, nor relations, who might have turned him aside and caused him to deviate from his path, take Socrates and consider a man who had a wife and young children, but didn't regard them as being his own, and had a country, in so far as it was his duty, and in the way in which that duty required, and had friends and relations, all of this subject to the law and to obedience to the law. That is why, when it was his duty to serve as a soldier, he was the first to set it out, and exposed himself to the dangers of war without sparing himself in the least.[54]

Is Epictetus being inconsistent? Does he just have some specific grievance against national loyalties he overlooks in his admiration of Socrates? There must be some missing piece that would make these views fit together.

Let us consider the first passage against the construct of "two cities," which Seneca elucidates as "the one, which is great and truly common, embracing gods and men, in which we look neither to this corner nor to that, but measure the boundaries of our state by the sun; the other, the one to which we have been assigned by the accident of our birth."[55] Epictetus echoes Seneca's perspective, adding that the earthly community is "a microcosm of the universal city."[56] When the Stoics discuss humans as a microcosm of something greater, it is almost always within the context of these two most salient communities. The resulting dichotomous framing is usually sufficient for whatever point the author is trying to make, but as a conceptual model it is also implicitly limited, priming us for zero-sum thinking: we struggle to comprehend we might give to one without taking from the other. Further, we are predisposed to wrongly map the two tiers of role-based duties onto what appear as two tiers of community, which I discussed earlier as a misreading of Epictetus.

---

52 Ibid. 1.9.1–3.
53 E.g., Ibid. 1.12.7, 2.10.4, 2.13.8, 2.23.36–9, 3.7.21.
54 Ibid. 4.1.159–60.
55 Seneca, *On Leisure* 4.1 = LS 67K.
56 Epictetus, *Discourses* 2.5.26.

What is missing from these accounts is provided well by Hierocles. Demonstrating a broader Stoic perspective obscured in the simplistic framing of an earthly and cosmic city, he emphasizes that the relationship between the individual and the cosmos is not a simple dichotomy but a continuum. Between myself and my city lie my family and neighbors, and between my city and my country are the surrounding cities. The number of circles is infinite, limited only by where I choose to draw the lines. If I can extend my moral horizon to encompass each circle in sequence, then zero-sum thinking is exposed as an illusion—there is no real limit to what I can consider *oikeiōn*.

Although his work describes it more vividly than any other surviving Stoic text, Hierocles did not invent the idea that communities exist in a continuum. Cicero, for example, describes the extension of social morality from the family unit to one's fellow citizens and ultimately to the gods as a reflection of natural law.[57] As with much of Cicero's philosophy, it is reasonable to suppose these ideas derive from the lost writings of Panaetius. These foundational notions likely shaped the perspectives of later Stoic thinkers, including both Epictetus and Hierocles.

Understood in light of a continuous, not dichotomous model of community, Epictetus is not saying one is wrong to be a citizen of any particular city or state any more than he says one is wrong to belong to a specific family. Instead, he insists it would be wrong to stop there. Nation-states, in his view, are no less arbitrary as points of reference than our neighborhood, our family, or even the corner of whatever sordid room facilitated "the accident of our birth." Personal affiliation should encompass all these touchpoints and ultimately transcend them.

The resulting system of nested microcosms resembles a Russian matryoshka doll. Just as a finger is part of a hand, which is part of an arm, and so on, each circle in Hierocles' model is both a microcosm to larger circles containing it and a macrocosm to the smaller ones it contains.[58] Each circle represents a scale of community, each an organic member of a larger whole. Even the individual human is a type of community, consisting of the physical body and the mind, which itself includes the ruling center and subordinate processes. Upon this structure, the natural property of Self-Similarity snaps into place, whereby communities, as natural systems, exhibit the features of their members across various scales. As I discussed in Chapter 1, the life processes and wisdom of an individual human mirror the life processes and wisdom of the organic universe, much like the smallest corner of a fractal image reflects the structure and complexity of the whole.

What does this say about the problem of partiality? Even if my moral horizon is not subject to zero-sum limitations, my attention and actions are very much so. As I have said, I cannot fulfill the role of a friend, a mate, a son, a daughter, or a

---

57 Cicero, *On Duties* 3.28; cf. 1.53.
58 Wedgwood, "Hierocles' Concentric Circles," 293–332.

protector to all the world's people with any degree of effectiveness. Although all of the world's people may become *oikeiōn* to me, meaning their welfare gives me reasons to act, this does not mean I am compelled to act the same way toward all of them nor does their welfare compel my action to the same degree. In all cases, my duties toward any one of them must be considered in light of all other duties that compete for my action. In other words, *oikeiōn* is not simply *oikeiōn*—even for a sage.

Although Hierocles only deals with this issue in passing, his circles of concern offer a uniquely compelling framework for examining problems of partiality. In short, the appropriate action or what most aligns with nature is likely the action that maximizes the overall welfare of all the circles I inhabit.[59] For example, suppose I am faced with the choice to either save the life of my sibling or to save a distant stranger. The life of my brother or sister seems to contribute more to the welfare of my immediate family (we might say it contributes more to the achievement of the family's natural purpose) than the life of a distant stranger contributes to the welfare of the entire human race. Using Hierocles' anatomical analogy, for a family to lose a child is like a body losing a limb, whereas for the whole of humanity the loss of any individual is more akin to losing a hair. Thus, even if I manage to serve both inner and outer circles equally, this doesn't necessarily demand I treat their respective members equally.

This framing can also provide clarity in questions of self-sacrifice. For instance, sacrificing my own life to save two siblings may be justified because it significantly benefits my family, outweighing the loss of my own life. However, sacrificing myself for just one sibling is less clearly justified, since my family still loses one member, and I fail to preserve my own life. Similarly, in the context of warfare, to preserve my comrades or my country at the cost of my own life would show me to be "both dear to the gods and equipped with rational arguments," as Hierocles puts it.[60] Still, this is not to say I should throw my own life away in pursuit of lost causes or vainglory. Again, what most accords with nature is arguably that which best contributes to the net welfare of all the circles I occupy.

While this approach helps clarify how we should prioritize obligations toward individuals within our various circles, a larger question arises: how should we conceive our duties toward *an entire circle*—such as a country? An even greater question follows: how should we respond to the obligations *of a circle*—such as a country—to which we belong? The Stoics' extant writings hardly acknowledge such questions, but Hierocles' continuum of nested communities seems purpose-built to address them, providing a much-needed structure for examining the moral obligations that emerge at each level.

---

59 Ibid., 335–38.
60 Hierocles, (51,5–10), from Wedgwood, "Hierocles' Concentric Circles," 293–332.

Recall that when something is deemed *oikeiōn*, it is generally understood one has a responsibility to see to its well-being. We might say we bear responsibility for the fulfillment of its natural purposes. Illustrating this, Hierocles draws a parallel between members of a family and the parts of a single body. He explains that just as the eyes, hands, and legs are integral to a person, each reliant on the others to function properly, so too are siblings connected within the family unit. Echoing Chrysippus, he notes if each part of the body were possessed with consciousness, it would naturally care for the others, recognizing its own well-being is tied to theirs.[61] In the same way, as human beings with reason and understanding, we should recognize our connection to the whole and strive to care for our fellows, knowing their welfare is essential to the whole and therefore to our own. The example is not about familial duty so much as it is about the parallel purposes that exist between communities at each tier of the continuum.

The same principles and patterns are reflected in the relationships between the city and its surrounding regions, extending further to the broader human species and, ultimately, to the connection between humanity and the organic cosmos. As with relationships between siblings, these connections imply responsibilities: a city should care for its citizens and citizens should cooperate for the good of the city. This construct of parallel purposes and responsibilities should be familiar to anyone with experience inside a hierarchy; one has responsibilities up and responsibilities down. From this reading of Hierocles, then, we can describe the responsibilities between circles systematically.[62] We observe the *telos*, or mission of each circle (i.e., community) "C" to subsist on three levels:

- First, this circle C should preserve itself and its constitution (that is, its physical and moral integrity) for as long as possible.
- Second, if there is a smaller circle, C-, contained within circle C, C should support this smaller circle in fulfilling its mission (i.e., to preserve itself and its constitution) too.
- Finally, if there is any larger circle, C+, containing circle C, C should cooperate with any other circles contained within C+ to fulfill the mission of C+ as well.

Under normal circumstances, each circle can simultaneously work to preserve itself, support the smaller circles it contains, and cooperate with peer circles to fulfill the purposes of the larger circles to which they all belong (Figure 6). This implies that while individuals should care for their own well-being and that of their immediate family and city, they should also consider their contribution to the flourishing of the larger wholes they are a part of. Consequently, a kind of

---

61 Cf. Epictetus, *Discourses* 2.6.8–10, where Epictetus echoes Chrysippus similarly.
62 The following framework is adapted from Wedgwood, "Hierocles' Concentric Circles," 333–34.

cosmopolitan moral imperative emerges, where moral actions are those that align with the natural purposes of all the circles involved. This is the very logic Marcus Aurelius invokes when he states that, between Rome and the world, "it's only things that benefit these communities that are good for me."[63] Occasions for self-sacrifice would be considered abnormal circumstances, yet they can be resolved using the same reasoning discussed earlier.

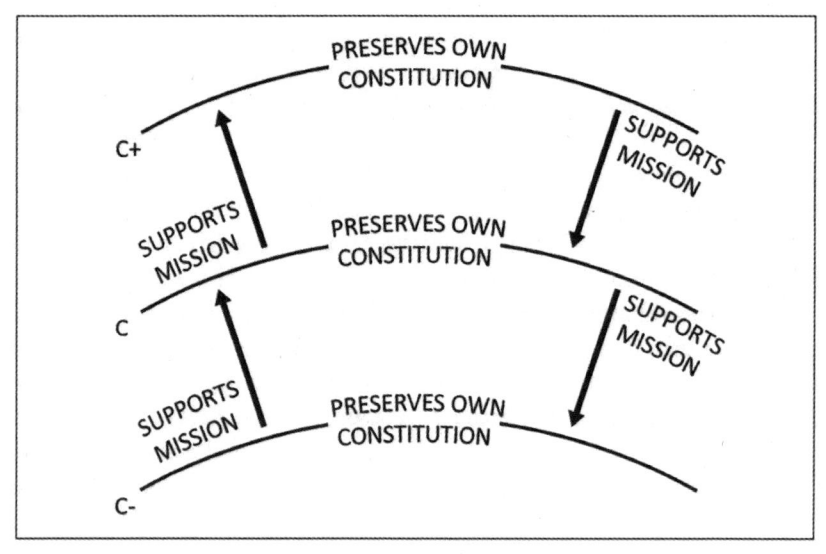

Figure 6. The mutually supporting missions of Hieroclean circles.

It is clear Hierocles sat atop a gold mine of philosophical potential, particularly in recognizing the existence of responsibilities between different social circles. The truly intriguing questions arise when we consider the implications of collective responsibilities. If we accept Hierocles' suggestion an entire community can bear responsibility or be the recipient of certain responsibilities from others, then does it become necessary to view that community's behaviors as manifesting a form of collective agency? Furthermore, how do the moral entitlements and responsibilities borne by a community distribute to its individual members, if they distribute at all?

I speculate that if the Stoics had continued as a philosophical movement and expanded specifically on Hierocles' ideas, such questions would have arisen and a theory of collective moral agency would have naturally emerged. The development of such a theory might have enriched human understanding of group dynamics and international relations centuries ahead of modernity. However, while it is intriguing to ponder what might have been, the reality is we have little evidence of activity that

---

63 Marcus Aurelius, *Meditations* 6.44.

can be definitively called "Stoic" after Hierocles and Marcus Aurelius. Therefore, I must emphasize that what follows is my own inference, grounded in the interpretation of Hierocles I have presented above. These concepts will be particularly relevant in the final chapter, where I examine the warrior's unique moral duties in the context of a collective.

Collective Duty

In the previous chapter, I established the Stoic equivalent of duty as that which bears *consequentiality*—the degree to which a given action follows, or is consequent, from nature. Duties can arise from specific roles or from virtue itself, but when the duties of a specific role contradict virtue, they lack *reasonableness* and therefore do not constitute appropriate action. In this sense, all appropriate actions are duties, but not all duties are appropriate actions.

Importantly, this Stoic concept of duty refers to an obligation to do what is *kathêkon*—what is appropriate—but not necessarily a *moral* obligation. To be subject to moral obligation, one must possess moral agency, which at a minimum requires the capacity for moral deliberation and moral action.[64] However, animals, plants, and infants, despite lacking moral agency, still perform appropriate actions, therefore they have natural duties. As Hierocles demonstrates, collectives can also have appropriate actions and, by extension, duties, even when they lack moral agency.

Today, sophisticated theories of collective moral agency have arisen to address questions of responsibility for collective actions such as pollution, wars, and genocides. According to one representative example, a collective must possess several things to be considered a candidate for moral agency: an identity that is more than the sum of the identities of its constitutive parts (and therefore one that does not rely on determinate membership); a decision-making structure; an identity over time; and a conception of itself as a unit.[65] I propose the first of these criteria alone suffices to say that a collective has appropriate actions, even if it lacks moral agency. For example, a city, possessing an identity greater than the sum of its constituents, has

---

64 After Erskine, *Can Institutions Have Responsibilities?*, 6.
65 Ibid., 24. Cf. Phillip Pettit's argument that a system constitutes an agent if it forms and adjusts its desires for how the environment should be, develops corresponding beliefs about how the environment actually is and then acts to align reality with its desires. Stephanie Collins suggests that for a collective to be considered an agent, it must have a decision-making process allowing it to reason, i.e., to maintain beliefs and desires as objects and, further, that the ability to produce coordinated action (she calls it multilateralism) confers duties to groups that no individual member of the group bears. See Pettit, "Responsibility Incorporated," 171–201; Collins, "Duties of Group Agents and Group Members," 38–57. All these thinkers are indebted to the work of Peter A. French in corporate moral agency.

appropriate actions, as does a school of fish, even if the latter lacks the deliberative faculties necessary for moral agency.

Using a conventional definition of duty, some argue assigning duties to a collective that is not a moral agent is an incoherent exercise because it fails to effectively allocate responsibility. For instance, calls for "the international community"—which is not a moral agent by the above criteria—to intervene on behalf of the Tutsi during the 1994 Rwandan Genocide could neither compel specific action nor establish a basis for holding anyone accountable.[66] However, in the Stoic view, it remains the case that an international community exists and is capable of performing collective actions that can be judged as appropriate or inappropriate, just like a school of fish. It would have been appropriate, even if infeasible given the existing state of international relations, for the international community to intervene and put an end to the Rwandan Genocide; its failure to do so reflects a deeper failure to realize human nature. In other words, the existence of collective actions—and therefore collective appropriate actions—is not contingent on the present state of effective mechanisms to compel them.

Now, according to the Hieroclean framework, if I am conceivable as a discrete social circle C, whose boundaries end at my own skin, then I have appropriate actions *as* C. These responsibilities concern not only me but also members of larger circles C+, C++, and so forth. Similarly, C+ has specific responsibilities toward me, toward C+ itself, and toward C++. There is no particular reason we must draw the boundaries of these larger circles exactly where Hierocles did, around tribes, city-states, and such. Indeed, today's social structures are more complex than anything Hierocles could have imagined.[67] Epictetus indicates, in defining our largest circle, we should "choose the place that is more sovereign," suggesting the lines can be drawn anywhere.[68] I propose anywhere we might act with collective *consequentiality*, that is, collective duty, can be recognized as a Hieroclean social circle.

Although existing literature on collective moral responsibility tends to emphasize the roles of states or business enterprises, military hierarchies also naturally provide a framework for collective identity. Suppose, for example, that I am a United States Marine in an Assault Amphibian Battalion, and that we call this battalion C+. As a member of C+, my actions directly influence not only my fellow Marines within the battalion and the Ground Combat Element but also extend far beyond,

---

66 Erskine, *Can Institutions Have Responsibilities?*, 35. Cf. Hannah Arendt's argument that collective responsibility can extend to all humanity, in Arendt, "Organized Guilt and Universal Responsibility," 146–56.
67 Pointing to shared natures common to living things, some ecologically conscious theorists have proposed an expanded conception of Hierocles' circles to include all life on earth. See Whiting et al., "Sustainable Development."
68 Epictetus, *Discourses* 1.9.1–3.

affecting the greater Marine Corps (C++), my entire country (C+++), and even the wider species of humanity (C++++). The consequences of my actions and decisions manifest through various channels: the success or failure of my assigned tasks; the effect I have on fellow Marines; the influence I exert on the moral and material trajectory of my country; and, of course, the outcomes experienced by enemy forces as a result of my actions.

Within C+, I am bound to follow the unit's rules and protocols, which are designed to comply with policies established by C+++, my country. These regulations are not arbitrary; they represent the collective will of the country, shaped through deliberative processes that aim to protect both national and global interests. The moral origin of these laws lies in the collective agency of C+++, where citizens, including myself to a minuscule degree, contribute to the creation of regulations that define the character of my service and my country.

My obligations toward distant members of C++++ are accessed through the layers of community to which I belong, from my immediate professional environment to broader national and global contexts. While my individual participation in C+++'s deliberative processes may have a minute effect on these distant communities, the collective actions of C+++ exhibit significant influence on outcomes for C++++. My obligations toward members of C++++ are therefore mediated through my roles within C+, C++, and C+++. As a member of C+, I must execute all lawful orders in service to the greater mission of C++, the Marine Corps. As a visible member of C++, I have an outsized influence on the collective character of my country, C+++, and I must exercise that influence with intentionality. Finally, as a citizen of C+++, I bear responsibility for participation in the deliberative processes that establish policy, which affects C+, C++, and C++++.

It is clear my degree of moral responsibility for, say, the actions of C+ or C+++, is to some extent a function of my relative influence within those organizations. For instance, I am more responsible for the actions of C+ if I am a high-ranking officer with significant influence than if I am a new recruit. Still, it seems I bear some degree of responsibility by virtue of my membership in the organization alone, regardless of my position. If I choose to quietly exist within the organization, to abstain from planning or training responsibilities, to decline promotions to more influential roles, or to remain silent when assigned questionable or ambiguous tasking, all of these are moral decisions even if they are of a negative type. Of course, competing duties will impact the accessibility and costs of such choices but, as I have established, there is always a choice.

The entanglement of choice and duty deepens when we introduce time to the calculus. C+ existed as a collective entity long before I was recruited and will exist long after my service ends. To the extent C+ is responsible for its actions, it is physically a "Ship of Theseus": it remains an entity even while all of its constituent parts are replaced.[69] This raises the question of how much responsibility, if any, I bear for actions C+ performed before I was recruited—or even before I was born. This question applies to activities both virtuous and vicious—if I'm going to take pride in my unit's past accomplishments, then I should be ashamed of its past shortcomings. What appropriate actions attend these impressions is another matter. We know "I" only exist as a moral agent in the present, but we also know this does not make it any less appropriate for me to repay a debt or to visit a doctor. This same logic presumably extends to C+++ and to whomever shares or inherits moral responsibility for C+++. It weighs heavily on decisions about what we owe to future generations, what sacrifices should be made for their well-being, and what comforts we might enjoy at their expense.

Obviously, these are all very worthy questions with far-reaching consequences. All of them have been asked before in one form or other and they have yielded volumes in analysis and debate. Many of them remain fiercely contested as their implications weigh upon the most heated issues within modern discourse. We cannot grapple with them here. For our purposes, it is sufficient to assume Stoics would agree in general terms with the Hieroclean concept of collective duty as discussed above. This idea is highly adaptable; for example, in the next chapter, I will consider its implications on personal identity within a combat unit and the impact this has on the concept of moral freedom.

What a Country Owes

If we suppose a Hieroclean circle is responsible for supporting the natural purposes of those circles within it, then it is only right to ask what that support entails. Specifically, if this circle represents an entire country, we will encounter difficult questions about the extent of this support, who has the authority to define and execute these obligations, and how those individuals are chosen. This inevitably leads to broader questions about the ideal structure and attributes of governance, steering us—if not forcing us—onto the field of Stoic political philosophy.

As we have said, there is ample room for disagreement between reasonable Stoics when it comes to matters of collective policy. For example, the most basic natural

---

69 The "Ship of Theseus" is a philosophical thought experiment first described by Plutarch around the 1st century BCE, in which the components of a ship are gradually replaced until none of the original parts remain, prompting the question of whether it is still the same ship. Thomas Hobbes later revisited this dilemma, suggesting if the original parts were gathered and reconstructed, we should then question which of the two assemblies is the true ship. A widely accepted resolution to this problem is the idea the material from which the ship is constructed is distinct from the ship itself, meaning the two entities—ship and material—exist simultaneously in the same space, implying the whole is something more than just the sum of its parts. See Plutarch, Life of Theseus 23.1; Hobbes, *Elements of Philosophy: The First Section, Concerning Body*, 100–101; Wasserman, "Material Constitution."

purpose of an individual, be they an infant or a senator, is to preserve their own constitution—their life. For their country to support this would imply an obligation to provide for safety and security. But how these are to be provided and what higher individual purposes might be compromised in their provision would be subject to differences in opinion, to say nothing of tradeoffs between what is due to an individual and what is due to a collective.

If the most basic natural purpose is the preservation of life, then the most advanced would be the fulfillment of humanity's rational nature. For the individual, this would mean the acquisition of moral knowledge, so, for the country, some obligation to educate the populace is implied. Although beliefs that virtue can be taught and states have a duty to teach it have been around since well before Zeno, these views become especially salient in light of the Stoic claim that humans are designed by nature to make moral progress.

A fair and equitable system of justice would also seem to be implied in the duties of a state. Furthermore, whatever its form, leadership should be motivated by the selfless performance of duty rather than greed or vainglory. This would be especially relevant to those in position to bend the powers of law to personal ends; as Cicero states, "the well-being of the people shall be the supreme law."[70] Furthermore, while "well-being" is a notoriously contentious concept, attention to the public good does seem to require a degree of material provision for the general welfare. For instance, Posidonius, as cited by Seneca, reflects upon wise and just rulers who:

> … restrained aggression, protected the weaker from the stronger, advised and dissuaded, and indicated what was advantageous and what was not. Their prudence saw to it that their people lacked for nothing, their courage averted dangers, and their generosity enabled their subjects to progress and flourish.[71]

Cicero, likewise, indicates an obligation toward some form of prudent resource distribution. Specifically, he juxtaposes a wasteful magistrate who squandered the treasury with extravagant dispensations of grain against a prudent administrator who provided modest yet appropriate distributions, thereby fostering "the well-being of both the citizens and the state." In apparent tension with this perspective, he goes on to argue the primary concern of government should be the preservation of private property, ensuring "that the individual keeps what is his."[72] In context, this supports into a broader narrative about liberty, which, for the Romans, was distinctly contrasted with slavery in the legal right to own property. Essentially, one could either own property or *be* property, with little in between. In any case, this vision is far removed from Zeno's utopian ideal of universal community property among sages.

---

70 Cicero, *On the Laws* 3.8. Cf. Cicero, *On Duties* 1.85.
71 Seneca, *Letters* 90.5–7 (Posidonius fragment 284, part) = LS 67Y.
72 Cicero, *On Duties* 2.72–3.

If we were to ask a modern legal scholar what a country owes its people, independent of this discussion, we would likely encounter answers resembling those outlined above. These might include references to natural rights—life, liberty, and the pursuit of happiness—and the notion that governments derive their legitimacy from serving the collective good. Pressed to name the origins of such ideas, a scholar would likely point to Enlightenment figures such as John Locke, Jean-Jacques Rousseau, or Baron de Montesquieu. However, such thinkers owe a tremendous intellectual debt to classical philosophers, even if the concept of "natural rights" are a decidedly post-Stoic idea. Among these classical influences, Cicero stands out as particularly impactful to later political philosophers.

For our purposes, Cicero's most relevant political contributions involve the idea a country, its government, and the people are different things. While Romans had long referred to their state as *res publica*, meaning the "property of the people," Cicero invests this phrase with new meaning, emphasizing its nature as an emergent whole, greater than the sum of its individual parts. Unlike a disorganized mob—or what he calls a "multitude"—a country is different in that *this* multitude "forms a society by virtue of agreement with respect to justice and sharing in advantage."[73] In other words, the country is a *qualified* multitude, whose progression to something greater is a function of justice and an achievement of its own doing. The "agreement" that facilitates this transformation is described in distinctively legalistic terms, providing substance and structure to the "property metaphor."[74]

As to the proper administration of this entity, Cicero promotes a "mixed" government where powers are divided between a lawmaking Senate and executive "magistrates" who implement and enforce the law. Presaging Epictetus, Cicero emphasizes the special obligations attendant to these specific roles.[75] When one performs in a public role, some degree of personal liberty is sacrificed for the collective interest. Incidentally, Cicero's early writing suggests military forces, such as soldiers, sailors, and a fleet, are understood as an instrument or resource of the country, like fields or harbors.[76] These, too, would have a specific role to play in the collective interest.

Whereas the country itself is like an article of property, its government is understood as something more like a legal guardian appointed to manage the affairs of a minor.[77] While a minor—the people—may be legally free and entitled to own property, they would still lack the ability to govern their own affairs effectively. The people, then, should voluntarily accept certain constraints on their behavior

---

73 Cicero, *On the Republic* 1.39.
74 The term "property metaphor" is attributed to Malcolm Schofield. See Schofield, *Saving the City*, 164.
75 Wood, *Cicero's Social and Political Thought*, 135.
76 Cicero, *On Invention* II, 168–69.
77 Klink, "Legal Analogies," 9–11.

to ensure their long-term well-being, much like a minor can flourish under the tutelage of a wise guardian.

In this arrangement, the Senate and magistrates should receive prestige and executive power respectively. The people, for their part, would receive precious liberty.[78] These benefits follow from the precise and balanced arrangement of powers. In Cicero's thought, then, we find a framework for the transition of an unthinking collection of humans into a deliberating moral agent. Furthermore, if we can agree moral progress occurs for collectives like it does for individuals, then the emergence of collective moral agency would be analogous to an individual human's transition from a pre-rational phase to an age of reason. As such, it would mark the most important juncture in the collective agent's moral development. "When virtue governs the Commonwealth," reflects Cicero's interlocutor, "what can be more glorious?"[79]

However, collective moral regression is always possible. Any disruption to the critical geometry of powers might collapse the reaction, leading to the disintegration of prestige, power, and liberty. One way for this to happen is through the rise of mob rule, as when an unreasoning people reject the guardianship of representative government entirely. In such a scenario, the populace would no longer resemble a minor under guardianship but rather an insane person—a *furiosus*—legally deemed incapable of managing their own affairs and thus stripped of control.[80] This analogy builds upon Cicero's theory of natural law, which holds that one cannot be rightly considered the proprietor of something they lack the knowledge or ability to manage.[81] The key point is that in Cicero's view, placing the powers of government directly into the hands of the people would, counterintuitively, result in the loss of their liberty.

The other path to liberty's annihilation is more direct: the consolidation of governing power into the hands of a single individual, eliminating the checks and balances of divided government. In this scenario, the people would no longer resemble a *furiosus* but rather a slave—stripped of the right to manage their affairs, not due to madness, but by the arbitrary force of law. Without the ability to own property, the very foundation of the *res publica*—the property of the people—would disintegrate.[82] The country, in any meaningful sense, would cease to exist.

---

78 Cicero, *On the Republic* 2.33. Regrettably, the "people," in Cicero's construct, referred to propertied heads of households, excluding women, minors, foreigners, and slaves. See Wood, *Cicero's Social and Political Thought*, 127.
79 Cicero, *On the Republic* 1.34.
80 Klink, "Legal Analogies," 13–6. Cf. *On the Republic* 3.33, where Cicero expresses through the Stoic Laelius that nothing deserves to be called a country less than an unruly mob.
81 Cicero, *On the Republic* 1.27.
82 Klink, "Legal Analogies," 7–8. Cf. Plutarch, On Listening to Poetry 33D (SVF 1.219) = LS 67O. Despite their differences, a unifying point of agreement from early to late Stoa is that an individual is free if one so chooses, even their body is enslaved by a tyrant. We do not have evidence, however, of Stoic contemplation of *prohairesis*, or moral choice, at a collective level.

Cicero, having served as a consul of Rome and experienced the rise of Julius Caesar, remained unwavering in his dedication to the Roman Republic and its divided powers of governance. He resisted Rome's slide into authoritarianism, a stance that would ultimately lead to his death. In stark contrast stands Seneca, who, as tutor to the mad emperor Nero, sought to rationalize monarchy. Then, of course, there is Marcus Aurelius, who ruled as an emperor himself. Especially considering the anarchism of the early Stoics, it seems the features of ideal governance were among the most varied of opinions within ancient Stoicism. The views of the middle Stoics, insofar as they can be reconstructed, are best represented today within the classical Republicanism promoted by Cicero.

When compared to Cicero's views, Seneca's political philosophy offers an intriguing alternative. Particularly notable is his work *On Mercy*, a fragmentary letter addressed to Nero. In this often overlooked text, Seneca appears to draw on Stoic principles to argue that living under a monarchy—previously equated with slavery—should instead be understood as liberty, provided the monarch is virtuous. He further insinuates Rome's true oppressors had been the regime toppled by Nero's predecessors. Specifically, the Roman life had been a form of servitude under a dominant faction, but liberty was restored by the benevolent monarch Augustus.[83]

At first glance, *On Mercy* appears to be a sincere effort by Seneca to guide the young Nero toward virtuous leadership. However, one of its most striking features is the excessive and recurring flattery bestowed upon the self-absorbed emperor.[84] The letter opens with Seneca's imagined account of Nero's own presumably justified reflections:

> Have I, of all mortals, found favor with the gods and been chosen to act on earth in their stead? I am the judge with the power of life and death over nations, and the fate and condition of everyone rests in my hands. My verdict is what gives people and cities cause to rejoice. No region anywhere flourishes but by my will and favor. These swords in their countless thousands, sheathed through the peace that I bring, will be drawn at my nod. The extermination or relocation of nations, the granting or loss of their liberty, the enslavement of kings or their coronation, the destruction or rise of cities—all this falls under my jurisdiction.[85]

The passage doubles as a chilling commentary on unchecked executive power. We can imagine an excited Nero clutching Seneca's letter, rapt with attention upon contact with the introduction. *Yes, tell me more.* Seneca's flattery sets the stage for an effort to lead Nero to virtue through Stoic philosophy. His chosen path to the heart of a narcissist is a mirror. "No one seeks an example for you to imitate," Seneca reassures the teenaged emperor, "except for yourself."[86]

---

83 Stacey, "Princely Republic," 135.
84 Martina Russo, "Seneca's Flattery of Nero": *De clementia,* Flattery in Seneca the Younger: *Theory & Practice* (Oxford Academic, 2024), 134–69.
85 Seneca, *On Clemency* 1.1.3–4, trans. Braund.
86 Ibid. 1.1.6.

Understood only as a letter to Nero, *On Mercy* appears to be little more than Seneca's attempt to make the best of a bad situation, using any method of persuasion that might gain traction to transform his pupil into a benevolent monarch—an end that would seem to justify even the most degrading means. However, scholars discern something entirely different in Seneca's letter, which, like other epistolary writings of the time, was apparently crafted with a broader audience in mind. Specifically, Seneca is engaging in political philosophy, seemingly with the intent to encourage wider acceptance of monarchy as an ideal form of government. Under the steady hand of a virtuous leader, Seneca argues, the populace will want for nothing except "the license to ruin itself."[87]

This claim places Seneca in direct opposition to the political views of Cicero and, as far as we can infer, to those of the middle Stoics as well. Seneca, rejecting the polite fictions of his day, ultimately dispenses with pretenses the monarch is beholden to the same system of justice as ordinary citizens. Especially relevant to our project, he endeavors to discredit notions that, in the absence of a dominant executive, the populace might be regarded as a cohesive entity capable of rational agency.[88] *On Mercy* has even been described as marking the "final collapse" of the Roman republican concept of liberty.[89]

Notably, many self-identified Roman Stoics continued to resist the consolidation of executive power during Seneca's time. This so-called Stoic Opposition included figures such as Thrasea Paetus and Helvidius Priscus, statesmen who were put to death under the emperors Nero and Vespasian respectively, and of whom Epictetus and Marcus Aurelius later spoke admiringly.[90] We do not have records of these figures' philosophical thinking, but it is not as simple as saying Seneca fully represents the Stoic political philosophy of his time. Whether his or Cicero's politics are more or less authentically "Stoic" must rest upon interpretive factors.

On one hand, Seneca might seem to veer from Stoic principles by playing to the power dynamics of a despotic regime. There is certainly something out of alignment in his obsequiousness—verging on sycophancy—toward the emperor. On the other hand, his focus on the personal virtue and ethical responsibilities of those actually in power could be understood as a pragmatic application of Stoic acceptance to the political realities of his time. Marcus, for his part, seems to perceive his emperorship as an assigned role he is obligated to play well, with a focus on avoiding abuses of power rather than any particular ambitions to alter the inherited power dynamic.[91]

---

87 Ibid. 1.1.8.
88 Stacey, "Princely Republic," 150.
89 C. Wirszubski, *Libertas as a Political Idea at Rome during the Late Republic and Early Principáte* (Cambridge University Press, 1950), 151.
90 See Epictetus, *Discourses* 1.1.26; Marcus Aurelius, *Meditations* 1.14.
91 See Marcus Aurelius, *Meditations* 1.14n26, 9.29.

Even if Seneca genuinely believes monarchy is the ideal form of government, it is notable he felt it necessary to present this belief wrapped in layers of obeisance that strain credibility. The claim is inherently compromised; when a message is delivered in a suspicious vessel, there might be something wrong with the message. As to Cicero, though he is no stranger to the arts of persuasion and politics, there can be little doubt about his patriotic fervor or sincerity of commitment to the Roman Republic.

The purpose of this venture into political philosophy is ultimately about contemplating a Stoic theory of collective moral agency. To that end, Cicero's ideas are more helpful than Seneca's, but only incidentally so. It would be convenient if we knew precisely where to draw the line between Cicero's independent thoughts and those of his Stoic influencers, but it is almost just as well we don't. We are fully capable of drawing independent conclusions based on Stoic moral precepts and, with so much on the line, it is best we do our own thinking.

Furthermore, while certain concepts may rightly be identified as Stoic ideas, that does not automatically make them good ideas. This is something we should always bear in mind, but it is especially important when it comes to matters as consequential as political philosophy. For example, should frustrations with the inefficiencies of divided powers and representative government ever tempt us to dabble in alternatives, Seneca's letter serves as a sobering reality check. To observe one of history's most celebrated moral thinkers lavishing flattery on the likes of Nero tells us everything we need to know about the implications of absolute power.

A Stoic Patriotism

The overarching purpose of this chapter has been to describe a moral relationship between a Stoic and their country. Additionally, it has sought to defend patriotism as a qualified Stoic virtue, opposing out-of-context readings that, contrary to historical evidence, would suggest Stoics are properly antipatriotic or indifferent to national affiliation. On the contrary, I have suggested that Stoics, far from rejecting patriotism, understand a properly regulated version of it as an expression of humanity's rational nature. It is, as Cicero put it, where "nature has given to mankind such a compulsion to do good, and such a desire to defend the well-being of the community," that these fundamental expressions of nature are inseparable.[92]

To support this discussion, I have introduced the lesser known late Stoic Hierocles, who provides valuable insights into the theory of *oikeiōsis* and Stoics' social worldview in general. Integrating his theories, I have come to several key conclusions about Stoics. First, they possess a profound sense of social morality, which necessarily involves partiality toward specific people and groups. While Stoics understand moral

---

92 Cicero, *On the Republic* 1.1.

progress to include an expanding moral horizon, this does not imply everyone within that horizon should be treated equally or without distinction. Furthermore, extreme cosmopolitanism, where empathy is distributed equally among all individuals (i.e., a flat empathy gradient), would be unjust and is not the ideal outcome of *oikeiōsis* or Stoic moral progress. Second, Stoicism involves a balance, or moderation, between communitarian and cosmopolitan principles, rather than the exclusive emphasis of one over the other. Finally, Hierocles' near-approach to a theory of collective agency implies a Stoic framework for understanding moral obligation both between a citizen and their country and between countries themselves.

We can now directly confront the question of patriotism. We should start by clarifying what it is. Even without venturing into the cliched differentiation of patriotism from nationalism, we find patriotism itself can be understood in various senses—as an emotional love for one's country, a desire for what is best for one's country, a sense of belonging to one's country, a sense of duty toward one's country, or a belief in the inherent superiority of one's country. Each of these interpretations represents a distinct moral position and interacts with Stoic ethics in a different way. Therefore, to fully explore how patriotism might be perceived by the Stoics, and particularly to consider whether it can be regarded as a proper Stoic virtue, let us review what we know of Stoicism in light of each of these interpretations:

Patriotism as love for my country. Like the love of one's parents or children, under normal circumstances, Stoics would consider a love of country as *eupatheia* or "rational emotion." The validity or rationality inherent in the emotion would depend on the truth of whatever underlying impression produced it. It would be wrong, for example, to say my country is *good* or that its welfare is a *good thing*. These are preferred indifferents in the Stoic view. A Stoic would say it is rational to feel joy in the presence of my beloved country, just as it is rational to feel joy in the presence of a beloved friend. But it would be inappropriate to get *carried away* by emotion so as to lose control of my actions or to desire inappropriate things.

Patriotism as a wish for my country's welfare. As the correct selection among indifferents, it would be virtuous under normal circumstances to prefer my country's welfare. Likewise, apathy or antipathy toward my country, as appears in the so-called anti-patriotism of some extreme cosmopolitans, would be vicious. As we discussed in Chapter 2, virtue is largely realized through the correct recognition and selection of what is preferred or dispreferred. Under normal circumstances, the welfare of one's country is objectively in the preferred category; for example, Seneca categorizes it with joy, peace, victory, and well-behaved children.[93]

Whatever moral reasoning I would apply to the welfare of my family, I should also apply to the welfare of my country. I would not wish for my child to unjustly thrive at the expense of others; as we have said, I would be wrong to bribe school

---

93 Seneca, *Letters* 66.5, 36–7.

administrators to advance them over others more deserving. Likewise, I would not wish for my country to thrive unjustly—a wish for welfare is fundamentally a wish for *moral* welfare. As a member of the community circle that is my country, then, I should support the fulfillment of its natural purposes, which entails both moral progress and the preservation of its (physical *and* moral) constitution.

Patriotism as a sense of belonging to my country. Contrary to the antipatriotic reading of Epictetus' "citizen of the universe" statement, I think Stoics would agree that to identify with my country is a step in the right direction on a path of moral progress. Epictetus might say it is an early step. Like being a member of my own family, I would be correct to claim membership within every community to which I belong. I would be wrong, however, to claim nothing greater than that. I would be most correct to identify as a member of 'that which is most sovereign', which is the rational universe.

Patriotism as a sense of duty or obligation toward my country. As an application of communitarian principles, Stoics would agree specific obligations follow from belonging to the community that is my country—just as they do from family.[94] As a function of my own natural purposes, I am required to support the fulfillment of my country's natural purposes. It does not necessarily follow that I am obligated to take up any particular role within this community aside from citizen, which, as we have suggested, entails plenty of its own obligations. More specific roles, such as parent, teacher, or warrior will be assigned through some combination of choice, uncontrollable circumstances, and my own natural abilities.

Patriotism as a belief in my country's inherent superiority. It is reasonable to believe my country is better than others at some specific things. I might justifiably believe it has the best national parks, or that it produces the best Olympic swimmers or the best pickup trucks, but such factors are plainly irrelevant to the question of what makes one country 'better' than another. Reaching for something determinative, I might claim its economic system, its form of government, or its intrinsic cultural values are better aligned to the achievement of humanity's natural purposes than those of its fellow countries. I might even be able to substantiate and defend these claims.

None of these arguments would convince a Stoic philosopher. And although it might seem appropriate to clarify 'better at what?' in a 'whose country is better' contest, this is not the question a Stoic would ask. A Stoic would inquire, in binary formulation, whether the countries in question are virtuous or vicious. Recall from

---

94 For equivalence of familial and patriotic belonging, consider DL 7.108: "Actions belonging to duty are those that reason prescribes our doing, as is the case with honoring one's parents, brothers, country, and spending time with one's friends." Cicero, in contrast, subordinates the family to the country: "... none of these affinities has more weight and induces more affection than the allegiance which we each have to the state. Our parents are dear to us, and so are our children and relatives and friends, but our native land alone subsumes all the affections which we entertain." Cicero, *On Duties* 1.57.

Chapter 2 that Stoics are moral perfectionists, believing any individuals falling short of moral perfection are equally imperfect. If we apply the same standard to countries, then we would have to conclude that all imperfect countries (that is, all countries) are equally deficient in virtue; that which is not 'straight' is properly 'crooked'. While I might acknowledge my country has made more moral progress than others, these claims remain irrelevant to the country's status as virtuous or vicious.

As I previously acknowledged, the Stoics' moral perfectionism is a minor paradox that seems to run against basic intuitions and a functional concept of progress. However, there are some practical takeaways from the perfectionist perspective that are relevant to any competitive evaluation. First, all countries are works in progress; none is entitled to win any contest. As with any prolonged endeavor, be it of a solitary or collective nature, a constant-improvement effort is required just to maintain steady performance. As it is put in the old saw of coaches and drill sergeants, if we're not getting better, then we're getting worse. Furthermore, it is the business of the weak and insecure to measure oneself against an obviously deficient neighbor. Those who are truly interested in virtue recognize all parties are flawed and success is earned through efforts that are sincere, consistent, and relentless.

With all of this in mind, is patriotism a Stoic value or not? I suggest that a sophisticated kind of patriotism is. Like conformity, courage, generosity, or any other discrete virtue requiring moderation, there are right and wrong ways to be patriotic. As a citizen, I should want what is best for my country, as long as that is just. I will recognize certain obligations toward my countrymen that I do not extend to others, just as my country, as a collective moral agent, will have special obligations toward its specific citizens. I will perceive my country's welfare, realized appropriately, as consistent with the welfare of all people. As a function of my individual moral duties, I will do my part to advance my country toward that ideal.

A Perfect Society

At the beginning of this chapter, we discussed the hypothetical Republic of Zeno, which, according to our painfully limited sources, describes a society in which everyone is perfectly wise. Seneca suggests real communities can and do exhibit virtuous behaviors: "Sometimes virtue is widespread, governing kingdoms, cities, and provinces, creating laws, developing friendships, and regulating the duties that hold good between relatives and children."[95] Collective actions thus demonstrate a community scale sense of social morality—exercising prudent generosity toward fellow communities as well as their own members, refraining from exploitation or aggression, and so on. I submit that Zeno's Republic, speculative as it is, describes one man's conception of community scale sagacity.

---

95 Seneca, *Letters* 74.28. Cf. Epictetus, *Discourses* 4.1.30–1.

As a counter offer to Zeno's community of sages, I think a real community, were it to be "governed by virtue" as Seneca says, would need to deal with the unwise rather than presume to eject or exclude them. Indeed, the just treatment of the unwise is among the most basic functions of a civil society. As Epictetus suggests, the unwise are among us and should be dealt with in terms they can understand—or perhaps more pertinently, they are us. To acknowledge this, however, is to acknowledge perfection is unattainable and, as we have said, this is beside the point of sagacity as a theoretical concept. The sage exists to describe perfection.

What, then, would a sage society really look like? If we dare indulge in some conjecture of our own, we may not arrive at a vision exactly like Zeno's, but we still might draw some important conclusions. I propose, for example, that a society of perfect sages would still require some social institutions to organize collective efforts. This is because sages, even if perfectly wise, would not be omniscient nor would they possess telepathic abilities. Individuals would still be exposed to different information at different rates and times, and opinions would form in the breaches. As a result, while decisions would be made quickly and dispassionately, deliberative processes and some form of adjudication would still be necessary.

Still, a society of sages would be completely alien to conventional sensibilities. Education, for example, would be prioritized for its own sake with little concern for competitive outcomes. Occupational roles would naturally optimize to individual abilities, with no need for external incentives or measures of exclusion. Prestige or pay would contribute no motivational influence. Physical fitness would be universal, but only as a means to maintain health, without any concern for vanity or competition. Everyday problems like obesity and self-inflicted disease would not exist, as everyone would happily subsist on healthy and constructive habits. Competitive customs, such as sports, would disappear, as there would be no desire to win or to experience excitement as a spectator.

Sex would be sanitized of passion and animal urges, serving only for reproduction. Art and music would vanish, as they would be understood as mere arrangements of shape, color, or frequency with no intrinsic value. Tradeoffs between liberty and equality would become meaningless, as no one would desire more than what they had. Exploitation, addiction, poverty, and crime would also cease to exist, as individuals would naturally act in the interest of the community. Borders would become unnecessary. Warriors would become unnecessary.

We could go on. The point, as I see it, is clear enough, with two key takeaways on offer. First, for all the good things we might say about such a society, most of us would not want to live in that world. Our various idiosyncrasies, defects, irrationalities, and the elaborate structures we create to deal with them are not just incidental—they are a vital part of what it means to be human. They are at least as important to who and what we are as the faculty of reason; if we were offered a magical button that could make such unreasonable features of our species disappear, we would not press it.

The second takeaway is that we assuredly do not live in that world. Ours is a world of passion, imperfection, improvisation, complexity, and chaos. It is a world where clashing visions, clashing interests, and clashing wills produce moments of the most sublime beauty and the most profound ugliness, sometimes in the same instant, and sometimes in the same soul. It is not the clinical world of theory, but the filthy world of practice. It is in that context, then, that we contemplate the role of the warrior—the ultimate moral practitioner. For that, we will need a new chapter.

CHAPTER 6

Warrior

> There are four species of the beautiful, namely the just, the courageous, the orderly, and the knowledgeable; for it is under these forms that beautiful actions are achieved.
>
> DIOGENES LAERTIUS, 7.100.

Rising starkly from the heart of Rome's Piazza Colonna, the Column of Marcus Aurelius towers over the surrounding forums. Commissioned by his son Commodus, the column was completed 13 years after Marcus' death, serving as a funerary monument and a celebration of his victories in the Marcomannic Wars (166–180 CE). With meticulous detail, its spiral reliefs wrap around the column to depict grueling campaigns along the Danube frontier. The subjects' heads are slightly exaggerated to emphasize facial expressions: disciplined Roman legions in relentless pursuit of their terrified enemies; the emperor himself a calm, commanding presence, overseeing an efficient military operation. At nearly 100 feet tall, it is an impressive landmark today, but in 193 CE it would have been one of the tallest and most imposing structures in Rome.

Considering his aversions to both grandiosity and bloodshed, there is little doubt Marcus would have despised it. At best, it is an unflinching acknowledgment of the awful price of imperial order. Less charitably, it is a "pornography of political violence": villages set ablaze, corpses arranged in piles, captives beheaded by collaborating tribesmen under the supervision of Roman victors.[1] Noncombatants are not spared from suffering; children are herded like cattle while women are stabbed or dragged by the hair toward unseen fates.[2] Perhaps the bleakest detail is that none of this indicates a breakdown in discipline; on the contrary, the Roman soldiers appear to be in complete control. This is simply war: brutal, filthy, methodical, and inevitable. Here, the cost of empire is laid bare in all its grim detail (Figure 7).

It is hard to imagine anything else quite so profoundly ugly as the scenes depicted on the triumphal column. Their vulgarity shatters the fascistic notion that war itself

---

1 Birley, *Marcus Aurelius*, 192; Ferris, *Hate and War*, 110.
2 Ferris, *Enemies of Rome*, 88–98.

ennobles a country or the people who wage it.[3] But for all of its depredations, war and its preparations can be occasions of sublime virtue and, to Stoics, that is synonymous with beauty. Accordingly, war's community of practice—the military—is at its highest functioning when it finds and cultivates individuals who are just, courageous, orderly, and knowledgeable. "Wherever it's possible to live," says Marcus, "it's possible to live well."[4] But the profession of arms does not develop virtuous qualities so that they may be deployed in service of the general collective good. It develops them for specific and pragmatic purposes of combat efficiency.[5]

Figure 7. Engravings on the Column of Marcus Aurelius. (Gary Lee Todd/Wikimedia Commons)

The profession of arms, then, would seem to be conflicted at a fundamental level, marrying the most exquisite skills and traits of character to the most terrible ends. Considering this inherent tension, which some might call incoherence, it is far from

---

3 Benito Mussolini famously said that "war alone brings all human energies to their highest tension and sets a seal of nobility on the peoples who have the virtue to face it." Of this claim General Sir John Winthrop Hackett counters, "This is rubbish." Specifically, he endorses Immanuel Kant's view that warfare likely corrupts more people than it kills; however, Hackett qualifies this thought to suggest that, perhaps ironically, *preparations* for war do tend to make those so enculturated more virtuous. See Hackett, "Society and the Soldier," 82–83; Toynbee, *A Study of History*, 4: 644; Kant, *Zum Ewigen Frieden*, 57. Cf. Shay, *Achilles in Vietnam*, Introduction.
4 Marcus Aurelius, *Meditations* 5.16. Cf. Epictetus, *Handbook* 24.4–5.
5 See Hackett, "Society and the Soldier," 82.

a given that Stoicism is conducive or even compatible with such a profession. On the contrary, there are many reasons one might argue military service is fundamentally antithetical to Stoic principles.

Such arguments generally align to one of three broadly overlapping themes. The first is an appeal to *anti-patriotism*: the idea that Stoics would reject patriotic loyalty or allegiance to a particular nation-state, citing a higher allegiance to universal reason and humanity as a whole. I spent much of the previous chapter investigating this claim. The second is an appeal to *nonviolence*, pointing again to Stoic cosmopolitanism to suggest it is never justifiable to harm or kill one's fellow humans on account of a shared rational nature. The third is an appeal to *individualism*, claiming Stoics would never consent to following orders, particularly orders of great moral consequence, as doing so would forfeit their individual freedom and reduce them to mere instruments of another's will. This chapter will address these two latter claims.

These arguments are intuitive, supported by evidence, and deserving of serious consideration. To address them properly, I will first survey the extant Stoic perspectives on war and warriors, with particular emphasis on Marcus Aurelius, who provides the most remarkable evidence of a true Stoic at war. I consider whether his actions, and acts of war more broadly, are consistent with his purported beliefs or if they were mere acts of hypocrisy. After briefly introducing the key tenets of established just-war thinking, I examine the rationality of state-sanctioned violence in light of Stoic moral concepts. My analysis leans on the concept of competing and overriding responsibilities to suggest warfare is sometimes appropriate within a Stoic moral system just as it is in many others.

I then pivot to the issue of moral freedom and appropriate collective action, building on the theory of collective duty outlined in the previous chapter. This exploration centers on the distinctive role of the warrior in society, highlighting the extraordinary extent to which a warrior's duties and their moral consequences are intertwined with the collective action of a nation. This analysis leads to wider discussions of moral autonomy and collective action, considering how these can coexist within the fragmented responsibilities of modern, technologically advanced warriors. I specifically consider how Stoics might evaluate the practical challenges of constrained information, task specialization, and hierarchical organization in modern warfare.

Balancing these challenges against the primacy of moral freedom, I turn to the question of obedience, specifically examining when it is appropriate for a morally autonomous warrior to disobey orders, independent of the prevailing moral framework. From there, I pivot to the topic of guilt and remorse—sometimes described as moral injuries—exploring how Stoicism might mitigate these hardships and where it might fall short. Finally, to conclude this project, I synthesize insights from this and previous chapters to construct an image of the ideal Stoic warrior: one who harmonizes personal virtue, moral responsibility, and collective duty while navigating the ethical complexities of war.

According to the Evidence

Stoic attitudes toward war range from ambivalence to disgust. On the one hand, the destruction wrought by war is plainly recognized as a dispreferred indifferent—something to be avoided but not inherently evil in itself. Seneca remarks, "Of course I prefer that war should not occur; but if war does occur, I shall desire that I may nobly endure the wounds, the starvation, and all that the exigency of war brings."[6] On the other hand, and despite its apparent inevitability, war is no force of nature. As Epictetus suggests, it is always the result of human failures to correctly interpret impressions.[7] Regardless of who starts it, human irrationality and stupidity are invariably at root, and these are contrary to nature.

True to form, Marcus is unimpressed by the famous warriors who preceded him, remarking not upon what they "accomplished" but the utter futility of the violence: "Alexander, Pompey, and Julius Caesar wiped out entire cities by the dozen, and slaughtered hundreds of thousands of horsemen and foot soldiers in battle, and one day they too passed away."[8] Epictetus' mentor Musonius Rufus lectures soldiers on "the blessings of peace and the dangers of war," much to their irritation.[9] More forcefully, Seneca condemns the "much-vaunted crime of slaughtering whole peoples."[10] With biting irony, he notes such acts, when carried out under the banner of the state, are not only sanctioned but celebrated, while individual murderers are put to death—a practice he finds abhorrent and deeply hypocritical.[11] Violence, in general, is a perversion of human nature.

But despite their shared distaste for war and violence, the Stoics make extensive use of military metaphors and the imagery of battle. Musonius lauds the warrior race of Amazons to argue that women can be capable philosophers, just as they are capable warriors.[12] Epictetus likens the process of mental assent to a sentry who turns away irrational impressions.[13] Seneca, Epictetus, and Marcus all compare the vicissitudes of fate to the orders given to soldiers and sailors—commands that must be carried out without complaint.[14] They all elevate the warrior archetype, particularly the Spartans (or *Lacedaemonians*), as exemplars of resilience and acceptance, idealizing their discipline and ability to endure hardship.[15]

---

6 Seneca, *Letters* 67.3; cf. Epictetus, *Discourses* 1.28.14–6.
7 Epictetus, *Discourses* 1.28.12–3, 2.22.22.
8 Marcus Aurelius, *Meditations* 3.3.
9 Tacitus, Histories, III.81.
10 Seneca, *Letters* 95.30.
11 Ibid. 7.4.
12 Lutz, *Disdain Hardships*, 16.
13 Epictetus, *Discourses* 3.12.15.
14 E.g., Seneca, *Letters* 120.12; Epictetus, *Discourses* 3.24.31–5; Marcus Aurelius, *Meditations* 8.25.
15 E.g., Marcus Aurelius, *Meditations* 11.24; Epictetus, *Discourses* 1.2.2, 2.20.26; Seneca, *On Benefits* 6.31; Musonius Rufus, *Discourses* 20.

Seneca specifically employs the Spartans to highlight a distinction between useful philosophy and mere academic prattle. He points to martial valor as an example of virtue inherent in human nature, which philosophy is meant to reveal rather than to suppress or confuse:

> I point out to you the Lacedaemonians in position at the very pass of Thermopylae! They have no hope of victory, no hope of returning. The place where they stand is to be their tomb. In what language do you encourage them to bar the way with their bodies and take upon themselves the ruin of their whole tribe, and to retreat from life rather than from their post? … You see, then, how straightforward and peremptory virtue is; but what man on earth can your deceptive logic make more courageous or more upright? Rather does it break the spirit, which should never be less straitened or forced to deal with petty and thorny problems than when some great work is being planned. It is not [only] the Three Hundred, it is all mankind that should be relieved of the fear of death.[16]

Intriguingly, Epictetus, who probably never met Seneca, also invokes the Spartan stand at Thermopylae to make precisely the same point. He contrasts them with the Athenians, who twice abandoned their city rather than defend it from invaders, which he suggests is illustrative of the emasculating philosophies he opposes.[17] These comparisons are particularly curious considering the Spartans were not Stoics—the battle at Thermopylae took place approximately 180 years before Stoicism was founded. Yet, if the quality of a philosophy can be judged by the qualities it inspires, then a sound philosophy should produce individuals like the Spartans, embodying courage, discipline, and resilience, whereas an unsound philosophy would foster equivocation and infirmity. This powerfully reinforces the point that martial virtues, so to speak, are not distinct from moral virtues—they are simply virtues.

As discerned from their words, then, the Stoics seem to admire warriors but despise war. What little we know about their lives generally supports this impression. While there is no record of military service for Seneca, Epictetus, Hierocles, or Musonius, other figures provide more illustrative examples. Epictetus' student Arrian, who recorded the *Discourses* and compiled the *Enchiridion*, became a Roman military commander. The Stoics' revered philosophical forebear, Socrates, was a heroic veteran who served with distinction in the Peloponnesian War.[18] The much-admired Roman statesman Cato, himself a Stoic, also had extensive military experience. Although not traditionally remembered as a philosopher, Cato's example reflects the Roman nobility of his time, many of whom were Stoics and for whom pacifism or anti-patriotism were far from normative values.

Yet no historical example better illustrates this relationship than Marcus Aurelius himself. Uniquely positioned in history, he bore both the authority and the responsibility to make agonizing decisions of immense consequence. To the extent he was

---

16 Seneca, *Letters* 82.20–3.
17 Epictetus, *Discourses* 2.20.26.
18 Epictetus specifically lauds Socrates' courage in battle, e.g., Ibid. 4.1.

a philosopher-king, he was also a warrior-king, with actions and character not only described in third-party accounts but also, remarkably, preserved in his most intimate personal writings. This rare combination of external and internal perspectives offers an incomparable view into the mind of the most powerful man in the world as he struggles to govern a fraying empire while adhering to philosophical principles.

As with all powerful figures who are admired for their moral convictions, Marcus has no shortage of critics eager to expose any perceived hypocrisy. Lacking the sensual or temperamental vices of comparable figures, critics hold him to account for behaving precisely as an emperor was expected to behave. For example, despite the Stoics' emphasis on justice as preeminent, Marcus did not move to abolish slavery, eliminate economic disparities, or align Roman society more closely with egalitarian gender ideals.[19] However, within the context and economic framework of imperial Rome, such undertakings would have been futile at best and extravagant at worst. The Roman Stoics, products of a society defined by well-established and revered institutions, were not predisposed to contemplate radical social reform or economic upheaval in the way we might today.

This is not to suggest Stoics are inherently resigned to the social status quo—they are not—but rather that they recognize the imprudence of tilting at windmills, accepting that the feasibility of reform depends on the circumstances and opportunities for change in a given time and place. Marcus steels himself for frustration when he writes, "Don't expect to create Plato's ideal state, but be satisfied if you make even the slightest progress, and regard that in itself as no small achievement."[20] Lasting change, he recognizes, is impossible unless the people comprehend it and actively participate in the transformative process—something that cannot be achieved by fiat.[21] Moreover, even when ostentatious action succeeds, it risks fostering "pompous affectation" and self-righteousness in the actor. Regarding political progress, Marcus reminds himself, "The work of philosophy requires simplicity and modesty."[22]

In the Stoic view, the most effective way to exert influence usually lies in the conscientious fulfillment of one's responsibilities as reason would recommend. For Marcus, this meant attending to the often banal but essential duties of governance: adjudicating disputes, writing letters, and persuading the Senate to cooperate with his agenda. His chief policy interests were not some grandiose national project but rather the mundane issues of just governance: appointing proper guardians for orphans and minors, selecting competent local governors for distant provinces, and ensuring the previously enslaved could maintain their freedom.[23] Relentlessly dedicated to

---

19 See Aikin and McGill-Rutherford, "Stoicism, Feminism and Autonomy."
20 Marcus Aurelius, *Meditations* 9.29.
21 See Annas, "My Station and its Duties," 117–18.
22 Marcus Aurelius, *Meditations* 9.29.
23 Birley, *Marcus Aurelius: A Biography*, 154–58.

his duties, Marcus avoided the indulgences and leisure activities customary of elites, instead working late into the night with a degree of commitment some considered excessive.

Of key relevance to this project, of course, is Marcus' foreign policy. It is not as simple as determining whether or not he governed in accordance with cosmopolitan principles. As I discussed in the previous chapter, *Cosmopolitanism* can lead to perverse moral outcomes when it is taken to extremes or treated as an end in itself. For example, the ultimate cosmopolitan dream is a post-national world free of borders and the armed forces that fight over them. But the most realistic path to such a world is *hegemonic globalism*, wherein a dominant world power would subsume all others within its jurisdiction, establishing a powerful and unified world government.[24] With such a system in place, cosmopolitan ambitions such as universal education and an equal distribution of resources might then be extended to all the world's people. Over time, the world's unified military forces would transition into a policing role, gradually dismantling their most destructive capabilities and consuming an ever-decreasing share of global productivity. It is an outcome seemingly transcendent of its origins in conquest, illustrating why utopian ideologies become hazardous when wielded by those in power. The pursuit of an unconstrained greater good can justify nearly any act.

As sovereign of the largest empire on earth and a major force for economic, intellectual, and cultural development, it would not have been out of the ordinary for Marcus to subscribe to the hegemonic globalist worldview. He might even intuit a specific role among nations for Rome as a catalyst of species-wide moral progress. Notably, commentators who preceded him drew parallels between Zeno's theoretical Republic—a vision of a unified and cosmopolitan society—and what might have been achieved through the historical conquests of Alexander the Great.[25] This demonstrates the notion of global unity through imperial dominance was neither foreign to ancient minds nor universally regarded as incompatible with Stoic principles.

But Marcus Aurelius did not evince these views. His writings and his actions demonstrate no grand vision but to do his job as the emperor to the best of his ability. He was no expansionist, nor did he venture abroad in search of monsters to destroy. His foreign policy was defensive, focused on preserving the integrity of his inherited empire from foreign incursions and internal unrest.

The first major trial of Marcus Aurelius was the Roman–Parthian War of 161–166 CE, which reclaimed lost territory and influence in the east, in present-day Iraq and Iran. Marcus did not visit these battlefields in person; the campaign was carried out under the command of his brother and co-emperor, Lucius Verus, while Marcus

---

24 Nathanson, "Is Cosmopolitan Anti-Patriotism a Virtue?" 73.
25 Plutarch, *On the Fortune of Alexander* 329A–B (SVF 1.262, part) = LS 67A; Long and Sedley, *The Hellenistic Philosophers*, 1: 435.

remained in Rome as the senior ruler. Lucius died before the campaign ended, possibly from a plague carried by the returning legions. The disease would devastate Marcus' empire for years to come.

Just as the Parthian campaign concluded, tensions with the Germanic tribes to the north escalated into full-scale invasions of the Roman frontier, ushering in the so-called Marcomannic Wars commemorated in spiral relief on Marcus' Column. These conflicts consumed the remaining 14 years of his life, much of which he spent in a command post or enduring the hardships of constant travel, no longer able to divide the burdens of emperorship. Amid these grueling campaigns, the popular general Avidius Cassius, who had derisively referred to Marcus as a "philosophizing old woman," capitalized on domestic unrest to declare himself emperor.[26] Marcus moved quickly to address the rebellion, but a loyalist centurion assassinated Cassius before battle could be met, causing the movement to collapse. Far from conquest, then, Marcus' reign was instead defined by the relentless challenge of preserving stability in the face of both external threats and internal discord.

The way Marcus approached these tasks is informative. For example, in response to his wife Faustina's urging against mercy for the family and accomplices of Cassius, Marcus wrote, "There is nothing that can commend an emperor to the world more than clemency."[27] Marcus was under no illusions about the criticisms leveled against him, but responding with passion or bravado would have been beneath him. His framing of clemency not merely as a personal aversion to violence but as a prudent and effective act of governance is consistent with a disposition that seeks harmony between official duties and philosophical principles. As he lamented, "If my wishes had been followed in respect to the war, not even Cassius would have been slain."[28]

But Marcus was neither naive nor pacifistic. Rather, his governance is characterized by a stark political realism. He employed shrewd diplomacy, carefully balancing the temperamental Germanic tribes against one another while decisively crushing opposition when it arose. In keeping with Roman custom, potential upstarts were presented with a stark choice between swift and assured destruction or a peaceful and prosperous existence within Roman law.[29] When order was restored, Marcus

---

26 *The Correspondence of Marcus Cornelius Fronto*, Vol. 2, trans. Charles Reginald Haines, Letter of Verus to Marcus.
27 Ibid. Answer of Marcus to Faustina.
28 Ibid.
29 Of Roman power in general, Hans Morgenthau observes, "Isolated revolts would be dealt with swiftly and efficiently by preponderant Roman power, thus increasing Rome's prestige for power. The contrast between the dismal fate of those who dared to challenge Rome, and the peaceful and prosperous existence, under the protection of Roman law, of those who remained loyal, increased Rome's reputation for moderation in the exercise of its power." Morgenthau, *Politics Among Nations*, 84.

strove to ensure Roman governance was as legitimate as possible, aiming for lasting peace and stability.

The integration and "Romanization" of defeated enemies was a key component of Marcus' strategy.[30] He relocated barbarian tribes within the empire's boundaries, especially to repopulate regions devastated by the plague. Whenever feasible, he adhered to the Roman tradition of integrating non-Italian outsiders as full citizens, affording them the corresponding rights, privileges, and responsibilities of Roman society. There was no value in creating or declaring permanent enemies; instead, the goal was to bring unstable regions under control and transform adversaries into contributing members of society.[31]

Given the particular set of problems Marcus Aurelius inherited and his overriding belief that 'good' can only mean what's good for 'both communities'—the empire of Rome and the universal community of human beings—it is hard to recommend a radically different approach to governance than the one he took. Such an approach was neither indifference, nor helplessness, nor duplicity, but a thoughtful and pragmatic attention to duty, informed by a clear and dispassionate appraisal of his situation. If we are to criticize Marcus based on what we find in the *Meditations*, it might be for his apparent failure to fully accept or acknowledge that the duties of human virtue could conflict with the duties of empire, and for not thinking through how such conflicts might be resolved.

But what if he had? Specifically, if Marcus Aurelius—or the Stoics more broadly—had given deliberate and systematic attention to the morality of war, what frameworks of evaluation might they have developed? After all, their actions and attitudes can only reveal so much. It is always possible Stoics were simply unwilling to stick to their principles when tested, making them hypocrites. It is also possible they were unable to do so, which would incriminate Stoicism as an untenable philosophy.

To tackle these questions, we need to think about the morality of war—"just war" in academic shorthand—like Stoics. Since the literature on just war is vast, it's important to confine the discussion to a few key points of interest. We also don't need to invent a new vocabulary for justified war—existing frameworks are more than sufficient to capture the main issues. But since not all readers will be familiar with the just-war tradition, I will start with a quick overview of some of its key principles to make sure we're all on the same page for what's ahead.

---

30 Marcus is severely criticized on this point, which some regard as "the beginning of the barbarization of the empire." Birley, *Marcus Aurelius: A Biography*, 185.
31 Martha Nussbaum writes, "All Stoics took cosmopolitanism to require certain international limitations upon the conduct of warfare—in general, the renunciation of aggression and the resort to force only in self-defense, when all discussion has proven futile; also the humane treatment of the vanquished, including, if possible, the admission of the defeated people to equal citizenship in one's own nation." Nussbaum, "Kant and Stoic Cosmopolitanism," 12–13.

The Just-War Tradition

The morality of war is much like a rocky, fog-shrouded path that winds precariously between two perilous extremes. On one side lies pure violence, unrestrained by law or humanity. On the other is pacifism: an ideological opposition to violence under any circumstances. While the former is easily recognized as a moral abomination, the latter is also wrong, despite its claims to a moral high ground. Specifically, pacifism fails to adequately address situations where the use of force could prevent real and imminent greater harms, or where force is called for as a matter of principle. Furthermore, it inevitably results in free-riding and the deflection of moral and physical hazards onto others.

Navigating a morally defensible course between these extremes requires thinking about the conditions under which fighting can be justified—or when the refusal to fight would itself be a moral failure—as well as the proper conduct by which the fighting is done. Thus, war is always judged on two levels: first, for the reasons nations go to war (*jus ad bellum*); and second, for the ways they prosecute it (*jus in bello*).[32] Recent discussions have introduced concepts such as *jus ante bellum* and *jus post bellum*, which address the moral responsibilities of combatants before and after conflict respectively. Together, these principles seek to reconcile the awful necessities of war with ethical reasoning, toward the ultimate goal of making war as infrequent and humane as possible. Such deliberations are not meant to rationalize evils but to establish a framework for evaluating the reasons and conduct of war so those evils might be meaningfully reduced.

While advanced theories of just war only developed after Stoicism declined as a dominant philosophy, they are by no means recent innovations. The most influential just-war theorist is the 4th-century Christian theologian Augustine of Hippo. Drawing on the ideas of earlier thinkers such as Plato, Aristotle, and Cicero, Augustine articulated the foundational principles of just-war thinking, including the concepts of just cause, legitimate authority, and right intention. He argued wars should only be fought to secure peace, protect the innocent, and restore justice. Augustine's contributions laid the groundwork for later philosophers such as Thomas Aquinas, who refined and systematized these ideas into the more comprehensive framework we recognize today. Upon the foundation laid by these thinkers, a consensus has crystallized around several key principles of just war, each of which continues to inspire debate and refinement:

Jus ad bellum criteria refer to the conditions under which it is justifiable to engage in war:

- Legitimate authority. Only duly constituted and recognized authorities can commit a nation to wage war.

---

32 Walzer, *Just and Unjust Wars*, 21.

- Just cause. War is only justified when waged for legitimate reasons, such as self-defense or protecting innocent lives from aggression.
- Right intention. The true intention behind a decision to wage war should be to achieve a just outcome, not for self-gain, revenge, or pride.
- Probability of success. The lives of combatants should not be squandered on vainglory or lost causes.
- Last resort. War should be undertaken only when no peaceful alternatives can succeed.
- Proportionality. The anticipated moral benefits of waging war should outweigh its expected harms.

If all of the above are satisfied then, according to the traditional view, a nation may be justified in deciding to wage war. In contrast, *jus in bello* criteria refer to the conduct of combatants in waging war:

- Discrimination and noncombatant immunity. Combatants must distinguish between military targets and noncombatants, minimizing harm to civilians and never targeting them intentionally.
- Necessity. The use of force is only appropriate as necessary to achieve legitimate military objectives.
- Proportionality. The use of force must be appropriate to the military objective sought, avoiding unnecessary suffering and destruction.
- Humane treatment of the vanquished. Prisoners of war and wounded soldiers should be treated with dignity and humanity, prohibiting torture and cruelty.

One important result of the separation between *jus ad bellum* and *jus in bello* criteria is what modern theorists call the *moral equality of combatants*. This idea suggests individual warriors on both sides of a conflict are morally justified to kill one another, as long as they adhere to *jus in bello* principles like discrimination and proportionality. This justification is independent of either side's war aims, regardless of whether or not these aims satisfy *jus ad bellum* criteria, because these factors are generally beyond the responsibility of individual combatants.[33]

Some theorists challenge the moral equality of combatants on the grounds it unjustly absolves those who fight for immoral causes of responsibility for their actions.[34] In this view, combatants on both sides cannot be moral equals when one side is fighting for a manifestly unjust cause. For instance, soldiers protecting their homeland in a justified defense should not be morally equated with those participating in an unprovoked invasion. On the contrary, the justice of the cause (*jus ad bellum*) should influence the moral characterization of individual combatants' actions. Because this is such a significant point of contention, theorists who take

---

33 See Walzer, *Just and Unjust Wars*, 34–41.
34 E.g., McMahan, *Killing in War*, 123–54.

this view consider themselves revisionists of just-war thinking, while those who continue to support the moral equality of combatants are just-war traditionalists.

As long as there have been theories of just war, there have been critics who claim just-war thinking is a tool for mythmaking and the rationalization of great evils. Some argue the very notion of a justified war makes all war more permissible—as if heads of state have ever particularly cared about the thoughts of moral philosophers. What such individuals do care about are the institutions that constrain their freedom of action: treaties and international laws, such as the Geneva Conventions and the broader Law of Armed Conflict, which are established in times of stability and are themselves products of the just-war tradition. Realized through behavior-shaping mechanisms like military Rules of Engagement, such developments have undeniably reduced the suffering and destruction wrought by war. We can debate the effectiveness or fairness of their enforcement, but it is difficult to argue the world would be better without them.

Modern warriors widely recognize the value of these institutions, even if chafing at legal impediments and the criticism of academics are clichés of the modern military experience. A morally conscious approach to warfare does not just mitigate the suffering of warriors and noncombatants on all sides. Thanks to global advancements in education, shifting public attitudes, and the ubiquity of modern media, the moral dimension is crucial to any contemporary theory of military victory.[35] Just-war thinking, therefore, offers a vital space where mechanistic military duty and human moral duty intersect, arguably representing a key dimension of humanity's moral progress as a species.

Stoic Just War

Had the Stoics endured as an identifiable school, the evidence suggests they would largely align with the core principles of just war that enjoy consensus today. Like modern moral theorists, Stoics would likely disagree and debate at the margins, challenging one another with urgency. On some specific points, they would veer sharply from conventional just-war thinking, with reasons and caveats I will address shortly. But first, we should acknowledge a rather obvious question: why would Stoics even bother moralizing about war?

If death and misery are actually indifferents, we might wonder why Stoics would perceive any obligation to offer protection to noncombatants or to exercise any degree of restraint toward enemy combatants. A warrior might ask, "If I am to regard my own life as indifferent, then why should I hold any regard whatsoever for the lives of noncombatants or of my enemy? Why must I turn the Stoic knife on myself but

---

35 Michael Walzer observes, "I will call this the usefulness of morality ... Its wide acknowledgement is something radically new in military history." Walzer, *Arguing about War*, 10.

not on them?" It is a fair question. The restrictions we, as a society, impose upon our warriors come at real costs both to their safety and their immediate combat effectiveness.

Readers should recognize this question as a repackaging of the *problem of other peoples' indifferents*, which we addressed in the previous chapter. In this instance, the question fallaciously compares the way I should *feel* about one thing with what I should *do* about another. Even if I am to regard my own life as a moral indifferent, it does not follow that I should forgo all effort to preserve or improve it, as would be expressed through the appropriate selection of preferred indifferents. Likewise, even if I am to regard the welfare of my neighbor as a moral indifferent, it again does not follow that I can deny any moral responsibility concerning it. The specific balance to be struck between my neighbors' interests and my own is a different moral calculation and, by all available evidence, Stoics expect both can be served in harmony when interests are identified correctly. Problems arise when someone misidentifies what is actually good.

Even when I interpret my impressions with sagacious precision, I might have cause to war on account of my neighbor's foolish actions. A common view of such circumstances is that war becomes a "necessary evil" or a "lesser of two evils."[36] Stoics would plainly reject this; specifically, they would deny the possibility an appropriate action can be considered evil. For an action to be appropriate, it must have both consequentiality and reasonableness, which means it is defensible according to the standard of a sage. If a given action is justified in light of all available information, then it is simply the right thing to do, regardless of any apparent wrongs "conditioned by" the circumstances.[37]

Instead of viewing war as a necessary evil, Stoics would regard it as the potential winner among competing moral duties. As discussed in Chapters 2 and 4, certain indifferents, such as poverty or sickness, are typically dispreferred unless their preference is "conditioned by" exceptional circumstances.[38] Likewise, certain behaviors, such as telling the truth, are also normally appropriate in that they are *consequent*—meaning they follow from nature—when considered in isolation from important contextual factors. Such behaviors might lack *reasonableness* in light of exceptional circumstances, such as villainous secret police at the door. In such cases, *consequentiality* can be overridden by the prevailing circumstances.[39]

---

36 Childress, "Just-War Theories," 261.
37 Cf. McKenna, "Ethics and War: A Catholic View," 650.
38 E.g., DL 7.104, 7.109.
39 James Childress applies the concept of prima facie duty, as originally articulated by W. D. Ross, to explain how serious moral obligations can be overridden in the face of competing imperatives during war decisions. The discussion that follows adapts his approach to a Stoic framework of moral reasoning. See Childress, "Just-War Theories," in *War, Morality, and the Military Profession*, 256–76.

As a fundamental function of reason, all humans are bound by a duty of non-maleficence—an obligation to avoid causing harm—against which all war decisions must be evaluated.[40] This duty is inherently binding and carries significant moral weight, typically outweighing other ethical obligations, such as the duty to provide aid. However, non-maleficence is not absolute; it can be overridden by sufficiently compelling circumstances. For instance, a justified belief that refraining from the use of force would lead to even greater harm or loss of life might warrant an exception. Alternately, non-maleficence might be overridden by the belief capable nations should respond with force when malevolent actors disrupt the international system. One might justifiably desire such action as a universal law if they truly believed a better and more-stable world would result. Notably, none of this would apply in a world of sages.

On these bases, pacifism and absolute commitments to nonviolence create perverse moral outcomes upon contact with the real world. It is not just that humans can't be pacifists because they are imperfect, it's that even perfect humans could not be pacifists while other humans are imperfect. This would be as true in a Stoic moral system as it is in any other and, accordingly, war and military service are no less morally compatible with Stoicism than they are with any other peace-promoting philosophy. It is why virtually every country possesses some capabilities of self-defense, while exceptions to this rule subsist under the aegis of powerful security guarantors. Notably, this says nothing about the appropriate level of investment in such capabilities or how they should be employed, which are questions of policy that merit individual evaluation.

Because it follows from nature for all reasoning humans, the fundamental duty of non-maleficence is self-evident and role independent. Within the Epictetan framework, this means it cannot be overridden by the obligations of specific roles. As a warrior, then, my duty to pull the trigger, to service the target, or to order the launch of a missile—my duty to kill—cannot follow from my role as a warrior. Instead, my duty to kill must originate from within my identity as a virtuous and rational human being. Where specific roles might come into play is in tipping the balance between conflicting human duties, such as the duty of non-maleficence as weighed against a duty to defend an ally from invasion—both of which follow directly from reason. If killing is what I must do, it must not be because I am a good warrior, but because I am a good human. The fact I am a good warrior helps define what kind of good human I am.

Any claim that non-maleficence has been overridden must overcome a high burden of proof. Reasoning through this justification naturally leads to a set of necessary and sufficient conditions for such an override. At the scale of collective action, these conditions inevitably resemble what are traditionally recognized as just-war criteria.

---

40 After Ross, *Foundations of Ethics*, 75, 130, 272; *The Right and the Good*, 21–22, 26.

Consider, for example, the decision to wage war, which requires the subordination of individual preferences to the judgment of a collective. Suppose it is clear to me that waging war is the appropriate action for my country, a larger Hieroclean circle of which I am but one member. I cannot independently act on this belief. Instead, such decisions must be made by a *legitimate authority* vested with the power to act on behalf of the collective within the established system of governance. Modern theorists argue legitimate authority is a prerequisite for satisfying any other *jus ad bellum* criterion because it is specifically this authority that must evaluate and apply those criteria.[41] If the deciding authority is not legitimate, then it is impossible to say that other *jus ad bellum* criteria have been correctly evaluated.

When committing a country to war, the legitimate authority must do so for a *just cause*. This means the duty or obligation said to override non-maleficence must be a serious one. Frivolous glory projects and opportunistic acts of aggression hardly meet this standard. Likewise, actions driven by pride or desires for vengeance fall short of just cause, as there is no corresponding duty strong enough to outweigh the fundamental obligation to avoid harm. Moreover, non-maleficence cannot be overridden without a *reasonable chance of success*; indeed, it would be imprudent to undertake even a morally neutral endeavor without a realistic prospect of achieving the desired end. When the endeavor involves overriding a fundamental moral duty, the burden of justification becomes that much higher.

Tightly linked to just cause is the requirement its pursuit genuinely motivates the deciding authority, a principle embodied in the criterion of *right intention*. This demands freedom from ulterior motives or passions such as fear, pride, greed, or hatred, which undermine integrity—the alignment of virtues, values, and actions—at both the societal and individual levels. Such contaminants poison the decision-making process, distorting judgment and obstructing paths to a just resolution of conflict.

If there is a realistic way to address the overriding duty without compromising the duty of non-maleficence, that path should be chosen. As Cicero says, "There are two types of military dispute, the one settled by negotiation and the other by force. Since the first is characteristic of human beings and the second of beasts, we must have recourse to the second only if we cannot exploit the first."[42] Therefore, the decision to wage war must be reserved as a *last resort*. Discussions of last resort often intersect with the concept of a formal declaration of war, which some view as a final measure of persuasion.[43] Cicero preempted later theorists on this point as

---

41 Childress, "Just-War Theories," 263. Cf. Cécile Fabre's argument that a requirement for legitimate authority denies the rights of individuals or non-state actors to defend their own interests. Fabre, *Cosmopolitan War*, 142–48.
42 Cicero, *On Duties* 1.34.
43 McKenna, "Ethics and War: A Catholic View," 650.

well, arguing "no war is just unless it is preceded by a demand for satisfaction, or unless due warning is given first, and war is formally declared."[44]

While few serious theorists defend this view, an intuitive argument suggests that once war is underway, all methods are justified to bring it to an end. This perspective has been echoed by various figures throughout history and is perhaps best captured in the expression of General William T. Sherman before destroying the city of Atlanta: "War is cruelty, and you cannot refine it."[45] This view is often paraphrased "War is hell." Such reasoning flows naturally from the belief war is a necessary evil. If war is inherently evil, it disconnects entirely from moral reasoning, such that all actions are equally impermissible and therefore none are worse than others.

This view, however, is deeply deficient. For one, peace, when treated as an end in itself, is a bad priority. The shortest path to peace is surrender, and the second shortest is to "create a desert and call it peace."[46] Both options are readily available, especially in modern times, and they grow more tempting with every setback or frustration. Yet, as has been observed since at least the time of Cicero, only a just peace is lasting and all war decisions should support its achievement. Even from a purely pragmatic standpoint, then, violence that is unnecessary, indiscriminate, or disproportionate should be eliminated.

Practical observations aside, the view that war is always unmitigated cruelty is simply lazy. Stoics, who would reject the concept of a justified evil, would argue no activity is exempt from moral reasoning, including the conduct of war. Even if war can never be made perfect (that would be peace), it can still be waged in ways more or less destructive depending on the choices made. In other words, the duty of non-maleficence is not a binary feature overridden once and then discarded; rather, it must be overridden continuously, with case-by-case evaluations of every potential violent act, prohibiting those that do not meet the burden of proof.

For example, noncombatants are unequivocally off-limits from direct attack.[47] As unwilling participants in conflict, they are properly regarded as its victims and this burden cannot be overridden by mere suspicions they harbor or sympathize with the enemy. Furthermore, even though I have a role-based duty to preserve the

---

44 Cicero, *On Duties* 1.36.
45 General William T. Sherman to the mayor and councilmen of Atlanta, 1864.
46 The expression *ubi solitudinem faciunt pacem appellant* is attributed to Calgacus, a Caledonian chieftain who resisted Roman dominion. See Tacitus, *Agricola*, 30.
47 "Collateral damage" to noncombatants is traditionally justified under the "doctrine of double effect." Rooted in the thinking of Thomas Aquinas, this principle suggests an action that has both a good effect and a harmful side effect can be morally permissible if certain conditions are met. These conditions include that the action itself must be morally good or neutral, the harmful effect must not be intended (even if foreseen), and the good effect must outweigh the harmful consequences. In the context of war, this principle is often invoked to justify military operations where harm to noncombatants is a foreseen but unavoidable consequence of achieving a legitimate military objective. See Walzer, *Just and Unjust Wars*, 151ff.

lives of my troops, I cannot do so by clearing population centers with bombers and heavy artillery. Just as my troops cannot attack noncombatants to improve their own safety, I cannot authorize attack of noncombatants for that reason either.[48] These restrictions reflect the *jus in bello* principles of *discrimination* and *noncombatant immunity*. A distinctly Stoic contribution is the belief noncombatants are not just victims, but are fellow citizens of a higher, global community.

Broadly understood as Stoic cosmopolitanism, this belief illuminates the space between traditional *jus in bello* criteria and practical realities, where questions of immense moral consequence can arise. For example, even if I am not permitted to kill noncombatants to save my own troops, might I reduce their margin to safety?[49] Can I make them uncomfortable or miserable? Can I starve them or destroy their access to power, water, and medical care? How confident must I be that my actions do not result in their deaths, now or in the future?

It is not uncommon for two lawful and professionally competent commanders to reach different conclusions about what degree of hazard or misery for noncombatants can be justified in the interest of efficiency, mission effectiveness, or safety of one's own forces. It is precisely in these ambiguous trade spaces that moral wisdom—to include a cosmopolitan ethic—manifests with enormous consequence. Although certain special obligations do distinguish kin and fellow citizens from foreigners, as discussed in the previous chapters, these are generally functions of specific roles and, as such, they cannot override those duties attendant to one's fundamental role as a reasoning human. The result is that, for Stoics, all wars are civil wars, placing noncombatants among those to be protected, even at significant risk to life and mission.

A special category of noncombatant is the defeated enemy, who should be recognized as an ex-combatant when the fighting stops.[50] Even they would be regarded by Stoics as human beings apart from their roles as combatants, and fellow countrymen in a civil war. Naturally, *humane treatment of the vanquished* emerges as a separate *jus in bello* criterion. Once again, Cicero presages the theorists: "Consideration should also be shown to those who have been subdued by force, and men who lay down their arms and seek the sanctuary of our generals' discretion should be granted access to them, even if a battering ram has shattered their city wall."[51] He refers to

---

48 Ibid., 155. Walzer cites the difficult decisions faced by American officers in the Korean War as a real-world example of this dilemma.
49 A commonly cited historical case of such harm-shifting is the NATO air war in Serbia, where precision bombing runs were conducted from high altitudes, adding significant risk to noncombatants but improving margins to safety for pilots. See Shue, "Bombing to Rescue?"; Economides, "Kosovo," in *United Nations Interventionism, 1991–2004*, 85–105; Roberts, "NATO's Humanitarian War over Kosovo"; Wheeler, *Saving Strangers*, esp. chap. 8.
50 Childress, "Just-War Theories," 267.
51 Cicero, *On Duties* 1.35.

Julius Caesar's promise not to destroy a besieged city if surrender came before the battering ram was applied, which it regrettably did not.[52]

For any act of violence, a thoughtful assessment of its costs against the proposed tactical, operational, or strategic benefit is required. These include the second- and third-order effects that may transpire over generations. If a specific use of force is not essential to achieving legitimate military objectives aligned with the broader moral goals of the war, then the act lacks *necessity* and fails to override the duty of non-maleficence. I cannot kill or destroy simply because I am in enemy territory or because my target may be an enemy combatant—the killing must serve a valid military purpose. Moreover, the military gain must be worth the human suffering it causes; otherwise, the *jus in bello* criterion of *proportionality* will not be satisfied.

In summary, I have addressed the question of whether Stoics can justifiably perform acts of violence by applying concepts of competing and overridden moral duties. I concluded they can—and, indeed, sometimes must—provided the appropriate criteria are satisfied, as outlined above. However, I have not yet examined the matter of collective action and whether participation in such actions might constitute a forfeiture of moral freedom. If it does, this would render such actions incompatible with Stoic principles, so it is to that question I now turn.

The Collective Duties of Warriors

When we left off in the previous chapter, I had introduced a Stoic concept of collective duty. Drawing on the writings of the Stoic Hierocles, I argued a group of individuals can be considered a collective entity—what Hierocles represents as a circle—if it possesses an identity greater than the sum of its parts, such that its collective actions might bear consequentiality. In this construct, the terms *circle*, *community*, or *collective* all refer to the same idea: a group with an independent identity capable of performing actions to fulfill its distinct *telos*, or mission. Within such a group, the interests of the individual and the collective are intrinsically connected, if not identical. As Hierocles states:

> In these matters, things may be summed up thus: that one must not separate the common interest from the individual interest, but it should be regarded as one and the same. For the interest of the country is common to each of its individual members (for the whole is nothing without the parts), and the interest of the citizen belongs to the city as well—at least if it is taken to be his interest as a citizen.[53]

This principle applies at all collective scales: what benefits the country benefits the citizen, and what benefits the species benefits the country. Accordingly, the appropriate actions of a collective align to three general imperatives: to fulfill its

---

52 Ibid., 134n35.
53 Hierocles, (51,10–9); trans. Wedgwood, "Hierocles' Concentric Circles," 293–332.

own natural purposes, including to preserve its own moral and physical constitution; to support the fulfillment of the natural purposes of the smaller collectives that comprise it; and to contribute to the fulfillment of the natural purposes of the larger collectives of which it is a member. Just like an individual, then, a collective's actions can either align with or contradict nature. In other words, its actions can have consequentiality. Associating duty with consequentiality, I concluded that collectives, like individuals, can have duties.

Continuing in that line of reasoning, we observe that the duties of a collective do not necessarily distribute evenly to its members if they even distribute at all.[54] An individual cannot stop a genocide, prevent nuclear proliferation, or preserve freedom of the seas, even if these are appropriate actions, possessed with both consequentiality and reasonableness. Individual contributions to these collective actions may bear no resemblance to the larger task they comprise. The collective *is* the actor, while individuals are responsible for behaving appropriately within their specific spheres of influence, as would comport with reason.

Early in this book, I established warriors do not enjoy a special system of morality apart from the societies they serve. However, for warriors, the collectivization of duty accepts a special significance, comprising a critical dimension of one's moral responsibility. While many social roles involve acting on behalf of a collective, few—if any—are collectivizing to the same degree. With little more than a uniform, a modest amount of training, and a task to perform, a single young individual comes to represent the collective will of an entire nation. But this critical dimension of responsibility intersects with another: the moral consequence of the warrior's tasks. While many professions involve decisions affecting life, death, or suffering, few—if any—produce consequences at the same scale or immediacy as those of the warrior.

Warriors, therefore, occupy the extreme end of both spectra, where the boundary between professional and moral competencies disappears. With such breadth of responsibility, moral incompetence is a professional deficiency. And given the stakes of failure, professional incompetence becomes a moral deficiency.[55] When clinical simplicity and freedom from consequence are the province of moral theoreticians, warriors are, by contrast, the ultimate moral practitioners.

The specific nature of warriors' responsibilities grants them the status of combatants, making them legitimate targets under the laws of war and subjecting them to the unique risks and responsibilities of armed conflict. But this legitimacy—their enemies' right to kill them—subsists at the moral level as well as the legal. It is specifically the warrior's subsummation into the collective effort that confers it, and this is no less

---

54 See Erskine, *Can Institutions Have Responsibilities?*, 22.
55 See Wakin, "The Ethics of Leadership II," 208, 211–14; Hackett, "Society and the Soldier: 1914–18," 82. Notably, in the same breath that he cites Arnold Toynbee as an impartial witness that military virtues and moral virtues are indistinguishable, General Hackett also recommends Cicero's *On Duties* as a military training manual.

true when their individual roles and tasks bear little resemblance to conventional notions of combat.[56] While the individual's identity is immutably reducible to the capacity for choice, warriors, as extensions of their collective, become something greater than themselves, in the same sense the collective becomes something greater than the sum of its members.

Consider, for example, how an individual sailor transcends their personal existence by acting as an organ of a larger, far more capable entity. A warship, as a formidable extension of the country's collective purpose, is able to perform tasks no individual could even contemplate. And yet to the extent the warship defines the crew, it is also defined by it. Without it, the warship is nothing more than a derelict structure—and this would still be true with hundreds of individuals milling about it aimlessly. It is the collectivization of purpose that transforms a disorganized crowd into a crew and an inert metal hulk into a powerful instrument of national will.

For its constitutive members, the warship is both a collective and a Hieroclean social circle. It has purposes to fulfill—for itself, for its crew, and for the larger fleets and joint forces of which it is an element. The ship is a microcosm of the nation, embodying its values, desires, and features of personality in both tangible and intangible ways. Likewise, the sailor becomes a microcosm of the ship and, by extension, the country it represents. Through various psychological processes, the ship and its crew come to supplant the sailor's preexisting communal ties, often fostering a sense of connection to distant circles—such as the country—stronger than anything previously experienced.[57]

Military training programs universally encourage this transformation, emphasizing the ancient principle that "what is useful to the individual is identical with what is useful to the community."[58] In many settings, 'individual' is treated as a slur, a derisive label for someone who fails to transcend the self-affirming comfort zones of childhood. The United States Navy's mantra of "Ship, Shipmate, Self" emphasizes the preeminence of the collective as the fundamental unit of action. Combat pilots are trained to rely on wingmen, and special forces emphasize extreme interdependence and teamwork—highlighting that an individual 'hotshot' is not just ineffective but is a liability. These principles of coordinated action scale to fleets and airwings and networked ground forces where combat advantage is no longer found in more

---

56 Noam Zohar frames this as a compromise, necessitated as an exigency of war, between individualistic and collective conceptions of morality. Zohar, "Collective War and Individualistic Ethics," 615–19. Cf. Nagel, "War and Massacre," 140; Walzer, *Just and Unjust Wars*, 145–46.
57 Social theorists have attempted to describe these processes in concepts like *identity fusion* and *depersonalization*. See Turner, "Social Categorization and the Self-Concept," 243–72; Garner, "Why Cosmopolitan War Is an Ethics of Fantasy?" 280–83; Conover, "The Influence of Group Identification," 761–85; Fredman et al., "Identity Fusion," 468–80; Hart and Lancaster, "Identity Fusion in U.S. Military Members," 45–58.
58 Cicero, *On Duties* 3.27.

powerful weapons but in multi-domain, combined-arms maneuver of ever-increasing scale and efficiency.

Although these military units possess moral agency within their own spheres of decision making, from the perspective of the country they are instruments—tools of the national will. Recall from Cicero's political philosophy that military forces are not considered participants in the power dynamics of mixed government but are rather a resource of the state, like fields or harbors. This 'instrumental' role reinforces the concept of military service, where the well-being of the people—expressed through collective agency and transformed into national policy through deliberating processes—must be upheld as the "supreme law."

If military institutions fail to prioritize the national will and instead come to serve their own ends, the societal affliction known as *militarism* takes root.[59] This condition resembles a cancer or autoimmune disorder, where essential systems of the body run haywire and consume the organism from within. Scholars of history have long recognized militarism as a destructive but inexorable impulse, described as "suicidal" for nations and repeatedly observed to facilitate catastrophic social collapse.[60] Thus modern institutions of government enshrine safeguards against it in the forms of law, regulation, and military culture. These include the inviolable supremacy of civilian authority over the military and the strict rejection of partisan political affiliations within its ranks.

Thus, as agents of their country rather than any faction within it, modern warriors bear a role-based duty to uphold standards of nonpartisanship and civilian control within their spheres of influence. These principles are essential to maintaining public trust and safeguarding the military's legitimacy as a servant of collective well-being. Furthermore, they protect against the military's exploitation by partisan political forces that might misuse it for purposes not legitimately representative of national will. Should the principles of nonpartisanship and civilian control ever appear to conflict, a commitment to enduring institutions, such as a national Constitution, rather than to individuals or factions, will clarify how they align.

I, Warrior

As demonstrated earlier, many traditional principles of just-war thinking follow naturally from Stoic morality. This is unsurprising as seminal just-war theorists like Augustine and Aquinas were deeply influenced by the Stoics. However, there are crucial points where Stoics would diverge from conventional just-war thinking, and some of these appear to challenge the entire project of just-war theory itself. Chief among these is that Stoics would deny a just war can even exist at all.

---

59 Hackett, "Society and the Soldier: 1914–18," 81.
60 Toynbee, *A Study of History*, 4: 388–402.

Intuitively, we might think this is a function of Stoic perfectionism: war is an intrinsically messy and imperfect enterprise. For example, the decision to take a country to war is never made by a single individual; even autocrats are influenced or supported by complicit advisers and staff, all of whom, we can be certain, are not sages. Responsibility is not even confined to one Hieroclean circle of community. Generals, captains, and squad leaders, alongside politicians, their electorates, and media organizations, contribute to a complex web of decisions that both initiate and sustain a conflict. Even if a nation's primary aim in going to war is a just cause, pursued with right intention, there will inevitably be ulterior motives and human passions involved.

Furthermore, the decision to engage in war is never confined to a single moment. Instead, it follows a long trajectory of choices that begins well before the first shots are fired and extends far beyond the ceasefire. What might begin as a just cause can easily devolve into cycles of vengeance and animosity. These complexities militate against the possibility of a purely just cause. This pattern is evident in every war throughout history, leading to the reasonable conclusion that vicious passions and hidden agendas are inherent to any conflict involving human beings.

Extending the logic of Stoic perfectionism, which holds that all non-sages are equally vicious, one might conclude that all wars lacking a perfect justification are equally unjust. This would align with some theorists who argue a war becomes unjust if it is contaminated by any ulterior motive or negative passion.[61] Since a "perfect" war—devoid of self-interest or passion—does not exist, this view would essentially prohibit all war on moral grounds. However, this same reasoning would also prohibit all collective endeavors, such as building cities, forming international agreements, or developing cures for diseases. While these activities do not approach the destructiveness of war, they too involve moral compromises, aggrieved parties, ulterior motives, and vicious passions. Yet, we do not declare such enterprises unjust on account of their imperfections.

Instead of perfectionism, it is ontology—the theory of what exists—that would lead the Stoics to deny the possibility of a just war. As briefly discussed in Chapter 1, early Stoics promote nascent concepts of *Materialism* and *Nominalism* that define their understanding of existence. Strictly speaking, Stoics would not only deny the existence of just wars but also of unjust wars. In their view, wars do not "exist" as morally salient concepts; rather, they merely "subsist," like all thoughts and abstract notions.[62] The term "war" refers to a series of individual events collectively identified as war by linguistic convention, but this practice of labeling does not confer existence. A practical result of this non-existence is we cannot look to wars, particularly the specious claim that any particular war is just, to rationalize our individual actions.

---

61 McKenna, "Ethics and War: A Catholic View," 652.
62 Konstantakos, "Stoicism and Just War Theory," 10.

External from the individual who performs each action, the events of war are morally indifferent, like the deaths of animals or the destruction of birds' nests.[63] A given action may be appropriate or inappropriate for the individual who performs it, but this evaluation is distinct from that of any other action, whether performed by others or the same individual, or even by the collective of which the individual is a member. These actions remain *heterogeneous*, meaning that even though they may follow from a common set of preceding events, to include acts of various motivations, they do not coalesce into some larger action with an overriding moral valence. Each choice must be made in the moment by an individual, according to that individual's judgment with consideration of all relevant contexts and contributing factors.

Concepts like just causes and right intentions similarly cannot exist, except within the physical substance of an individual who contemplates them. Therefore, the causes and intentions that motivate a decision to launch a specific collective action, such as a strategic bombing campaign, can say little about the intentions of an individual participant, such as a pilot or an ordnance handler. Reasonableness is not transferable between collectives and their members; at most, the perceived causes and intentions of some distant commander are moral indifferents that contribute to the context under which appropriate action is evaluated. Given this irreconcilable *heterogeneity* of individual moral actions, Stoics would plainly reject the notion of a "just combatant" or "unjust combatant," a convention some just-war theorists use to define a warrior by the collective actions they support.

However, this is not to say just causes and right intentions don't matter. Such things matter profoundly, but specifically within the ruling center of each individual actor, where the reasonableness of a given course of action is determined, in situ, 'all things considered'. Recall that a defining feature of reasonableness is its exclusive internality, wholly inaccessible and incomprehensible to outside observers.

An internal concept of justice expresses natural law. For the Stoic, it is personally binding, analogous to the written laws that govern civil and military conduct, yet ultimately superior in its claim on the conscience.[64] It completely overrides the judgment of any external authority, which to the individual is a moral indifferent. This is most clearly articulated in a dialogue by Cicero, where the Stoic Laelius is his mouthpiece:

> True law is right reason, in agreement with nature, diffused over everyone, consistent, everlasting, whose nature is to advocate duty by prescription and to deter wrongdoing by prohibition. Its prescriptions and prohibitions are heeded by good men though they have no effect on the bad. It is wrong to alter this law, nor is it permissible to repeal any part of it, and it is impossible to abolish it entirely. We cannot be absolved from this law by senate or people, nor need we look for any outside interpreter of it, or commentator. There will not be a different law at Rome and at Athens, or a different law now and in the future, but one law, everlasting and immutable,

---

63 Epictetus, *Discourses* 1.28.16–7.
64 Cf. Konstantakos, "Stoicism and Just War Theory," 83–93.

will hold good for all peoples and at all times. And there will be one master and ruler for us all in common, God who is the founder of this law, its promulgator and its judge. Whoever does not obey it is fleeing from himself and treating his human nature with contempt; by this very fact he will pay the heaviest penalties, even if he escapes all conventional punishments.[65]

Natural law, inherent in nature and accessible to human reason, does not only permit but fully *requires* individuals to discern right from wrong independently of external adjudicators. Its jurisdiction does not end at one's membership to a collective. Reflecting this independence, Seneca claims to "daily plead my cause before myself," a judge and jury of personal conscience, informed and animated as such by the universal *Logos*.[66]

Freedom, therefore, is always preserved, even when participating in collective actions. Building a bridge or fighting a forest fire are examples of collective efforts—undoubtedly imperfect in both conception and execution—that require me to follow orders. Yet, my participation in these efforts does not come at the cost of my freedom. Similarly, I can choose to join the military and support an imperfect war effort. In any case, my confidence in the appropriateness of collective actions provides essential context for deciding whether to perform individual contributing actions—a context that cannot be ignored. However, other contributing factors, mitigating circumstances, and competing duties must also be considered. At every juncture, I must decide whether to obey or disobey orders as reason recommends, based on the available information. I may not like the options before me, but there is always a choice, and choice is what I am.

That is to say, as a deciding moral agent, *I* remain nothing more than my instantaneous faculty of moral choice, even as a constitutive member of a collective, and even as a product of antecedent events. The collective, for its part, remains a separate and distinct moral entity. The compatibility of moral freedom and collective action, then, is similar to the compatibility between determinism and free will. As Epictetus insists, "someone is free if all that happens to him comes about in accordance with his choice and no one else is able to impede him."[67] With this individual freedom, however, comes responsibility. My choices place me where I am—whether I am holding a rivet gun or a machine gun. To point to an external actor as the cause for my actions is to abdicate responsibility and, as Epictetus would argue, to consent to coercion. In doing so, I surrender my freedom and become a slave.[68]

In this environment, the concept of moral equality among combatants cannot hold. While it may have its uses as a legal heuristic, it is fundamentally incompatible with the total moral autonomy of Stoics, placing them in company with just-war

---

65 Cicero, *On the Republic* 3.33 (SVF 3.325) = LS 67S.
66 Seneca, *On Anger* 3.36.
67 Epictetus, *Discourses* 1.12.9; cf. 4.1.1.
68 Ibid. 4.1.69–77.

revisionists on this particular point. The primary issue lies in its absolution of combatants from the broader contexts in which their appropriate actions must be evaluated, effectively circumscribing all factors that do not fall under the specific responsibilities of "warrior." But specific roles can never override the fundamental human duty to exercise reason, through which appropriate action must be determined in light of all available contexts and contributing factors. Combatants on both sides of a conflict may be justified in performing their wartime duties, but the fact they are combatants is far from the only reason.

Task Fragmentation

Even if we say that warriors are responsible for what they do, it cannot be true that responsibility is absolute. There are good reasons most figures in the just-war tradition only hold individual warriors to account for conduct *in bello*. Even the just-war revisionists, who expressly deny the moral equality of combatants, must acknowledge some mitigating conditions that would lessen the individual warrior's responsibility for collective war actions. While these conditions are typically discussed in an ex post facto context, such as a written legal judgment, they are also relevant to the warrior's present- and future-oriented evaluations of appropriate action.

Mitigating conditions, which just-war revisionists uncharitably call *excuses*, broadly fall into three categories: duress, epistemic limitation, and diminished responsibility.[69] Duress refers to situations where individuals may be compelled to perform war actions against their own agency, such as by threat of force or imprisonment, or even by social punishment. Epistemic limitation recognizes individual combatants may lack complete information about the reasons for their orders, or otherwise may be incapable of fully comprehending those reasons. Diminished responsibility acknowledges an individual's responsibility for the outcomes of a collective effort is, to some degree, a function of their specific responsibilities within that collective. When considering the interaction of these mitigating conditions with Stoic moral autonomy, we must remember the "reasonableness" of an appropriate action—its defensibility in light of all contributing factors—is always measured against the standard of the Stoic sage. This means that in evaluating the rightness of a given action, Stoics would make no allowance for human moral or intellectual limitations.

Thus, we can immediately dispense with duress as a mitigating condition, as Stoics would not recognize it. Stoics would reject the notion any order is compulsory; as we say, there is always a choice, including the option to disobey. Any punishment for disobedience, even death, would be properly classified as a dispreferred indifferent.[70]

---

69 McMahan, *Killing in War*, 115–22.
70 Cf. Michael Walzer: "Only a man with a gun to his head is not responsible." Stoics would not recognize even this excuse. Walzer, *Just and Unjust Wars*, 314.

As such, a sage would accept it over a compromise of integrity, which would constitute the destruction of the moral self. This is not to say the real consequences of disobedience, such as failing to defend one's post and the potential loss of life among comrades, would not factor into the evaluation of appropriate action. However, in such cases, as in all decisions, appropriate action is a moral judgment, not based on practicality or amoral self-interest.

The mitigating condition of epistemic limitation involves both access to information and the ability to process it, which can be hindered by factors such as immaturity, insufficient education, or time. It captures the common criticism that volunteer military service is morally compromising in that it involves willful immersion in forces of indoctrination, propaganda, and social pressures. Never mind the same should be said of membership in any ideologically tilted culture or organization; in any case, such influences would not affect a sage. Stoics, especially sages, are expected to diligently maintain an internal skepticism, withholding assent to impressions, including the impression "this person is telling the truth."

However, it is important to remember sages are not omniscient; they do not possess magical powers of perception. Sages can only make perfect decisions when perfect information is available; if they are provided with incomplete or incorrect information, they may make mistakes with serious consequences. This risk does not diminish their responsibility to make decisions. Appropriate action thus involves a justified trust in official authority such that the broader collective can function coherently, whether its purpose is to build a bridge or to project combat power. Accordingly, the sage's internal skepticism must also apply to impressions such as "this person is lying."

Closely related to the issue of information is the mitigating condition of diminished responsibility within a hierarchy. The higher one's position, the more information and authority they generally have, and thus the greater their contribution to the outcomes of collective actions. An important, though often overlooked factor in discussions of diminished responsibility is the fragmentation of war actions across a wide and growing set of contributing moral agents. Just-war theorists tend to underemphasize this phenomenon, partly due to the simplicity and clarity of traditional infantry-on-infantry thought experiments, and partly due to the relative novelty of some modern warfighting capabilities. This factor may be neglected in literature simply due to a lack of widespread exposure to the technologies and techniques involved. That said, it is not an entirely new phenomenon, as even a medieval longbowman must launch his arrow without personally knowing upon whom it will land.

In modern warfare, the execution of violent actions often distributes across a wide network of participants, the size of which depends on the complexity of the capability being employed. For instance, missile strikes and bombing missions involve targeteers, mission planners, firing-unit commanders, combat-system operators, as well as various technicians and ordnance handlers. As a practical matter, official responsibility for these collective war actions is typically assigned to the commander who gives the order. A traditional role of commanders is to shoulder the accompanying moral responsibility in hopes that subordinate operators may be relieved of moral burdens to the extent possible. However, moral responsibility is not so easily contained, especially when someone other than the commander selects the targets and yet another pulls the trigger.

The individual perceptions of participants are necessarily limited, not due to secrecy or hierarchical privilege, but because of technical realities. A vivid illustration of this is a roomful of sailors watching, via satellite-streamed news, the kinetic impacts of cruise missiles their warship launched only hours before. For these sailors, the targets existed merely as sets of coordinates until seen on a TV screen. This is not because of any deliberate effort to dehumanize the enemy, but simply because that's how the systems work.[71]

Because task fragmentation tends to increase with system complexity, it also tends to correspond with firepower. This creates a perverse relationship between destructive potential and the abstraction of those destroyed into impersonal data. Our most powerful weapons, in particular, are embedded within vast hierarchies of planning and authorization, where decisions originate at the highest levels of national leadership—as far as possible from the battlefield. However, somewhere in this intricate web of responsibility are not only those who give the orders, but also the weapons-system maintainers, network technicians who ensure communication, logisticians who supply repair parts and ammunition, and the cooks and medics and clerks who ensure those others are able to do their jobs.

While questions about "who does the killing" within such a distributed organization of responsible agents are interesting, they are not the point of the discussion here. Instead, my aim is to clarify how a Stoic would evaluate appropriate action and responsibility within such a system, and whether they would consent to be part of it. Regarding the latter, it is unlikely a Stoic would deny the necessity of such an organization, just as the Stoics did not deny the necessity of Rome's legions. Stoics remain steadfastly grounded in the real world and regularly acknowledge a need to deal with humans as they are rather than how we might wish them to be.

If warriors do indeed fulfill a necessary role, then normal military service must be reasonable—that is, defensible by reason against the standard of the sage. Again, there are no "villain roles" in Stoicism. This defensibility, however, might evaporate in the presence of extreme circumstances, such as manifestly unjust collective actions or an intolerable system of government. Furthermore, if conditions are severe enough

---

[71] A growing body of research shows that treating enemy forces as "non-human" amplifies the severity of moral injury and post-traumatic stress disorder. E.g., Shay, *Achilles in Vietnam*, Introduction, 115.

to render military service indefensible, then so also would normal civic acquiescence to those conditions also become indefensible.[72] In such cases, moral integrity would likely demand a contrarian role of active resistance to the prevailing system, likely involving great personal sacrifice.

Returning to the question of conditions mitigating accountability in war, we can assert that Stoics would dismiss duress as a valid consideration, but they would take the combined matters of epistemic limitation and diminished responsibility very seriously. Stoics would be keenly aware of the physical limitations on the availability of information and the realities of coordinated action in a complex environment. Stoics would recognize military organization and hierarchy as necessary accommodations to these limitations, understanding efficient action requires division of labor and justified trust in a chain of command. However, while Stoics would dutifully perform their specific roles within the hierarchy, their appropriate actions would always be conditioned by the circumstances and they would remain personally accountable for their own decisions. In other words, the role of warrior would never override the role of human.

Obedience and Disobedience

Even if we can say with confidence Stoics would recognize obedience as necessary for the accomplishment of coordinated action, there is still something incongruous about the idea of an obedient Stoic. It seems to run in the face of freedom and independent judgment, even if we insist moral autonomy is preserved in the capacity to disobey. This is particularly true in the case of military obedience, where the consequences of action or inaction take on a moral gravity unparalleled in other roles. However, it's possible this dissonance arises from a caricatured view of military obedience, so it would be worthwhile to say something about what obedience really means in a military setting.

In popular imagination, military obedience is often understood as blind, unthinking submission to authority. But "blind" and "unthinking" are unmistakably pejorative terms, and very few real military leaders would identify them as desirable qualities in a subordinate. Furthermore, going back to at least the time of Aristotle, the ability to disobey has been recognized as a precondition to calling obedience a virtue.[73] We can set the record straight, then, by saying blind or unconditional obedience is neither required nor desired in a warrior. Modern warriors are even purposefully trained to disobey unlawful orders, such as a command to directly attack noncombatants.

---

72 See Lazar, "Response to Moral Wounds," who argues that if armed forces are justified to exist, then members of the armed forces are justified in accepting the associated risks of wrongdoing.
73 See Aristotle, *Nichomachean Ethics*, Book III.

Normally, military discipline requires a presumption of competence and legitimate authority on the part of the commander.[74] But blatant illegality would void this presumption and carrying out such an order would not only be immoral but also harmful to broader war aims, which presumably include establishing a just peace. Justified disobedience, then, may not just protect immediate beneficiaries like noncombatants, it can also protect the wider organization and its strategic imperatives from internal malfeasance.

Sometimes even lawful orders are appropriately disobeyed. For example, in select circumstances, disobedience to a lawful order may be justified in the interest of achieving the commander's higher aims, which we might call "obedience by other means."[75] Such circumstances are most likely when the subordinate has access to information the commander lacks, as might occur in emergencies where the pace of events outstrips the flow of communication. Justification of such acts carries a high burden of proof, where disobedience must be done openly and with full acceptance of any consequences that might result. Such qualifications ensure the disobedience serves the commander's intent rather than simple defiance or personal agendas.

We can find an example of "obedience by other means" in the thinking of the Stoic Musonius Rufus. Specifically, he posits a situation where a father, ignorant in medical matters, instructs his ill son to follow a harmful regimen. If the son recognizes adhering to these instructions would undermine the father's ultimate intent—his recovery—it would actually be an act of true obedience for the son to disregard the harmful orders. Thus Musonius remarks, "refusing to do what one ought not to do merits praise rather than blame."[76] Real-world military equivalents are not hard to find; for example, consider these examples from the Allied landings at Omaha Beach during World War II:

- Two Navy lieutenants (junior grade), each in charge of landing craft responsible for launching amphibious tanks onto the beach, observed the tanks of neighboring craft were quickly swamped by high seas at the designated launch point. Without obtaining permission, they independently took the initiative to plunge through the defenses and crash-land their craft directly onto the beach.
- A group of Army Rangers ashore, recognizing an unexpected opportunity, deviated from their original tasking to exploit a gap in enemy defenses. They opportunistically destroyed key defensive positions they had successfully flanked, contributing significantly to the success of the wider assault.
- A destroyer captain, tasked with protecting the landing force from enemy vessels that never materialized, recognized the futility of his assigned position.

---

74 Huntington, *The Soldier and the State*, 74–76.
75 After Shanks Kaurin, *On Obedience*, 112ff.
76 Lutz, *Disdain Hardships*, 78.

Without orders, he moved his ship closer to shore to bombard enemy defenses in direct support of the landing force. His bold action was soon replicated by neighboring vessels and was eventually ordered retroactively by the shore-bombardment admiral.[77]

It is important to acknowledge the general exceptionality of such cases, as history offers far more examples where disobedience led to disaster. These quick-thinking warriors would be fully liable to administrative punishment had their superiors sought it after the battle and, given the stakes, we may assume they would still think their actions were worth it. The point here is that intellectual flexibility is just as crucial as obedience in defining the ideal warrior, while the notion of a zombie-like, blindly obedient super soldier belongs to the simplistic battlefields of science fiction. In the chaos of real-world military operations, such an individual would not only be a strategic liability—ready to commit atrocities just given an excuse—but also would be practically ineffective. They could not be relied upon to adapt to unforeseen developments and would require excessively detailed instructions to carry out even straightforward tasks.

Real warriors, in contrast, must be creative and resourceful in support of their commanders' intent. To properly understand what that is, they must employ both professional judgment and ethical reasoning, and they are obligated to speak up when concerns arise. Naturally, this practice requires discernment of the proper time and place for such exchanges—moments of crisis or battle conditions are typically not it. Nevertheless, the broader principle holds firm: military obedience does not mean suspending one's intellectual faculties; rather, it explicitly demands their engagement.[78]

For philosophers, such intellectual faculties are inseparable from moral faculties. Accordingly, Musonius' endorsement of principled disobedience extends from practical to moral bases: "whether one's father or the archon or even the tyrant orders something wrong or unjust or shameful, and one does not carry out the order, he is in no way disobeying, inasmuch as he does no wrong nor fails of doing right."[79] But how might such thinking find compatibility in the responsibilities of a warrior? We find a clue in the example of Socrates, warmly remembered for principled disobedience by Marcus Aurelius.[80]

---

77 Nightingale, "Combat, Orders and Judgement."
78 Some thinkers have proposed appending qualifiers like "enlightened" or "critical" to obedience to distinguish the behavior we describe here from pejorative forms, such as blind, unthinking, or malicious obedience. However, I consider this simply to be obedience, where any pejorative form is inherently a perversion of the concept and thus, in need of a qualifier. See Wakin, *Integrity First*, 67–68; Zwygart, "How Much Obedience Does an Officer Need?" 24; Shanks Kaurin, *On Obedience*, 231–37.
79 Lutz, *Disdain Hardships*, 78.
80 Marcus Aurelius, *Meditations* 7.66.

The specific event Marcus remembers occurred during a violent political purge orchestrated by a group of Athenian oligarchs known as the "Thirty Tyrants." Socrates, for his part, had been ordered to arrest an honest and respected opponent of the regime, an order he refused to carry out. Years later, in his defense before the Athenian court, Socrates cited the event as evidence of his own unwavering integrity. Specifically, he explained such orders had been deliberately calculated to create as many accomplices as possible to the oligarchy's criminal agenda, thereby entrenching their control. Fearing complicity in injustice more than death, he refused, and only escaped immediate punishment due to the oligarchy's subsequent collapse.[81]

Confronted with moral ambiguity like Socrates faced, the philosophical warrior can find clarity with reference to a virtuous country. Just as it is a tenet of virtue ethics that one should act as a virtuous individual acts, so also should a country act as a virtuous country does. The morality of collective actions, then, can be regarded in this light, which provides essential context when evaluating appropriate action for an individual. Thus Cicero cites Posidonius to describe some actions:

> … so degrading and others so criminal, that no man of wisdom would perform them, even to save his country … so the wise man will not undertake these on behalf of the state, and the state will not even wish to have them undertaken on its behalf. But happily enough, no situation can arise when it is in the interest of the state that a wise man should perform any such acts.[82]

Just as a virtuous individual would be destroyed as such by violating his moral integrity, so too might a virtuous country. To perform in the role of a country's moral agent, then, does not absolve one of responsibility for individual acts, rather, it burdens one with a share of responsibility in the collective moral fate. Paradoxically, this affords an escape from the dreadful dilemma of choosing between one's country and one's soul. If an act with terribly dispreferred consequences is justified by exceptional circumstances, then it is justified, period. On the other hand, a truly dishonorable collective action cannot save an honorable country, but it might well destroy it.

None of this is to say philosophical warriors can arbitrarily pick and choose which orders to follow. For disobedience to be justified, a high burden of proof must be overcome. Moreover, the legal standard for justified disobedience is different from the moral standard—that of natural law—and these are evaluated separately. Let us illustrate with a modern example.

Suppose an operator of an uncrewed aerial system (UAS) disagrees with her commander's decision to service a particular target, believing the attack poses excessive risk to noncombatants. Note that commanders are not required to eliminate all

---

81 Plato, *Apology* 32c–d. Coincidentally, the Thirty Tyrants' purge is referenced in Diogenes Laertius's commentary on Zeno, where it is noted that fourteen hundred citizens were executed at the very same painted porch from which the Stoics would later derive their name. See DL 7.5.
82 Cicero, *On Duties* 1.159.

risk to noncombatants, nor would it be feasible to do so. Their responsibility is to ensure any attacks meet the standards of necessity and proportionality, meaning the military value of destroying a target must outweigh the potential harm to noncombatants. While there are standardized frameworks for evaluating such decisions, the judgments involved are often ultimately subjective. Commanders must make reasonable determinations based on the information available to them, carefully balancing military objectives with the potential consequences. These consequences include not only the harm to noncombatants but also the likely downstream effects of failing to perform the mission.

Once a commander has determined the destruction of a target justifies the risks to civilians, subordinates are legally required to follow the order, even if they personally might have made a different judgment based on the available information.[83] In such situations, the commander's professional competence must be presumed, while coherence of collective action rests upon that presumption. The responsibility to disobey illegal orders does not grant individuals the license to disobey every order they find legally questionable. Similarly, moral autonomy does not necessarily give one reason to disobey every order they find morally questionable. A high burden of proof must be overcome in either event.

For our UAS operator, disobedience would plainly fall short of a legal justification, but it might still warrant a moral justification. For Stoics, this difference in standards maps onto Epictetan role ethics, particularly in the distinction between specific roles and the fundamental role of a reasoning human (Figure 8). Obligations attendant to the specific role of warrior would represent the legal standard—to obey all lawful orders is *consequent* from that specific role. That is a warrior's duty.

However, whether or not obedience is *reasonable*, given all available information and contributing factors, would specifically speak to the fundamental role—that "force of nature" articulable as natural law. It is according to this standard that a moral evaluation is conducted, and to independently conduct it is a *human's* duty. It is possible sufficient evidence might accumulate to make obedience to even lawful orders intolerable.

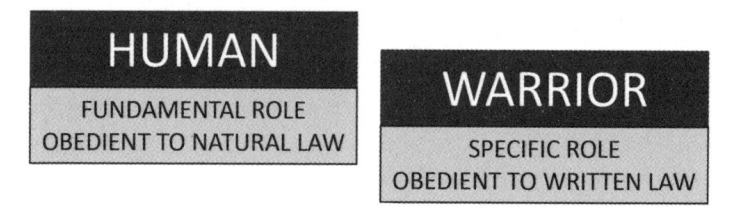

HUMAN
FUNDAMENTAL ROLE
OBEDIENT TO NATURAL LAW

WARRIOR
SPECIFIC ROLE
OBEDIENT TO WRITTEN LAW

Figure 8. Priority of roles and sources of legal authority.

---

83 Ford, "When Can a Soldier Disobey an Order?"

Virtually all thinkers in the just-war tradition agree warriors are morally justified—even if not legally justified—to disobey orders they find morally intolerable.[84] This is still an exceptionally high standard and the mere presence of uncertainty or disagreement is not necessarily sufficient to warrant disobedience. Even for a sage, avoiding the certain disruption to military order and the coherence of collective action might outweigh uncertain concerns about the necessity and proportionality of a specific decision.[85] This is more likely when those concerns are based on incomplete information and are weighed against the tangible negative consequences of failing to execute the mission. For a conflicted individual, the specific role of a warrior may "tip the balance" in determining the appropriate course of action for a reasoning human being.

A final note of caution regarding justified disobedience: while nearly all just-war theorists agree warriors are right to disobey orders they find morally intolerable, few, if any, make room for duplicity, subversion, or sabotage. Such underhanded activities are typically rationalized to avoid the consequences of disobedience—consequences the Stoics would regard as morally indifferent. True justified disobedience, on the other hand, must be executed openly, with clear and professional communication of the rationale behind it. It generally should not come as a surprise; instead, efforts should be made to persuade and consider alternatives before taking the step of refusal.

Critically, justified disobedience must be undertaken with full awareness and acceptance of the consequences, which, again, are morally indifferent from a Stoic perspective. Faced with undesired orders, a warrior's choices are clear: either execute the order *well* or refuse it and own whatever follows. There is no room for poor or begrudging execution. Making bad plans and incompetent superiors successful is part of being a warrior, but poor execution of an immoral or illegal order only creates more accomplices to it. Moreover, poor execution, in lieu of open refusal, subverts an essential feedback loop to higher echelons, undermining the opportunity for commanders to recognize and correct flaws in their plans or their people.

Remorse

When a fundamental human duty, such as non-maleficence, is overridden, many thinkers argue it should continue to impose a burden on the actor—if not through their actions, then in their mental attitudes and dispositions. Some modern philosophers refer to these residual effects as "moral traces."[86] The underlying idea, however, is not new. As far back as Augustine, it was argued the destruction of war—even

---

84 Cf. Martin Cook's assertion that principled disobedience is a high manifestation of military professionalism. Cook, *The Moral Warrior*, 63–64.
85 Cf. McMahan, *Killing in War*, 70–76.
86 Childress, "Just War Theories," 260–61.

when justified—should weigh on the conscience of its participants. For Augustine, wars should not only be just but also "mournful."[87]

The Stoics would likely approach this situation somewhat differently. Consider our earlier example of the conflicted UAS operator. Suppose that, despite her initial reservations, she ultimately chose to follow orders and engaged the targets in question. Later, she learns that while the intended targets were successfully destroyed, several noncombatants were also killed. Stoicism offers specific insights into how she might reflect on her actions. Two key Stoic claims weigh on this question:

- There is no such thing as a "justified" or "lesser" evil. An action is either appropriate, as "conditioned by the circumstances," or it is not.
- We exist in the present. The past, being beyond our power, can be neither good nor bad but indifferent.

Provided the operator was justified in performing her duties, Stoics would find later feelings of guilt or regret to be doubly nonsensical: once for regretting having done something appropriate, and twice for indulging regret at all. Even if the operator later concluded she really should have refused to obey orders, she would be mistaken to grant assent to the impression there is something bad about the past. The Stoic knife cuts away such events; they are as far removed from the person as the actions of a distant stranger.

On the surface, these claims are not especially surprising, and they follow straightforwardly from fundamental Stoic precepts. What makes them interesting is what they suggest about Stoic attitudes toward the experience of war and its long-term effects on the warrior. Widely accepted notions of appropriate remorse, necessary evils, and moral peril would find no purchase among Stoics.

For example, consider the concept of a warrior's moral risk. It is an ancient trope that warriors shoulder the dirty work of society, performing tasks repulsive on a moral level but nonetheless necessary. This idea has been adequately described as the "problem of dirty hands," where individuals, particularly in positions of power or in extreme situations, must engage in morally objectionable activities for the wider good. In this view, warriors' duties sometimes contribute to misery and death, and with that comes appropriate feelings of guilt and anguish. Just as warriors accept the physical dangers of combat, they absorb these moral burdens so others don't have to. The result is that warriors, by sacrificing their own moral purity, shield their societies not only from physical harm but from the emotional and ethical implications of the way of life they enjoy.

A recent development from the world of clinical psychology is the recognition of the lingering psychological consequences of morally objectionable experiences as a type of "moral injury," emphasizing the long-term effects of such events. While moral injury shares some features with Post-Traumatic Stress Disorder (PTSD), it is conceptually distinct. PTSD typically results from exposure to life-threatening events,

---

87 See Paolucci, *Political Writings of St. Augustine*, 162–83; Bainton, *Christian Attitudes toward War and Peace*, 98.

with symptoms like flashbacks and severe anxiety, whereas moral injury arises from a perceived violation of one's deeply held convictions or sense of human nature. This can stem not only from morally troubling actions taken but also from actions not taken, such as failing to intervene as appropriate to prevent an unjust act. Actions not taken might even refer to a failure to experience the expected emotions in response to extreme or shocking events. Symptoms of moral injury often include debilitating guilt, shame, and depression.

Some argue moral injury should be further divided into the subcategories of moral trauma and moral degradation, reflecting the different ways it can manifest. In this framing, moral trauma occurs when individuals are unable to function normally due to overwhelming feelings of guilt or shame, often tied to a specific past action or experience. In contrast, moral degradation refers to a long-term dampening of expected emotional responses to events that would typically evoke guilt, horror, or revulsion. If this latter category truly represents a kind of moral injury, then it is arguable the emotionally desensitizing aspects of combat training represent a deliberate infliction of moral injury onto military trainees.[88]

Stoics would probably reject this entire line of thinking. The effects of moral degradation, as described, would be indistinguishable from the emotional equanimity of a Stoic sage, who would regard the carnage and misery of war as dispreferred indifferents. For Stoics, these are external events that hold no bearing on one's moral character and should be met with rational detachment rather than emotional turmoil. Far from viewing such insensitivity as deficient, Stoics would actively cultivate it, rejecting the notion one should "try to feel" expected emotions or consider oneself defective for not experiencing them. Similarly, Stoics would interpret the effects of moral trauma as an internal failure to properly distinguish between the present, where the moral self exists, and the past, which is indifferent and beyond one's power. Even when past actions are indefensible, Stoics would argue those actions do not belong to us and might as well have been performed by another person. Consequently, they would reject the framing of remorse as a lasting injury, denying it is either necessary or reasonable for the effects of moral trauma to persist over time.

Consider, for example, the way Stoics might evaluate two very different real outcomes from a shared wartime action. Once again, our example is from the Second World War; this time, the action in question is the destruction of Hiroshima with an atomic bomb. Colonel Paul Tibbets, the pilot of the aircraft that dropped the bomb, was relatively untroubled by the experience, continuing his military career with distinction and retiring as a brigadier general in the United States Air Force. In stark contrast, Major Claude Eatherly, who commanded the reconnaissance aircraft that flew ahead of *Enola Gay*, spent the rest of his life haunted by his role in the mission. Eatherly suffered from recurring nightmares, attempted suicide, and was

---

88 Dobos, *Ethics, Security, and the War Machine*, 14–39.

compulsorily detained in psychiatric hospitals. He committed petty crimes with the apparent intent to get caught, such as check forgery for a trivial sum and a robbery in which he took no money. He would later write he felt happier in jail because the punishment allowed him a "release of guilt."[89]

What actually constitutes mental health and illness is an eternally debatable question, particularly considering the relative immaturity of psychology as a field of study. Without weighing in on these debates or making any comment on whether Hiroshima's destruction was justified, we can state with reasonable confidence that Stoics would evaluate Tibbets's disposition toward his wartime actions as healthy and appropriate while viewing Eatherly's as unhealthy and inappropriate. It is not unreasonable to argue Tibbets should have been deeply disturbed by his role in Hiroshima's destruction and was somehow deficient for not displaying the expected emotions. However, from a Stoic perspective, his ability and determination to carry on with a productive and harmonious life is precisely what "right" looks like. In contrast, Eatherly's pitiable and debilitated state—with significant consequences for anyone who might depend on him—clearly exemplifies the kind of internal disturbance and incoherence Stoics strive to eliminate.

It would be irresponsible not to acknowledge that the Stoics predated the formal discipline of psychology by millennia. While their insights into the human mind remain profound, we know far more today about how the mind works than the Stoics could have imagined, even if we still have only scratched its surface. As such, their teachings should not be interpreted as a replacement for clinical psychiatric care when such treatment is necessary. However, Stoic methods, patterns of thought, and reasoning closely align with many contemporary, evidence-based therapeutic practices. Their value may lie particularly in prevention—helping individuals build resilience and mental clarity before challenges or crises emerge—a possibility that will be revisited in the epilogue.

We should also acknowledge that many thinkers convincingly argue remorse plays an important role in regulating behavior and preserving moral accountability. From this perspective, remorse serves as an internal feedback system, helping individuals recognize when they have violated ethical norms and prompting reflection and a commitment to avoid similar actions in the future.[90] Similarly, the concepts of appropriate "mournfulness" and lingering "moral traces" of overridden duties provide a different regulative effect, acting as damping mechanisms or safeguards against excesses—even when performing actions accepted as necessary and appropriate.

The constructive aspects of these psychological processes are not suppressed in Stoicism but are instead delivered via other means, arguably with fewer negative side effects. The regulative function of "moral traces," for example, would be achieved through the constant reassessment of overridden duties at every juncture,

---

89 Glover, *Humanity*, 100–101.
90 Walzer, "Dirty Hands," 171–74.

as required when appropriate actions are morally heterogeneous. This persistent cycle of reevaluation would be mediated by a cosmopolitan ethic that views all humans as fellow citizens of the wider universe.

Similarly, the Stoic concept most akin to a "useful" or "regulative" guilt is the rational emotion of *aidōs*—a forward-looking sense of caution against behaviors that might invite justified condemnation. Epictetus refers to *aidōs* as "shame," and, in Chapter 2, I identified it as the Stoic counterpart to what we commonly call "honor" today. Instead of relying on remorse after the fact, a Stoic's conduct in war would be guided ex ante by honor—the constant and vigilant scrutiny of one's own moral witness. Backward-looking feedback would not manifest as emotions like guilt or regret but would instead take the form of disciplined and dispassionate reflection, as exemplified in the *Meditations* of Marcus Aurelius.

The Warrior-Philosopher

In writing this book, I have sought to present the ancient philosophy of Stoicism in a way both relevant and meaningful to members of my community of practice, the profession of arms. I have done so for several reasons, including to address unresolved questions about the compatibility of Stoic principles with this profession and as well as to highlight potential avenues for future exploration. Above all, however, my mission has been to inspire genuine warriors to become better in all of the ways that matter.

In many respects, we are the sum of what we consume, and this truth applies as much to our intellectual existence as it does to our physical bodies. When we engage with ideas, we are inevitably altered for better or worse. This reality places a profound moral responsibility on those who would put ideas into the world, requiring that those ideas are both sound and constructive. With this in mind, I have attempted to distill Stoic philosophy into a form that not only informs but also strengthens, offering tools for self-improvement and moral clarity for those who navigate the most hazardous terrain.

I do not claim Stoicism is without flaws, nor do I suggest anyone should accept its claims wholesale or on the authority of their vessels. No set of received wisdom should be accepted in that way. Ideas must stand on their own merits. As stated in this book's introduction, I advocate for an eclectic approach—one that incorporates claims and ideas independently of their source, provided the end result is a coherent and harmonious worldview.

It is the nature of philosophical discourse that the most important claims are often unverifiable. How, for instance, might we prove whether the events of fate are predetermined, or whether a collective possesses an identity beyond the sum of its parts? Such ideas can only serve as precepts—assumptions upon which broader and more sophisticated concepts are built. When these larger, macro-concepts are not only compatible but also mutually reinforcing, they give rise to a resilient and coherent philosophy. Stoicism, I suggest, is the premier example of such a philosophy.

If we aim to evaluate the virtue of a thing, be it a knife, a horse, or a human being, then we ask how well it does what it is supposed to do. We would do well, then, to ask the same of a philosophy, beginning with the degree to which it agrees with itself—that is, the degree to which its claims fit together. For a moral philosophy, the most crucial indicator of this internal coherence lies in its expression through action. This raises two distinct questions. First, what kinds of behaviors are *supposed* to arise from this philosophy? And, second, what kinds of behaviors *actually do* arise from it?

In the case of Stoicism, to answer the first question we would essentially describe a sage—the perfect "wise person" who embodies all Stoic principles to their fullest degree. Such an accounting would adequately summarize the principal ideas explored throughout this book. However, if we aim to present Stoicism in a way relevant to the profession of arms, it is more fitting to place the sage within this specific context. Stoic warriors, so described, would necessarily be philosophical warriors, defined by their appropriate actions as exemplars of virtue.

As I have emphasized, moral virtues and martial virtues are fundamentally inseparable—they are simply virtues. Using Stoicism as a point of departure for what a coherent philosophy looks like, then, we can describe the ideal philosophical warrior, or warrior-philosopher, with reference to the Stoic concept of a sage. To wit, this is what we can say about Stoic warriors:

- Stoic warriors are reverent of the rationality in nature, accepting all events as they occur. They carefully focus their energies on what they can control, dismissing what they cannot. They steel themselves for the dispreferred, thinking through every detail such that, when it occurs, it is as if they have been there before.
- Stoic warriors are fiercely committed to truth and reason. They question everything, exercising prudence as to the time and place of this questioning. They view knowledge as an unalloyed good, recognizing the tiny fraction of information they command is negligible compared to what they do not know. Recognizing professional competence as a moral obligation, they are relentlessly dedicated to mastering their craft.
- Stoic warriors identify their moral integrity as no less a part of who they are than their physical bodies, and they protect it with the same force of self-preservation. They attend to their duties as warriors in accordance with their duties as human beings, never prioritizing the former over the latter. When possible, they seek harmony between their various roles, making choices informed by all competing responsibilities. They hold themselves accountable, accepting no deficiency of character as permanent or beyond correction.

- Stoic warriors do not seek war. They view war as the result of human folly and its destructive consequences as dispreferred indifferents that are rationally to be avoided. They consider the profession of arms both honorable and necessary, even if not appropriate for everyone, yet they would welcome a just world where it is no longer required. To them, all wars are civil wars, as all humans—combatants and noncombatants alike—are fellow citizens of a higher country. When circumstances require violence, they act with a clear conscience, adhering to principles of necessity, proportionality, and discrimination to the best of their ability.
- Stoic warriors do not look to collective causes to justify their actions, because no external justification could ever suffice. Instead, they approach their duties with eyes open to all available information and willingly embrace responsibility for what they do. They do not indulge mournfulness or remorse about their past actions. Recognizing the past as indifferent, they do not harbor regret.
- Stoic warriors are naturally skeptical, withholding assent to impressions they cannot confirm and remaining cautious in their judgments. While they understand the limits of what they can possibly know, they also recognize the complexity of collective tasks and the necessity of justified trust in the institutions to which they belong. As warriors, they are predisposed to obey legitimate authority. However, they disobey when appropriate—whether in service of their commanders' intent, written laws, or a higher natural law. In all circumstances, they remain invulnerable to duress and coercion, with moral autonomy beyond compromise.
- Stoic warriors are deeply patriotic and devoted to the material and moral welfare of their country, which serves as their point of access to the greater human community. As citizens and warriors, they bear specific responsibilities toward their country that do not extend to others, just as they bear specific responsibilities toward close friends, family, and comrades-in-arms. Their patriotism is philosophically grounded and resistant to impulses of chauvinism or arrogance. They understand themselves as microcosms of their country and as determinative contributors to its collective character.
- Stoic warriors are indifferent to prestige or glory. They care nothing for external honors or reputation. Their concept of honor is a forward-looking protectiveness of self-respect and, as such, it is unassailable by outside forces. They are not motivated by vengeance and do not entertain anger or despair. They understand all virtues as applications of prudence, with courage being prudence in what is to be endured. They are not reckless but do not fear death.

Such qualities, it must be emphasized, represent an ideal. If we are to say anything meaningful about the underlying philosophy, we must first affirm this ideal is a good one. I unequivocally submit that it is, for it describes not only a heroic warrior but an impeccable human being—someone whose actions and behaviors would pass the test of coherence. To repurpose the favored exemplars of Seneca and Epictetus, these are the qualities we admire in the Spartans at Thermopylae, yet they transcend martial heroism to exemplify humanity itself. Whether this standard is realistically achievable is, in the end, beside the point. What matters is knowing where the standard lies.

Accepting this standard, we arrive at the second aspect of our evaluation: do the behaviors, the patterns of thought and action, promoted by this philosophy actually follow from its fundamental claims? Even if such a standard can never be fully achieved, does not the thoughtful consideration of its key precepts still move us closer to the ideal? When one interacts with these ideas, are they altered in a good way?

Answers to these questions will not be found in dust-covered tomes but in a mirror. As the Stoics repeatedly emphasize, the purpose of philosophy is not to provide essay topics for theorists or fodder for poseurs to talk about at parties. Philosophy is for practitioners, whose project is always a work in progress. To answer the question, then, we return to the language of Epictetus: *That*, the weathered old trainer would say, *is up to us*.

Epilogue

> There surely exists a medicine for the soul—it is philosophy. We must seek its help not from the outside, as we do with bodily ailments. We must exert ourselves intensely, deploying all our efforts and powers, so that we can act as our own healers.
> CICERO, *TUSCULAN DISPUTATIONS* 3.3 TRANS. CURTIUS.

Advanced societies across the globe are gripped by a crisis in mental health, driven by the convergence of new and modern pressures with timeless social ills. Inescapable news feeds are individually tailored to maximize anxiety and anger, while traditional spaces for interpersonal contact have been supplanted by virtual interactions that magnify these stressors. Social media, with its endless parade of curated perfection, exacerbates feelings of inadequacy and isolation. The impact of this crisis is particularly evident in the military, as growing emotional challenges among young adults shrink the pool of eligible recruits and erode the resilience of those already serving.

It is by no means assured humanity will fully recover from this state. Persistent epidemics like obesity and substance abuse illustrate that self-destructive patterns of thought and behavior can crystallize into a "new normal," even when ample resources and information are provided to counteract them. Throughout history, humans have sometimes failed to adapt effectively to their circumstances, resulting in prolonged periods of degraded societal health and diminished quality of life. The current mental-health crisis may represent yet another cycle of species-wide decline, as the forces driving it—social, economic, and technological—show no sign of abating.

Against this growing demand strains a vast and increasingly specialized mental-health industry. Practitioners include psychiatrists, who are medical doctors, and psychotherapists, who include the amalgam of psychologists, licensed counselors, social workers, and pastoral professionals. Psychiatrists diagnose mental-health disorders and prescribe medications to manage symptoms, while psychotherapists address emotional and psychological challenges through talk therapy and cognitive or behavioral interventions. Notably, most psychiatric treatments also integrate some form of psychotherapy, but the reverse is not true; psychotherapy is often appropriate for issues that do not require a medicalized approach.

The most extensively practiced and researched approach to psychotherapy is called Cognitive-Behavioral Therapy (CBT). A robust body of evidence supports its effectiveness for a wide range of mental-health conditions, including depression and anxiety disorders, and it is consistently endorsed in clinical guidelines specifically because of this strong empirical foundation. Authorities in the field consider it the "gold standard" of psychotherapy.[1] Fascinatingly, the most influential pioneers of CBT were deeply read in the Stoics; this is evidenced in their writings, quotations, and prescriptions. Many of CBT's fundamental practices are either paralleled by, or directly based upon, mental techniques the Stoics emphasized, although their philosophical origins are often obscured by technical lingo.

For example, the earliest forms of CBT emphasize the interruption of "autosuggestions" or "automatic thoughts," or, in other words, what Stoics would call the testing of impressions.[2] Additionally, a particularly influential form of CBT is called Rational Emotive Behavior Therapy (REBT), which stresses the role of irrational beliefs in emotional disturbances. A key tenet of REBT is recognizing emotions are shaped not by events but by our beliefs about them—a practice called "cognitive mediation."[3] Other techniques include resisting the judgment that adverse events are inherently bad—or "decatastrophizing"—and the mental exercise of visualizing future hardships, termed "rational-emotive imagery."[4] The therapist who developed REBT directly cited the writings of Seneca, Epictetus, and Marcus Aurelius as his inspiration.[5]

Despite these philosophical origins, it is important we do not infer psychotherapists are simply 'doing Stoicism'. While both Stoicism and CBT emphasize the importance of rational thinking and the management of emotions, CBT is a structured, evidence-based therapeutic approach developed through rigorous psychological research. Stoicism is nothing of the sort and does not claim to be. Consider that humans developed the practice of winemaking without knowledge of microbiology, and we recognized that chewing on the bark of a willow tree could relieve pain long before understanding that salicylic acid—the active compound—could be synthesized as aspirin. Like other ancient practices, Stoic mental techniques have been validated by time and evidence, even if the underlying mechanisms are only recently becoming understood.

It would be irresponsible, then, to prescribe Stoicism to someone in need of psychotherapy. Where Stoicism offers great promise, however, is as a preventive. A key component of all forms of CBT is the emphasis on self-treatment and proactive measures. By inculcating the tools to recognize and modify one's own thought

---

1 David, Cristea, and Hofmann, "Why Cognitive Behavioral Therapy Is the Current Gold Standard," Art. 4.
2 Robertson, *Philosophy of CBT*, 21ff. For senior military leaders, who must learn everything they can about mental health, Robertson's book may be particularly helpful.
3 Ibid., 117ff.
4 Cavanna, "Stoic Philosophy and Psychotherapy," 17–18.
5 Still and Dryden, *The Historical and Philosophical Context of Rational Psychotherapy*.

processes in situ, preventive therapeutic measures empower individuals to assert agency over their mental well-being, nipping potential crises in the bud. Stoicism does this as well and it further reinforces these tools with the force of a moral imperative. Stoics believe it is not just beneficial, but also morally *right* to practice healthy ways of thinking.

Viewed in this context, the rise of a popular Stoicism movement is a positive and exciting development. There's no denying popular Stoicism contains a faddish element, and fads come and go. The current surge of interest in Stoicism may recede like other popular philosophy trends and alternative belief systems. But, unlike other such trends, Stoic thinking inculcates empirically validated tools to cultivate resilience, emotional stability, and clarity of thought. Insofar as popular Stoicism is a reaction to modern pressures, then, it may not be a fad but an essential *adaptation*.

Recommendations for Scholars

If Stoicism is to have a future as a mainstream moral philosophy, then it must inevitably evolve. Even the most enthusiastic students of the Stoics acknowledge the limitations of the ancient perspective. Few today, for example, would defend the theory of *pneuma* as an explanation for life processes or would tolerate grave injustices as 'assigned roles' to be properly embraced. Would-be modern Stoics, therefore, must decide which aspects of the philosophy reflect enduring truths, which are merely useful frameworks to be selectively applied, and which are relics of historical ignorance.

This book has largely sidestepped the issue of appropriate revisionism by presuming Stoics exist solely in antiquity. Such an assumption simplifies the discussion but only works within the controlled environment of a single author's argument. In the broader and less regulated sphere of popular discourse, modern Stoics exist simply because they claim to. There is little consensus on the necessary or sufficient conditions to identify as Stoic, but such diversity of opinion is part of any philosophical movement's reality.

It may be tempting to suggest questions of Stoic identity and evolution should be addressed by academic scholars rather than bloggers or self-help writers. However, the truth is all of these voices influence the trajectory of Stoicism and will continue to do so. There is no unified Stoic *ecclesia* to arbitrate such matters, and any claims to centralized authority would, and rightly should, be eagerly dismissed by independent thinkers. In philosophy, disputes are not resolved by secluded magistrates but settled in the arena of open discourse. The best ideas tend to prevail, regardless of their source.

Popular influencers, then, may ultimately play a more significant role in shaping the future of Stoicism than academic theorists. Many of the concepts introduced in this project could contribute meaningfully to these broader conversations. For instance, the proposal of a responsibility heuristic and the equivalence of *aidōs* to honor might assist in translating complex moral concepts into accessible, practical terms. Additionally, as a metaphor for the utility of *prohairesis*, the Stoic knife illustrates Epictetan moral choice more comprehensively than the reductive and frequently misapplied 'dichotomy of control'. Each of these ideas has the potential to enrich Stoicism's ongoing evolution in both academic and popular contexts.

Still, certain questions involve specialized expertise and thus will likely remain the domain of professional scholars. One such area is the Stoic theory of emotions. Although Stoic mental practices and habits of thought are widely understood as healthy and therapeutic, the conceptual framework underlying them lacks the benefit of modern psychological research and may even conflict with empirical findings. Scholars who are sympathetic to Stoicism have acknowledged these shortcomings. Philosopher Nancy Sherman, for example, has drawn from her experience teaching military ethics at the United States Naval Academy to examine the relationship between Stoicism and military culture. Despite her broader endorsement of the Stoics as a positive influence on the military, Sherman cautions that strict adherence to an orthodox view can be counterproductive—or even harmful—when applied to complex psychological challenges like moral injury or post-traumatic stress.[6]

What, then, might a modernized Stoic theory of emotions entail? Philosopher Martha Nussbaum's cognitive-evaluative theory of emotions stands out as a compelling starting point. Deeply sympathetic to the Stoics, Nussbaum has described her approach as "neo-Stoic," fusing ancient philosophical insights with empirical evidence and contemporary psychological frameworks. She interprets emotions as intelligent, complex responses that *express* rationality as much as they complicate it, effectively rejecting the orthodox Stoic separation of passions from rational emotions.[7] She does not shy from disagreeing with the ancient Stoics, but if we are to think like philosophers, then neither should we.

Irrespective of popular Stoicism and its inevitable evolution, there are other areas of this project where additional investigation might yield valuable insights for scholars. For example, there is the Hieroclean approach to collective moral identity, which may have applications in fields like political science, international relations, or business ethics, particularly as synthesized with frameworks like Peter A. French's theory of corporate moral agency. For example, we might fully develop a Stoic-influenced concept of moral progress at the scale of a Hieroclean collective, such as when a community transitions from irrational group behavior to a conscious state of moral agency. Such investigations might shed light upon problems of social

---

6 See Sherman, *Stoic Warriors*, 122–29; *Stoic Wisdom*, 134–50.
7 See Nussbaum, *Upheavals*, 19–88ff.

responsibility and the tension between communitarian and cosmopolitan principles. Additionally, we might consider the existence of Epictetan social roles at the scale of nations, such as an economic power that catalyzes scientific and cultural progress, or a military power that preserves international law and order. Such roles would naturally impose obligations and prohibitions on the collective, grounded in virtue and guided by a community-scale faculty of reason.

Another promising area for further scholarly exploration is the Stoics' naturalistic concept of duty, which is rooted in the view that *consequentiality* is that which naturally follows from a given set of conditions. Recall that the pursuit of normally preferred indifferents, such as health or wealth, operates under the same logical structure as the performance of normally required moral actions, like preserving innocent life or telling the truth. In any event, the *reasonableness* of a given action may be overridden by specific circumstances, as negotiated by a fully informed faculty of reason. This closely parallels W. D. Ross's concept of prima facie duty, which similarly acknowledges that apparent moral obligations can yield to more important priorities under certain conditions. While we have applied this parallel to articulate a Stoic theory of just war, the same approach could be adapted to other moral problems involving competing principles and obligations.

Recommendations for the Military

Despite harboring deep personal sympathies for the Stoics and their way of thinking, I have sought to present their philosophy in as objective a light as possible. This book was written to inform, not to recruit or persuade, and certainly not to advocate for any institutional action. However, as a military officer addressing an institutional audience, it would feel remiss to conclude without offering some form of recommendation. To that end, I offer the following.

Military institutions should welcome any development that might improve the readiness and resilience of their people. However, there are many ways we might mishandle Stoicism. It would be a mistake, for instance, to heavy handedly integrate Stoicism into general training curricula. Such an approach would most likely elicit little more than eyerolls and disengagement. While there may be some room for Stoicism within tightly controlled performance-psychology programs, even this limited application should be considered with caution. A sensible approach in this case would be to acknowledge Stoic origins of proven mental exercises, leaving it up to trainees to investigate further on their own time if desired.

Specifically at issue is the appearance of promoting what some will inevitably interpret as a religious view. Despite the efforts of contemporary authors to downplay Stoicism's theistic elements, the inconvenient reality is that ancient Stoics spoke of God constantly—a fact apparent upon even the most cursory contact with the primary sources. In a pluralistic society, confessionally specific beliefs truly have no place within official military business, and the Stoics' theism might cross a line for some members. Today, even nonspecific religious traditions, like public prayers before official functions, are controversial and make many members uncomfortable. With due appreciation for the diversity of their charges, then, military leaders would be right to exercise caution when publicly engaging with or integrating Stoic principles into institutional practices.

A logical approach, it would seem, is to simply view Stoicism as the business of chaplains, who exist to address the military's religious requirements. In addition to providing direct ministry services to members within their respective traditions, chaplains advise and assist unit commanders with meeting the needs of their members. When individuals request reasonable accommodations, such as a regular time and space to discuss or practice religious functions with like-minded members, unit commanders tend to oblige with the support of the chaplaincy. For example, U.S. warships have long accommodated such requests from Wiccan or Norse crewmembers, alongside more mainstream groups such as Christians and Muslims.[8] If individual members desire it, Stoicism might be treated in just the same way, and such a development may be inevitable if its popularity continues to grow.

As both mental-health professionals and experts in ancient thought, chaplains should be familiar with the Stoics and would do well to have some Stoic literature on hand for interested parties. But anyone enthusiastic about Stoicism should resist the procrustean impulse to treat it as a religion. It is not one nor should it be encouraged to become one. A religious approach would needlessly place it in competition with established religious frameworks, many of which are shot through with Stoic ideas and would be complemented by deeper engagement with their own philosophical origins.[9] More importantly, a religious approach invites claims to doctrinal authority, which does not and cannot exist for Stoicism. A truly philosophical approach, in contrast, demands a fiercely independent mind, one that evaluates ideas on their own merits and challenges appeals to authority. Any compromise to that impulse would necessarily come at the expense of intellectual and moral integrity, which philosophers should view as inseparable.

For the institutional military, the appropriate response to the popular Stoicism movement should involve as light a touch as possible. Military leaders should have some familiarity with Stoicism—if not for their own personal development, then for situational awareness. Furthermore, there is ample room for unofficial, member-organized associations to explore the integration of military and philosophical

---

8 Simkins, "Heathens Hold Religious Services," *Navy Times*.
9 For example, parallels between Christian and Stoic morality are explored for a general audience in Kevin Vost's *The Porch and the Cross*. For a more academic survey of the relationship between Stoicism and early Christianity, refer to Elizabeth Cochran's *Stoicism and Christian Ethics*, available online. Cf. Grant, "St. Paul and Stoicism."

practice. There are important reasons that great warriors of history, from Pompey Magnus to James Mattis, have looked to the Stoics for guidance and inspiration. The story of James Stockdale, including his lectures and writings on Epictetus, should continue to be shared in its full, unabridged form. However, there is no need to formalize or institutionalize Stoicism within the military. Its proper place remains just under the surface, where it has always been.

Chronology of Key Figures

For quick reference, this section presents a chronological overview of prominent figures in ancient Stoicism, spanning its origins in Hellenistic Athens to its decline in imperial Rome. A graphic timeline is included for clarity, followed by brief biographical sketches of each figure (Figure 9). While a teacher-to-pupil lineage can be traced from Socrates to Chrysippus, scholarchs between him and Panaetius are excluded, as they are not discussed in this book. Regarding the late Stoics, apart from Musonius mentoring a young Epictetus, there is no concrete evidence any key figures of this period directly interacted. These concise summaries serve as a reference to situate individuals within the Stoic timeline. For further exploration, numerous online and scholarly resources are readily accessible.

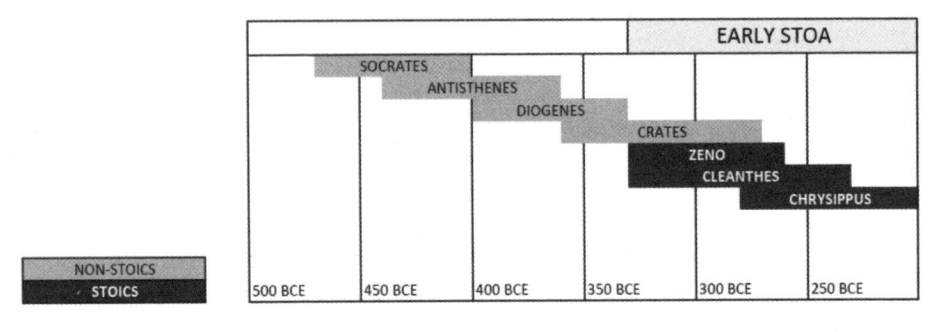

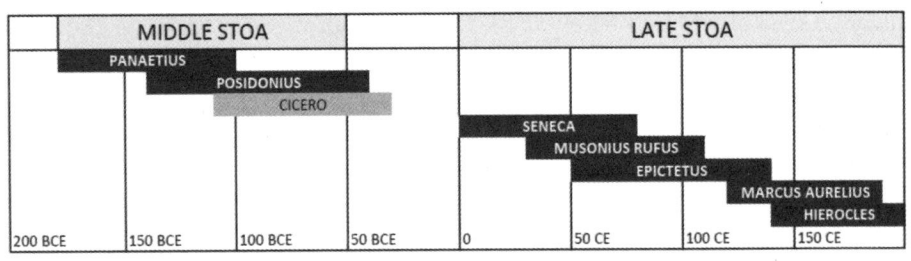

Figure 9. A timeline of key Stoic figures.

Socrates (470–399 BCE): A pivotal figure in Classical and Hellenistic philosophy, Socrates shaped the intellectual trajectory for numerous later schools of thought. Many of these groups, but particularly the Stoics, regard themselves as the rightful heirs to his philosophical legacy. Socrates demonstrated virtue is a form of knowledge and that external circumstances—such as wealth, power, or public recognition—are irrelevant to one's well-being. His emphasis on reason, virtue, and the pursuit of the good life became cornerstones of Stoic ethics. Furthermore, his steadfastness in the face of adversity, particularly during his trial and execution, exemplified the Stoic ideal of remaining rational and virtuous regardless of external conditions. Within the wider tradition of Western philosophy, Socrates' professed ignorance and practice of relentless questioning fostered a lasting emphasis on critical thinking and self-examination.

Antisthenes (444–365 BCE): A student of Socrates and the founder of Cynicism, Antisthenes emphasized virtue is the sole path to happiness and is achieved through rigorous self-discipline and moral integrity. Rejecting conventional desires for wealth, power, and pleasure, he advocated for an ascetic lifestyle free from the distractions of material possessions and societal conventions. Antisthenes believed virtue could be taught and true freedom comes from mastering one's own desires. His teachings laid the groundwork for the Cynic philosophy, which later influenced Stoicism, particularly its focus on virtue, self-sufficiency, and the rejection of external goods as necessary for a fulfilled life.

Diogenes of Sinope (400–325 BCE): The most notorious of the Cynics, Diogenes pushed the emphasis on self-sufficiency and simplicity to extremes, aggressively rejecting societal conventions and material encumbrance. Known for his provocative behavior and sharp wit, Diogenes was famously approached by Alexander the Great, who offered to grant him any wish. Diogenes, who was sunbathing at the time, replied, "Stand out of my sunlight." He used his life as a form of philosophical critique, challenging conventional values to highlight the importance of virtue and authenticity. Diogenes' uncompromising focus on living free from external status or material possessions significantly shaped the Stoic perspective, and he was admired by Epictetus as a monk-like radical.

Crates of Thebes (365–285 BCE): Born into a life of wealth, Crates chose to abandon his fortune and adopt the Cynic philosophy as a student of Diogenes. Together with his wife, fellow Cynic philosopher Hipparchia of Maroneia, he embraced a lifestyle of voluntary poverty. Crates exemplified the Cynic ideals of simplicity, self-control, and living in harmony with nature, rejecting societal norms and material wealth. His teachings emphasized personal integrity, detachment from external possessions, and the pursuit of virtue. As a mentor to Zeno, Crates significantly influenced the development of Stoicism, particularly its emphasis on virtue as the highest good and the value of inner strength over external conditions.

Zeno of Citium (335–263 BCE): The founder of the Stoic school of philosophy, Zeno established Stoicism around 300 BCE in Athens, teaching at the Stoa Poikile, which gave the school its name. Drawing on ideas from earlier thinkers, such as Socrates, Heraclitus, and the Cynics, Zeno developed the foundational doctrines of Stoicism, emphasizing the pursuit of virtue as the highest good, living in accordance with nature, and the importance of rationality and self-discipline. Zeno divided Stoicism into three parts: logic, ethics, and physics, integrating them into a unified framework. His most notable innovation beyond the Cynics, however, was accommodating a natural preference among moral indifferents, which made Stoicism sustainable as a widely practiced philosophy.

Cleanthes of Assos (331–232 BCE): Zeno's immediate successor as scholarch of the Stoic school, Cleanthes embodied perseverance and dedication, working as a water-carrier to sustain himself while dutifully advancing Stoic teachings. He emphasized the unity of nature and the concept of divine reason (*Logos*), depicting the cosmos as a rational, living entity governed by providence. Cleanthes is best remembered for his *Hymn to Zeus*, a poetic expression of Stoic principles that celebrates the interconnectedness of all things and the rational order of the universe. Although less innovative than his prodigious successor Chrysippus, Cleanthes played a crucial role in preserving and developing the Stoic tradition, grounding it firmly in both ethics and cosmology.

Chrysippus of Cilicia (280–207 BCE): The third and most influential scholarch of the Stoic school in Athens, Chrysippus is often considered a co-founder of Stoicism due to his substantial contributions to its development. Despite the near-total loss of his writings, Chrysippus reportedly authored over 700 works, primarily in defense against outside criticism. He expanded the teachings of Zeno and Cleanthes into a comprehensive philosophical system, making significant advancements in logic, ethics, and physics. Chrysippus systematized the core Stoic principles, such as the unity of virtue, the understanding of the cosmos as a rational, living entity, and the nuanced relationship between fate and free will. His intellectual rigor ensured the longevity of Stoicism, profoundly influencing later thinkers and cementing its status as one of the most enduring schools of ancient philosophy.

Panaetius of Rhodes (185–109 BCE): The eclectic middle Stoa began under the leadership of Panaetius, who infused Stoicism with beliefs from the Platonic, Aristotelian, and Academic Skeptic traditions. After studying with Stoics in Athens, he spent time in Rome, where he mentored a variety of key statesmen and likely aided the eventual rise of the late Stoa. Panaetius dismissed utopian political visions like Plato's *Republic*, instead supporting the Roman governmental structure and viewing imperialism as a justified means of imposing order. While his writings and much of his thought have been lost, his treatise *On Duties* endures indirectly through its profound influence on Cicero's masterful work of the same title. Panaetius is the last undisputed scholarch of the Stoic school in Athens, which effectively disintegrated amid the political turmoil of the First Mithridatic War.

Posidonius of Apamea (135–55 BCE): Panaetius' most famous pupil is Posidonius, a polymath who established a Stoic school in Rhodes after the fall of Athens. Renowned for his vast intellectual pursuits, Posidonius integrated Stoic philosophy with the scientific and cultural advancements of his era. As a philosopher, historian, and scientist, he explored fields such as astronomy, geography, and psychology, highlighting the interconnectedness of the cosmos and humanity's role within it. His studies on emotions, particularly their physiological and psychological dimensions, left a lasting impact on later Stoics like Seneca. In addition to his intellectual achievements, Posidonius was an accomplished statesman, serving as an ambassador for Rhodes and maintaining relationships with prominent Romans, including Pompey and Cicero. Although only fragments of his work remain intact today, he is widely praised by subsequent thinkers, including Seneca, as one of Western philosophy's most influential thinkers.

Marcus Tullius Cicero (106–43 BCE): Although formally an Academic Skeptic, this Roman statesman and philosopher admired the Stoics' ideas and incorporated many of their principles into his own eclectic philosophy, especially those regarding ethics, leadership, and natural law. Having served as consul during a time of political crisis, Cicero earned a reputation for fervent patriotism and unwavering dedication to the principles of the Roman Republic. His writings remain invaluable sources on the teachings of early and middle Stoics. Furthermore, his selective adaptations of Stoicism offer a compelling model for modern practitioners, demonstrating how to honor key principles while maintaining intellectual independence. His work *On Duties* (*De Officiis*) has long been esteemed as a fundamental text in leadership education, and it might be reasonably considered a work of middle Stoic philosophy.

Lucius Annaeus Seneca (Seneca the Younger) (4 BCE–65 CE): A Roman statesman and dramatist who wrote extensively on Stoic ethics, focusing on resilience, self-control, and the art of living. Like Cicero, he took an eclectic approach, often citing outside philosophers like Epicurus, but, unlike Cicero, he also personally identified as a Stoic. As an adviser to Emperor Nero, Seneca's life reflected the tensions between philosophical ideals and political realities. His writings, particularly the moral epistles, can probably be interpreted with some accuracy as works of a burdened man reflecting upon the vicissitudes of an intense and turbulent life. His experience of maneuvering and surviving at the highest levels of a hazardous political environment invests his thinking with a note of practicality not reflected by other Stoics. He is also a downright beautiful writer and his moral epistles are often recommended as an introduction to ancient Stoicism.

Musonius Rufus (30–100 CE): A Roman Stoic and mentor of Epictetus who emphasized the importance of practical ethics and virtue, demonstrating keen interest in family and social relationships. He advocated for philosophy as a way of life, focusing on the application of Stoic principles to everyday challenges. His teachings on gender equality, education, and moderation influenced the broader Stoic tradition by highlighting the role of virtue in fostering harmonious communities. Though less renowned today than his student Epictetus, Musonius' emphasis on practical wisdom and ethical conduct remains central to Stoicism's enduring appeal.

Epictetus (50–138 CE): A former Phrygian slave turned Roman philosopher who emphasized the power of mastering one's mind and desires to achieve true freedom. As a key figure of the late Stoa, his teachings, preserved in *the Discourses* and *the Handbook (Enchiridion)* profoundly influenced both ancient and modern thought on self-discipline and resilience. His focus on the distinction between what is within our power and what is not became a cornerstone of popular Stoic philosophy. Epictetus' legacy endures as a guide for personal empowerment and ethical living, shaping later philosophical traditions and contemporary practices such as Cognitive-Behavioral Therapy.

Marcus Aurelius (121–180 CE): Roman emperor and philosopher whose *Meditations* reflect a Stoic approach to duty, impermanence, and self-control. Recognized as the last of the "Five Good Emperors" of Rome, Marcus Aurelius exemplified the dutiful application of Stoicism, emphasizing rationality and virtue amid the immense pressures of political life. His *Meditations*, written as personal reflections and not intended for publication, became one of the most influential works in Western philosophy, inspiring leaders and thinkers throughout history. Revered as a model of the benevolent monarch and philosopher-king, his legacy punctuated and solidified Stoicism as a guide for ethical leadership. His life and writings continue to shape discussions on moral responsibility and the pursuit of inner peace.

Hierocles (exact years unknown; 2nd century CE): A lesser-known Stoic philosopher, who lived around the timeframe of Marcus Aurelius, whose writings on ethics and *Cosmopolitanism* contribute importantly to modern interpretations of the Stoics' theory of expanding moral concern. His influential model of concentric circles of community emphasized the importance of cultivating relationships and moral responsibility, starting with oneself and extending outward to family, neighbors, and all of humanity. Though much of his work has been lost, fragments preserved by later writers reveal his commitment to the Stoic ideals of universal wisdom and living in harmony with nature.

Bibliography

Aikin, Scott, and Emily McGill-Rutherford. "Stoicism, Feminism and Autonomy." *Symposion* 1, no. 1 (2014): 9–22.

Annas, Julia. "My Station and Its Duties: Ideals and the Social Embeddedness of Virtue." *Proceedings of the Aristotelian Society* 102 (2002): 109–23.

Arendt, Hannah. "Organized Guilt and Universal Responsibility." In *The Portable Hannah Arendt*, edited by Peter Baehr, 146–56. London: Penguin Books, 2003.

Aristotle. *Nicomachean Ethics*. Translated by W. D. Ross. Oxford: Clarendon Press, 1926. Internet Classics Archive, n.d.

Asmis, Elizabeth, Shadi Bartsch, and Martha C. Nussbaum. "Seneca and His World." In *Anger, Mercy, Revenge: The Complete Works of Lucius Annaeus Seneca*, edited by Robert A. Kaster and Martha C. Nussbaum. Chicago: The University of Chicago Press, 2010.

Bainton, Roland H. *Christian Attitudes toward War and Peace*. New York: Abingdon Press, 1960.

Baumeister, Roy F., and Jean M. Exline. "Virtue, Personality, and Social Relations: Self-Control as the Moral Muscle." *Journal of Personality* 67 (1999): 1165–94.

Beck, Aaron T. *Cognitive Therapy and the Emotional Disorders*. Oxford: International Universities Press, 1976.

Berger, Peter. "On the Obsolescence of the Concept of Honour." In *Liberalism and Its Critics*, edited by M. K. Sandel, 149–58. Oxford: Basil Blackwell, 1984.

Birley, Anthony R. *Marcus Aurelius: A Biography*. Taylor & Francis e-Library edition. London: Routledge, 2002.

Bobzien, Susanne. "Stoic Conceptions of Freedom and Their Relation to Ethics." *Bulletin of the Institute of Classical Studies* 41, no. S68 (1997): 71–89.

Bonhöffer, Adolf Friedrich, and William O. Stephens. *The Ethics of the Stoic Epictetus: An English Translation*. Revised edition. Revisioning Philosophy, vol. 2. New York: Peter Lang, 2021.

Brennan, Tad. "Stoic Moral Psychology." In *The Cambridge Companion to the Stoics*, edited by Brad Inwood, 257–94. Cambridge Companions to Philosophy. Cambridge: Cambridge University Press, 2003.

Brunschwig, Jacques. "Stoic Metaphysics." In *The Cambridge Companion to the Stoics*, edited by Brad Inwood, 206–32. Cambridge Companions to Philosophy. Cambridge: Cambridge University Press, 2003.

Card, Claudia. *The Atrocity Paradigm: A Theory of Evil*. Oxford: Oxford University Press, 2005.

Caruso, Gregg. "Skepticism About Moral Responsibility." *The Stanford Encyclopedia of Philosophy*. Edited by Edward N. Zalta. Summer 2021 Edition. Stanford: Metaphysics Research Lab, Stanford University, 2021. https://plato.stanford.edu/archives/sum2021/entries/skepticism-moral-responsibility/.

Cavanna, Andrea E. "Stoic Philosophy and Psychotherapy: Implications for Neuropsychiatric Conditions." *Dialogues in Philosophy, Mental & Neuro Sciences* 12, no. 1 (June 1, 2019): 10–24.

Childress, James F. "Just-War Theories: The Bases, Interrelations, Priorities, and Functions of Their Criteria." In *War, Morality, and the Military Profession*, edited by Malham M. Wakin, 2nd ed., revised and updated, 256–76. Boulder, CO: Westview Press, 1986.

Cicero, M. T. *The Academic Questions, Treatise De Finibus, and Tusculan Disputations*. Translated by C. D. Yonge. London: George Bell and Sons, 1875.

Cicero, M. T. *De Legibus (On the Laws)*. Translated by David Fott. Ithaca, NY: Cornell University Press, 2014.

Cicero, M. T. *De Natura Deorum (On the Nature of the Gods)*. Translated by Francis Brooks. London: Methuen, 1896.

Cicero, M. T. *On Obligations: De Officiis*. Translated and edited by P. G. Walsh. Reissue ed. Oxford: Oxford University Press, 2008.

Cicero, M. T. *Tusculan Disputations*. Translated by Quintus Curtius. Charleston, SC: Fortress of the Mind Publications, 2021.

Cicero, M. T., and Harry Mortimer Hubbell. *Cicero in Twenty-Eight Volumes. Vol. 2: De Inventione. De Optimo Genere Oratorum. Topica*. Loeb Classical Library 386, 1949.

Cochran, Elizabeth Agnew. "Stoicism and Christian Ethics." In *St. Andrews Encyclopaedia of Theology*, edited by Brendan N. Wolfe et al. University of St. Andrews, 2022. Accessed April 18, 2025. https://www.saet.ac.uk/Christianity/StoicismandChristianEthics.

Collins, Stephanie. "Duties of Group Agents and Group Members." *Journal of Social Philosophy* 48, no. 1 (March 2017): 38–57.

Conover, P. J. "The Influence of Group Identification on Political Perception and Evaluation." *Journal of Politics* 46, no. 3 (1984): 761–85.

Cook, Martin L., ed. *The Moral Warrior: Ethics and Service in the US Military*. SUNY Series, Ethics and the Military Profession. Albany, NY: State University of New York Press, 2004.

Copleston, Frederick Charles. *Greece and Rome*. Reprint. *A History of Philosophy*, Vol. 1. London: Continuum, 2011.

David, Daniel, Ioana Cristea, and Stefan G. Hofmann. "Why Cognitive Behavioral Therapy Is the Current Gold Standard of Psychotherapy." *Frontiers in Psychiatry* 9 (2018): Article 4.

De Harven, Vanessa. "How Nothing Can Be Something: The Stoic Theory of Void." *Ancient Philosophy* 35, no. 2 (2015): 405–29.

Diogenes Laertius. *Lives of the Eminent Philosophers*. Edited by James Miller. Translated by Pamela Mensch. New York: Oxford University Press, 2018.

Diogenes Laertius. *Lives of the Eminent Philosophers*. Translated by R. D. Hicks. Loeb Classical Library. Cambridge, MA: Harvard University Press, 1925.

Diogenes Laertius. *The Lives and Opinions of Eminent Philosophers*. Translated by C. D. Yonge. London: Henry G. Bohn, 1853.

Dobos, Ned. *Ethics, Security, and the War Machine: The True Cost of the Military*. Oxford: Oxford University Press, 2022.

Dyck, Andrew R. *A Commentary on Cicero, "De Officiis."* 4th printing. Ann Arbor, MI: University of Michigan Press, 1999.

Economides, Spyros. "Kosovo." In *United Nations Interventionism, 1991–2004*, edited by Mats Berdal, 217–45. LSE Monographs in International Studies. Cambridge: Cambridge University Press, 2007.

Epictetus, Robin Hard, and Christopher Gill. *Discourses, Fragments, Handbook*. Oxford World's Classics. Oxford; New York: Oxford University Press, 2014.

Erskine, Toni, ed. *Can Institutions Have Responsibilities? Collective Moral Agency and International Relations*. Global Issues Series. Basingstoke; New York: Palgrave Macmillan, 2003.

Fabre, Cécile. *Cosmopolitan War*. Oxford: Oxford University Press, 2012.

Ferris, Iain M. *Enemies of Rome: Barbarians through Roman Eyes*. 1st ed. Stroud: Sutton, 2000.

Ferris, Iain M. *Hate and War: The Column of Marcus Aurelius in Rome*. Stroud: History Press, 2009.
Ficarrotta, J. Carl. "Are Military Professionals Bound by a Higher Moral Standard?" *Armed Forces & Society* 24, no. 1 (October 1997): 59–75.
Ford, John. "When Can a Soldier Disobey an Order?" *War on the Rocks*, July 24, 2017. Accessed October 2023. https://warontherocks.com/2017/07/when-can-a-soldier-disobey-an-order/.
Frede, Dorothea. "Stoic Determinism." In *The Cambridge Companion to the Stoics*, edited by Brad Inwood, 257–94. Cambridge Companions to Philosophy. Cambridge: Cambridge University Press, 2003.
Fredman, Leah A., Michael D. Buhrmester, Angel Gomez, William T. Fraser, Sanaz Talaifar, Skylar M. Brannon, and William B. Swann. "Identity Fusion, Extreme Pro-Group Behavior, and the Path to Defusion." *Social & Personality Psychology Compass* 9, no. 9 (September 1, 2015): 468–80.
French, Shannon E. *The Code of the Warrior: Exploring Warrior Values Past and Present*. 2nd ed. Lanham, Boulder, New York, and London: Rowman & Littlefield, 2017.
Fronto, Marcus Cornelius. *The Correspondence of Marcus Cornelius Fronto, Volume 2*. Translated by C. R. Haines. London: William Heinemann Ltd; New York: G. P. Putnam's Sons, 1920. Accessed October 2023. https://en.wikisource.org/wiki/The_Correspondence_of_Marcus_Cornelius_Fronto/Volume_2/Miscellaneous_Letters_of_Marcus_Aurelius.
Garner, Renaud-Philippe. "Why Cosmopolitan War Is an Ethics of Fantasy?" *European Review of International Studies* 7, no. 2/3 (2020): 271–92.
Gettier, Edmund L. "Is Justified True Belief Knowledge?" *Analysis* 23, no. 6 (1963): 121–123.
Glover, Jonathan. *Humanity: A Moral History of the Twentieth Century*, 2nd ed. New Haven, CT: Yale University Press, 2012.
Godwin, William. *An Enquiry Concerning Political Justice*. Vol. 1. London, 1793.
Grant, Frederick Clifton. "St. Paul and Stoicism." *The Biblical World* 45, no. 5 (1915): 268–81.
Gray, J. Glenn. *The Warriors: Reflections on Men in Battle*. Lincoln and London: University of Nebraska Press, 1959.
Hackett, Sir John Winthrop. "Society and the Soldier: 1914–18" and "The Military in the Service of the State." In *War, Morality, and the Military Profession*, edited by Malham M. Wakin, 2nd ed., revised and updated, 80–9, 104–20. Boulder, CO: Westview Press, 1986.
Hadot, Pierre. *The Inner Citadel: The Meditations of Marcus Aurelius*. Cambridge, MA: Harvard University Press, 1998.
Hart, Roland, and Steven L. Lancaster. "Identity Fusion in U.S. Military Members." *Armed Forces & Society* 45, no. 1 (January 1, 2019): 45–58.
Hierocles. *The Ethical Fragments of Hierocles*. Translated by Thomas Taylor. London: A. J. Valpy, 1822.
Hobbes, Thomas. *Elements of Philosophy: The First Section, Concerning Body*. London: R&W Leybourn, 1656.
Houlgate, Laurence D. "Virtue Is Knowledge." *The Monist* 54, no. 1, Virtue and Moral Goodness (January 1970): 142–53. Oxford University Press.
Hume, David. "Essay XVIII: Of Moral Prejudices." *Essays, Moral and Political*. Hume Texts Online. Accessed May 22, 2025. https://davidhume.org/texts/emp/mp.
Huntington, Samuel P. *The Soldier and the State: The Theory and Politics of Civil-Military Relations*, 19th ed. Cambridge, MA: Belknap Press, 2002.
Ichikawa, Jonathan Jenkins, and Matthias Steup. "The Analysis of Knowledge." *The Stanford Encyclopedia of Philosophy*. Edited by Edward N. Zalta and Uri Nodelman. Fall 2024 Edition. Stanford: Metaphysics Research Lab, Stanford University, 2024. https://plato.stanford.edu/archives/fall2024/entries/knowledge-analysis/.
Inwood, Brad, ed. *The Cambridge Companion to the Stoics*. Cambridge and New York: Cambridge University Press, 2003.

Inwood, Brad. *Ethics and Human Action in Early Stoicism*. Oxford: Oxford University Press, 1985.
Inwood, Brad. "Rules and Reasoning in Stoic Ethics." In *Topics in Stoic Philosophy*, edited by Katerina Ierodiakonou, 95–127. Oxford: Clarendon Press, 1999.
Irvine, William Braxton. *A Guide to the Good Life: The Ancient Art of Stoic Joy*. Oxford and New York: Oxford University Press, 2009.
Jedan, Christoph. *Stoic Virtues: Chrysippus and the Religious Character of Stoic Ethics*. Continuum Studies in Ancient Philosophy. London: Continuum, 2009.
Johnson, Brian E. *The Role Ethics of Epictetus: Stoicism in Ordinary Life*. Lanham, MD: Lexington Books, 2014.
Kamtekar, Rachana. "ΑΙΔΩΣ in Epictetus." *Classical Philology* 93, no. 2 (1998): 136–60.
Kant, Immanuel. *Zum Ewigen Frieden*. Translated by M. Campbell Smith. London, 1903.
Klein, Jacob. "Making Sense of Stoic Indifferents." In *Oxford Studies in Ancient Philosophy, Volume 49*, 227–81.
Klink, Maarten. "Legal Analogies in Cicero's Political Thought." *Journal of the History of Ideas* 85, no. 1 (January 1, 2024): 1–17.
Konstantakos, Leonidas D. "Stoicism and Just War Theory." *FIU Electronic Theses and Dissertations*, no. 4999, 2021.
Kropotkin, Petr Alekseevich. *Anarchism: A Collection of Revolutionary Writings*. Dover ed. Mineola, NY: Dover Publications, 2002.
Lapidge, M. "Stoic Cosmology." In *The Stoics*, edited by J. Rist, 161–85. Berkeley: University of California Press, 1978.
Lazar, Seth. "Response to Moral Wounds." *Boston Review*, October 28, 2013. Accessed November 18, 2024. https://www.bostonreview.net/forum_response/seth-lazar/.
Long, A. A. *Epictetus: A Stoic and Socratic Guide to Life*. Reprint. Oxford: Clarendon Press, 2010.
Long, A. A., and D. N. Sedley. *The Hellenistic Philosophers. 1: Translations of the Principal Sources with Philosophical Commentary*. Reprint. Cambridge: Cambridge University Press, 2010.
Lossky, Nikolay, and Natalie Duddington. "The Metaphysics of the Stoics." *Journal of Philosophical Studies* 4, no. 16 (1929): 481–9.
Lutz, Cora E., trans. *That One Should Disdain Hardships: The Teachings of a Roman Stoic*. By Musonius Rufus. With contributions by Gretchen J. Reydams-Schils. New Haven, CT and London: Yale University Press, 2020.
Mandelbrot, Benoit B. *The Fractal Geometry of Nature*. San Francisco: W. H. Freeman, 1982.
Mansfeld, Jaap. "Diogenes Laertius on Stoic Philosophy." *Elenchos* 7 (1986): 297–382.
Mattis, James. "Remarks by Secretary Mattis at the Virginia Military Institute, Lexington, Virginia." September 25, 2018.
Marcus Aurelius. *Meditations*. Annotated edition. Edited and translated by Robin Waterfield. New York: Basic Books, 2021.
McKenna, J. C. "Ethics and War: A Catholic View." *American Political Science Review* 54, no. 3 (1960): 647–58.
McMahan, Jeff. *Killing in War*. 1st paperback ed. Uehiro Series in Practical Ethics. Oxford: Clarendon Press, 2011.
Morgenthau, Hans J. *Politics Among Nations: The Struggle for Power and Peace*. New York: Knopf, 1954.
Motto, Lydia. "Seneca on Trial: The Case of the Opulent Stoic." *The Classical Journal* 61, no. 6 (1966): 254–8.
Nagel, Thomas. "War and Massacre." *Philosophy & Public Affairs* 1, no. 2 (1972): 123–44.
Nathanson, Stephen. "Is Cosmopolitan Anti-Patriotism a Virtue?" In *Patriotism: Philosophical and Political Perspectives*, edited by Igor Primoratz and Aleksandar Pavkovic, 69–82. Aldershot: Routledge, 2007.

Nightingale, Keith. "Combat, Orders and Judgement." *Small Wars Journal*, May 7, 2017.
Nisbett, Richard E., and Dov Cohen. *Culture of Honor: The Psychology of Violence in the South*. Boulder, CO: Westview Press, 1996.
Nussbaum, Martha C. "Kant and Stoic Cosmopolitanism." *Journal of Political Philosophy* 5, no. 1 (1997): 1–25.
Nussbaum, Martha C. *Upheavals of Thought: The Intelligence of Emotions*. Cambridge: Cambridge University Press, 2003.
Olsthoorn, Peter. *Honor in Political and Moral Philosophy*. Albany, NY: State University of New York Press, 2015.
Paolucci, Henry, ed. *The Political Writings of St. Augustine*. Chicago: Regnery, 1962.
Parfit, Derek. "Theories That Are Directly Self-Defeating." In *Reasons and Persons*, by Derek Parfit, 87–110. 1st ed., Oxford: Oxford University Press, 1986.
Pettit, Philip. "Responsibility Incorporated." *Ethics* 117, no. 2 (2007): 171–201.
Pinker, Steven. *The Better Angels of Our Nature: Why Violence Has Declined*. New York: Penguin Books, 2012.
Pinker, Steven. *The Blank Slate: The Modern Denial of Human Nature*. Nachdr. Penguin Books. London: Penguin, 2003.
Plato. *Complete Works*. Edited by John M. Cooper and D. S. Hutchinson. Indianapolis: Hackett Publishing Company, 1997.
Reydams-Schils, Gretchen. "Human Bonding and Oikeiōsis in Roman Stoicism." *Oxford Studies in Ancient Philosophy* 22 (January 1, 2002): 221–52.
Reydams-Schils, Gretchen *The Roman Stoics: Self, Responsibility, and Affection*. Chicago: University of Chicago Press, 2005.
Roberts, Adam. "NATO's 'Humanitarian War' over Kosovo." *Survival* 41, no. 3 (1999): 102–23.
Robertson, Donald. *The Philosophy of Cognitive-Behavioural Therapy (CBT): Stoic Philosophy as Rational and Cognitive Psychotherapy*. London: Karnac, 2010.
Ross, David. *Foundations of Ethics*. Oxford: Oxford University Press, 1939.
Ross, David. *The Right and the Good*. Edited by Philip Stratton-Lake. Oxford: Oxford University Press, 1930.
Rotter, Julian B. "Generalized Expectancies for Internal versus External Control of Reinforcement." *Psychological Monographs: General and Applied* 80, no. 1 (1966): 1–28.
Russell, Bertrand, and John Skorupski. *The Problems of Philosophy*. Oxford: Oxford University Press, 2001.
Russo, Martina, "Seneca's Flattery of Nero": *De clementia*, *Flattery in Seneca the Younger: Theory & Practice*. Oxford Academic, 2024. https://doi.org/10.1093/oso/9780192858115.003.0007.
Santas, Gerasimos. "The Socratic Paradoxes." *The Philosophical Review* 73, no. 2 (1964): 147–64.
Sartre, Jean-Paul, John Kulka, Arlette Elkaïm-Sartre. *L'Existentialisme Est Un Humanisme; Explication de L'Étranger* [Existentialism Is a Humanism; Including, A Commentary on The Stranger]. New Haven, CT: Yale University Press, 2007.
Schmekel, August. *Die Philosophie der mittleren Stoa: in ihrem geschichtlichen Zusammenhange dargestellt*. Berlin: Weidmann, 1892.
Schofield, Malcolm. *Saving the City: Philosopher-Kings and Other Classical Paradigms*. Issues in Ancient Philosophy. 1st paperback ed. London: Routledge, 2012.
Schofield, Malcolm. *The Stoic Idea of the City*. Chicago: University of Chicago Press, 1999.
Seneca, L. Annaeus, and H. M. Hine. *Natural Questions*. Chicago: The University of Chicago Press, 2010.

Seneca, L. Annaeus. *Ad Marciam de Consolatione* [Of Consolation: To Marcia, IX]. In *Minor Dialogs Together with the Dialog "De Clementia" (On Clemency)*, translated by Aubrey Stewart, 162–203. Bohn's Classical Library Edition. London: George Bell and Sons, 1900.

Seneca, L. Annaeus. *De Beneficiis* [On Benefits]. Translated by Aubrey Stewart. London: G. Bell and Sons Ltd., 1912.

Seneca, L. Annaeus. *Epistulae Morales Ad Lucilium* [Moral Epistles]. Translated by Robin Campbell. The Penguin Classics L210. Harmondsworth: Penguin, 1969.

Seneca, L. Annaeus. *Minor Dialogs Together with the Dialog "On Clemency."* Translated by Aubrey Stewart. Bohn's Classical Library Edition. London: George Bell and Sons, 1900.

Seneca, L. Annaeus. *Moral Essays, Volume II: De Consolatione ad Marciam (On Consolation to Marcia). De Vita Beata (On the Happy Life). De Otio (On Leisure). De Tranquillitate Animi (On the Tranquility of Mind). De Brevitate Vitae (On the Shortness of Life). De Consolatione ad Polybium (On Consolation to Polybius). De Consolatione ad Helviam (On Consolation to Helvia)*. Translated by John W. Basore. Loeb Classical Library 254. Cambridge, MA: Harvard University Press, 1932.

Seneca, L. Annaeus, and S. H. Braund. *De Clementia*. Oxford: Oxford University Press, 2009.

Seneca, L. Annaeus, and Roger L'Estrange. *Seneca's Morals Abstracted in Three Parts: I. De Beneficiis (Of Benefits), II. De Vita Beata, De Ira, De Clementia (Of a Happy Life, Anger, and Clemency), III. Epistulae Morales (A Miscellany of Epistles)*. Translated by Roger L'Estrange. Oxford, 2004.

Seregin, Andrei. "Stoicism and the Impossibility of Social Morality." *ΣΧΟΛΗ. Ancient Philosophy and the Classical Tradition* 13, no. 1 (2019): 58–77.

Shanks Kaurin, Pauline. *On Obedience: Contrasting Philosophies for the Military, Citizenry, and Community*. Annapolis, MD: Naval Institute Press, 2020.

Shaver, Robert. "Egoism." *The Stanford Encyclopedia of Philosophy*. Edited by Edward N. Zalta and Uri Nodelman. Spring 2023 Edition. Stanford: Metaphysics Research Lab, Stanford University, 2023. https://plato.stanford.edu/archives/spr2023/entries/egoism/.

Shay, Jonathan. *Achilles in Vietnam: Combat Trauma and the Undoing of Character*. New York: Simon & Schuster, 1994.

Sherman, Nancy. *Stoic Warriors: The Ancient Philosophy behind the Military Mind*. New York: Oxford University Press, 2005.

Sherman, Nancy. *Stoic Wisdom: Ancient Lessons for Modern Resilience*. New York: Oxford University Press, 2021.

Shue, Henry. "Bombing to Rescue? NATO's 1999 Bombing of Serbia." In *Fighting Hurt: Rule and Exception in Torture and War*. Oxford: Oxford University Press, 2016. Online edition, Oxford Academic, March 24, 2016.

Simkins, J. D. "Heathens Hold Religious Services Rooted in Norse Paganism Aboard Aircraft Carrier." *Navy Times*, January 8, 2019.

Singer, Peter. *The Expanding Circle: Ethics, Evolution, and Moral Progress*. 1st Princeton University Press, 1st paperback ed. Princeton: Princeton University Press, 2011.

Sommers, Tamler. *Why Honor Matters*. New York: Basic Books, 2018.

Sorabji, Richard. *Emotion and Peace of Mind: From Stoic Agitation to Christian Temptation*. Oxford: Oxford University Press, 2000.

Sorabji, Richard. *Gandhi and the Stoics: Modern Experiments on Ancient Values*. 1st ed. Oxford: Oxford University Press, 2012.

Stacey, Peter. "The Princely Republic." *The Journal of Roman Studies* 104 (2014): 133–54.

Still, Arthur, and Windy Dryden. *The Historical and Philosophical Context of Rational Psychotherapy: The Legacy of Epictetus*. London: Routledge, 2012.

Stockdale, James B. *Courage under Fire: Testing Epictetus' Doctrines in a Laboratory of Human Behavior*. Hoover Essays, no. 6. Stanford, California: Hoover Institution, Stanford University, 1993.

Stockdale, James B. *Thoughts of a Philosophical Fighter Pilot*. Hoover Institution Press Publication, no. 431. Stanford, California: Hoover Institution Press, 1995.

Stockdale, James B. "The World of Epictetus: Reflections on Survival and Leadership." *The Atlantic*, April 1978.

Stockdale, James B., and Sybil Stockdale. *In Love and War: The Story of a Family's Ordeal and Sacrifice during the Vietnam Years*. 1st ed. New York: Harper & Row, 1984.

Tacitus. *The Annals*. Book XV, 60–4. Edited by E. H. Blakeney. Translated by Arthur Murphy. Vol. 1. New York: E. P. Dutton and London: J. M. Dent & Sons, 1908.

Taylor, Charles. "The Politics of Recognition." In *Multiculturalism: Examining the Politics of Recognition*, edited by A. Gutmann, 25–74. Princeton: Princeton University Press, 1994.

Toynbee, Arnold. *A Study of History*. Vol. 4. 1939.

Turner, J. C. "Social Categorization and the Self-Concept: A Social Cognitive Theory of Group Behavior." In *Rediscovering Social Identity*, edited by T. Postmes and N. R. Branscombe, 243–72. New York: Psychology Press, 2010.

United States Army. "Army Values." Accessed October 21, 2024. https://www.army.mil/values/index.html.

United States Navy, Naval Sea Systems Command, 1976. *SSN-688 Class Ship Systems Manual*.

United States Navy. "Our Core Attributes." Accessed October 21, 2024. https://www.navy.mil/About/Our-Core-Attributes.

Visnjic, Jack. *The Invention of Duty: Stoicism as Deontology*. Boston: Brill, 2021.

Vost, Kevin. *The Porch and the Cross: Ancient Stoic Wisdom for Modern Christian Living*. Brooklyn, NY: Angelico Press, 2016.

Wachsmuth, Curt. "Stichometrisches und Bibliothekarisches." *Rheinisches Museum* 34 (1879): 38–51.

Wakin, Malham M. "The Ethics of Leadership I and II." In *War, Morality, and the Military Profession*, 2nd ed., revised and updated, 181–218. Boulder, CO: Westview Press, 1986.

Wakin, Malham M., ed. *War, Morality, and the Military Profession*. 2nd ed., rev. and updated. Boulder, CO: Westview Press, 1986.

Walzer, Michael. *Arguing about War*. New Haven, CT: Yale University Press, 2004.

Walzer, Michael. *Just and Unjust Wars: A Moral Argument with Historical Illustrations*. 4th ed. New York: Basic Books, 2006.

Walzer, Michael. "Political Action: The Problem of Dirty Hands." *Philosophy & Public Affairs* 2, no. 2 (1973): 160–80.

Walzer, Michael. "Spheres of Affection." In *For Love of Country: Debating the Limits of Patriotism*, edited by Martha C. Nussbaum and Joshua Cohen, 125–7. Boston: Beacon Press, 1996.

Wasserman, Ryan. "Material Constitution." In *The Stanford Encyclopedia of Philosophy*, edited by Edward N. Zalta. Fall 2021 Edition. Stanford: Metaphysics Research Lab, Stanford University, 2021.

Wedgwood, Ralph. "Hierocles' Concentric Circles." In *Oxford Studies in Ancient Philosophy, Volume 62*, edited by Victor Caston and Rachana Kamtekar, 293–332. 1st ed. Oxford: Oxford University Press, 2023.

Wheeler, Nicholas J. *Saving Strangers: Humanitarian Intervention in International Society*. Oxford: Oxford University Press, 2000.

White, Michael J. "Stoic Natural Philosophy (Physics and Cosmology)." In *The Cambridge Companion to the Stoics*, edited by Brad Inwood, 124–52. Cambridge: Cambridge University Press, 2003.

Whiting, Kai, Leonidas Konstantakos, Angeles Carrasco, and Luis Gabriel Carmona. "Sustainable Development, Wellbeing and Material Consumption: A Stoic Perspective." *Sustainability* 10, no. 2 (February 2018): 474.

Wirszubski, C. *Libertas as a Political Idea at Rome during the Late Republic and Early Principate*. Cambridge: Cambridge University Press, 1950.

Wood, Neal. *Cicero's Social and Political Thought*. Berkeley: University of California Press, n.d.

Zohar, Noam J. "Collective War and Individualistic Ethics: Against the Conscription of 'Self-Defense.'" *Political Theory* 21, no. 4 (1993): 606–22.

Zwygart, Ulrich F. "How Much Obedience Does an Officer Need? Beck, Tresckow, and Stauffenberg—Examples of Integrity and Moral Courage for Today's Officer." *Combat Studies Institute, U.S. Army Command and General Staff College*. Accessed February 18, 2024. https://www.armyupress.army.mil/portals/7/combat-studies-institute/csi-books/ObedienceOfficerNeed_Zwygart.pdf

Index

addiction, 86, 94n. 6, 162, 205
afterlife. *See* soul
agency, 66–67, 82–84, 95–96, 104, 130, 185–89
   collective agency, 148–52, 185
Alexander the Great, 168, 171, 214
altruism, 132–34
amor fati, 8–9
anger, 68–72, 203
animals, 13–15, 42–43, 95–97, 127–28
Antisthenes, 24, 214
apatheia, 70–73, 77
appropriate action (*kathêkon*), 32–33, 92–98, 135, 149–50, 182–89
Aquinas, Thomas, 174, 180n. 47
Arendt, Hannah, 150n. 66
Aristotle and Aristotelianism, 27–28, 35, 62n. 24, 192
assent, discipline of, 56–68, 71, 91
Athens and Athenians, 23, 40, 115, 169, 195
attention (*prosochê*), 51–3, 64–67, 81–86
Augustine of Hippo, 174, 197–98
authoritarianism, 155–58

Brennan, Tad, 40n. 53, 95n. 9, 127n. 11, 132n. 2. 4
Buddhism, 52, 81

Caesar, Augustus, 156
Caesar, Julius, 119–20, 156, 168, 182
Caesar, Nero, 156–58, 216
Caesar, Vespasian, 157
Card, Claudia, 133n. 27
Cato, Marcus Porcius, 120, 169
caution (as rational emotion), 48, 69, 74, 201
Chalmers, David, 59
Childress, James F. 177n. 39
choice (*prohairesis*), 63–68, 155n. 82. *See also* Stoic knife

Christianity, 7, 174, 210
Chrysippus of Cilicia, 11, 33, 41, 46, 71, 82–83, 93, 100, 123–24, 131–32, 147, 215
citizenship, 18, 73–75, 104, 113, 153, 173, 203
   See also communitarianism
   universal citizenship, 17–18, 101, 123–24, 129–38
Cleanthes of Assos, 215
Cochran, Elizabeth, 210n. 9
Cognitive Behavioral Therapy (CBT), 57n. 10, 200, 205–7
coherency. *See* integrity
collectivism, 124, 140
Collins, Stephanie, 149n. 65
Commodus, Lucius Aurelius, 165
communitarianism, 16, 126, 129–38, 142–45
comprehension (*katalêpsis*). *See* impressions
conflagration (*ekpyrosis*), 12–13
conformity, 115–20
consequentialism, 98n. 18, 138–39
consequentiality, 96–99, 112–15, 149–50, 177, 183
Cook, Martin, 197n. 84
cosmopolis, 136–37, 144
cosmopolitanism, 17–18, 136–43, 171, 173n. 31
cosmos, 7–8, 12, 17, 145
courage, 27–28, 69, 115, 169
Crates of Thebes, 24, 110, 214
Croesus of Lydia, 30, 39
Cynics and Cynicism, 18, 24, 36, 109–10, 140

death, 16, 64, 67, 77–78
   as punishment, 115, 157, 168, 195n. 81
dehumanization, 191
Delphic maxim, 99, 106
deontology, 98n. 18, 174
depression, 85–86, 199, 206
Descartes, René, 99

desire, discipline of, 57, 81. *See also amor fati*
determinism, 5–6, 83–85, 188
Diogenes of Sinope, 18, 103, 123, 124n. 6, 140, 214
disobedience. *See* obedience
double effect, 180n. 47
duress, 189
duties, prima facie. *See* Ross, David

eclecticism, 3, 201, 215–16
egoism, 25, 50, 93, 131
emotions, 68–77
Epicureans and Epicureanism, 9, 35, 72, 128, 216
eupatheia. *See* emotions

Fabre, Cécile, 179n. 41
fate. *See* determinism
Faustina, Annia Galeria, 172
fitness. *See* training
fortitude. *See* courage
fractals. *See* self-similarity
freedom, 46n. 73, 51, 55, 66–68, 84n. 87, 124, 185–89
French, Peter A., 149n. 65

Galilei, Galileo, 115
genocide, 149–50, 183
Gettier, Edmund, 59n. 13
globalism, hegemonic, 171
Goldman, Alvin, 59
God(s), 2, 5–15, 48, 67n. 41, 84n. 85, 103, 111, 123, 143, 188, 209
Godwin, William, 139n. 42
Gray, J. Glenn, 49n. 89

Hackett, John Winthrop, 166n. 3, 183n. 55
Hadot, Pierre, 9n. 16, 38n. 49, 57n. 10, 66n. 37, 81n. 78
happiness (*eudaimonia*), 23, 34–35, 46, 70, 81, 93, 154
Hierocles the Stoic, 124, 129–32, 135–8, 145–49
Hipparchia of Maroneia, 110–12, 214
Hiroshima, 199–200
Hobbes, Thomas, 152n. 69
honor (*aidōs*), 27, 44–49, 69, 201
Hume, David, 73n. 62

impressions, 59–63, 65, 70–73, 94, 90
imprisonment, 55, 107, 200

indifferents, 35–44
injury, moral, 191n. 71, 198–201
insanity, 61, 155
integrity (*homologia*), 44–47, 120, 179, 190, 195
Inwood, Brad, 93n. 4
Irvine, William Braxton, 54n. 3, 65n. 32

Johnson, Brian E., 100n. 21, 111n. 54
justice, 27–28, 34n. 38, 47, 73, 123, 132, 134, 153
just war, theory of, 174–82

Kant, Immanuel, 92, 166n. 3
killing, 44, 143, 175, 178, 181–83, 191
Kropotkin, Petr Alexeyevich, 124n. 4

Lacedaemonians. *See* Spartans
law, natural, 131–32, 145, 155, 187–88, 195–96
Lazar, Seth, 192n. 72
liberty, 120, 132, 153–57, 162
Locke, John, 154
logos. *See* God(s)
Long, A. A. (Tony), 46n. 73
Lossky, Nikolay, 11n. 24

macrocosm. *See* microcosm
materialism. *See* ontology
Mensch, Pamela, 26n. 17
microcosm, 14, 67, 137, 144–49, 184–85
militarism, 185
Milo of Croton, 30
Mitchell, William "Billy," 115–16
moderation, 26–28, 48, 52, 117, 121, 142
Montesquieu, Baron de, 154
Morgenthau, Hans J., 172n. 29
Musonius Rufus, 132, 168–69, 193–94, 216
Mussolini, Benito, 166n. 3

Nathanson, Stephen, 138n. 40
Nietzsche, Friedrich, 9n. 16
nominalism. *See* ontology
Nussbaum, Martha, 35n. 41, 173n. 31, 208

obedience, 46n. 71, 192–97
obesity, 76, 162, 205 *see also* training
oikeiōn and *oikeiosis*, 126–32, 134–39, 142–46
ontology, 10–11, 19, 81, 186
oracle, 6, 24, 103

pacifism, 174, 178
Paetus, Thrasea, 157
Panaetius of Rhodes, 29, 70, 100, 131, 145, 215
paradoxes, 24, 70, 142, 161
Parfit, Derek, 139n. 44
Parks, Rosa, 115
partiality, 134–38
passions. *See* emotions
Pettit, Phillip, 149n. 65
Pinker, Steven, 140n. 46
Plato, 24, 27, 123, 174
pneuma, 10–13
Pompeius Magnus, Gnaeus, 21, 168, 211
Posidonius of Apamea, 22, 82, 153, 195, 215
post-traumatic stress disorder (PTSD), 198–99
presentism, 81–86
Priscus, Helvidius, 157
progressor (*prokoptôn*), 33, 69, 93, 135, 142
providence. *See* God(s)
prudence, 26–28, 43, 73, 80, 119, 130, 134, 142
purification (*katharsis*), 62

reasonableness, 96–99, 114–15, 177, 187, 189, 209
Reydams–Schils, Gretchen, 142n. 50
right action (*katorthôma*). *See* sage(s)
rights, natural, 154
Robertson, Donald, 57n. 10, 206n. 2
Ross, David, 98n. 17, 177n. 39, 209
Rousseau, Jean-Jacques, 154
Russell, Bertrand, 20

sage(s) and sagacity, 14–16, 33–34, 70–71, 92–93, 190
  as a parent, 75–7
  as a warrior, 142–43, 202–3
  unreality of, 29, 50, 86
Sartre, Jean Paul, 99, 107–8
Schofield, Malcolm, 123n. 1, 132n. 23, 154n. 74
selection. *See* value, selective
self-similarity, 14–15, 136, 145 *See also* microcosm
Seregin, Andrei, 133n. 27, 134n. 32
Shanks Kaurin, Pauline, 194n. 78
Sherman, Nancy, 208
Sherman, William T., 180
slavery, 55, 153–56, 170, 188
Socrates, 23–27, 34, 67n. 41, 99, 103, 115, 144, 169, 195, 213–14

Solzhenitsyn, Aleksandr, 115
soul, 4, 12, 91 *See also pneuma*
Spartans, 168–69
Spinoza, Baruch, 84n. 85
Stockdale, James B. xvii–xviii, 46, 107, 211
Stoic knife, metaphor of, 53–55, 64–66, 76, 81, 101, 118, 127, 176, 198
suicide, 67, 129, 199

teleology. *See* God(s)
temperance. *See* moderation
Toynbee, Arnold, 166n. 3, 183n. 55, 185n. 60
training, 30n. 33, 57, 78, 162

U.S. Military Academy (West Point), 45
U.S. Naval Academy (Annapolis), xvii–xviii, 208
universals. *See* nominalism
utilitarianism. *See* consequentialism

value, selective, 37–44
virtues, cardinal, 26–28, 165
Visnjic, Jack, 95n. 9–10, 96n. 13
Vost, Kevin, 210n. 9

Wakin, Malham M., 46n. 71, 194n. 78
Walzer, Michael, 140n. 46, 176n. 35, 181n. 48, 189n. 70
war, nuclear, 180, 191, 199–200
wars
  American Civil (1861–65), 180
  Korean (1950–53), 181n. 48
  Kosovo (1998–1999), 181n. 49
  Marcomannic (166–180 CE), 165–66, 172
  Mithridatic, First (89–85 BCE), 169, 215
  Peloponnesian (431–404 BCE), 23, 169
  Roman–Parthian (54–217 CE), 171–72
  Second World (1939–45), 193–94, 199–200
  Vietnam (1955–75), xvii
Washington, George, 120
Wedgwood, Ralph, 147n. 62
wisdom. *See* prudence

Xenophon, 24

Zeno of Citium, xxii, 3, 15, 24, 36, 43, 75n. 66, 103, 123–26, 214
Zohar, Noam, 184n. 56